The Influence of Federal Grants

A publication of the Joint Center for Urban Studies of the Massachusetts Institute of Technology and Harvard University

The Influence of Federal Grants

Public Assistance in Massachusetts

Martha Derthick

Harvard University Press
Cambridge, Massachusetts
1970

Acknowledgments

From beginning to end, my work on this book was supported by the Joint Center for Urban Studies of the Massachusetts Institute of Technology and Harvard University. I started during the directorship of James Q. Wilson, who headed the Joint Center from 1963 to 1966, and finished in that of his successor, Daniel P. Moynihan. Being enlightened executives, both men managed to show, as friends, an agreeable interest in my progress and, as bosses, no interest whatever. I am grateful to them both.

If the Joint Center's subsidy was crucial, so too was the cooperation of many public officials. As the reader will see, I could not have written the book had they not freely provided access to files and other sources of information.

At the federal level, I am indebted to Douglas I. McIntyre of the Division of State Merit Systems and especially to Ruth M. Pauley, of the New England regional office of the Social and Rehabilitation Service, whose care and candor were immensely helpful.

At the state level, Commissioner Robert F. Ott of the Massachusetts Department of Public Welfare helped in every conceivable way, giving me access to his files, the run of his department, and, not least, an introduction to Joseph W. Chamberlain who, as director of research and statistics, was keeper of the department's facts. I could not possibly have had more congenial hosts than Mr. Chamberlain and Agnes B. Sullivan, then supervisor of research and statistics, in whose office much of my research was based. No matter what the time of my arrival (I never made an appointment), they greeted me cheerfully; no matter how crowded the of-

v

fice, they always found desk space for my use; no matter how harassed the moment or obscure the information I sought, they always responded promptly and with utmost good humor. Also in the state welfare department, Mary Darragh, the in-service training supervisor, was notably helpful not merely as a source of information but also as a source of enthusiasm and sympathy for the enterprise of research.

I asked every local welfare director in Massachusetts for help at least once: they all received questionnaires from me, and more than two thirds, an exceptionally high proportion, replied. I asked many of them for other and more demanding kinds of cooperation, and nearly all responded, although—as the people who actually administered the assistance program and as the objects of much criticism from clients, newspapers, reformers, social-work professionals, and just about everyone else—they had more reason than most of my informants to be wary of what I was up to. Among many I might name, I must list at least three. Daniel I. Cronin, as director of the department in Boston and as an extraordinarily knowledgeable man, helped me to cope both with his city and with the subject in general. Stanley Lipp of Dedham, as chairman of the Public Welfare Administrators' Association's legislative committee, supplied answers to frequent questions about legislative politics. And I seemed fairly often to call Eunice Smith, director of the local agency in Framingham, for no reason that I can now remember except that she was especially friendly and eager to do what she could.

Several of these officials read the manuscript in whole or in part and commented on it, as did Professor Wilson and Professor Samuel H. Beer, also of Harvard.

Finally, I am happy to acknowledge the moral support and skilled editorial criticism of my father, Everest P. Derthick, which are none the less appreciated for the fact that I have been able to take them entirely for granted from the time I was old enough to sit down at a typewriter. In this case, his contribution was more singular as well. He built the desk on which the book was written, and I should add a word of appreciation as well to my mother, whose skills do not happen to run in the editorial direction but who discovered in the dim recesses of an Ohio barn the splendid expanse of aged walnut that crowns the desk.

I have benefited, in summary, from much assistance and advice, nowhere near all of which is explicitly acknowledged here, but I do not wish to deny what convention and the facts of the matter dictate that I admit: I am solely responsible for what I have said.

M. D.

Belmont, Massachusetts
January 1969

Contents

Abbreviations

ADC—Aid to Dependent Children
ADC-UP—Aid to Dependent Children, Unemployed Parent
BFS—Bureau of Family Services
BPA—Bureau of Public Assistance
DA—Disability Assistance
FS—Family Services
FSA—Federal Security Administration
HEW—Department of Health, Education, and Welfare
MA—Medical Assistance or Medicaid
MAA—Medical Assistance to the Aged
NASW—National Association of Social Workers
OAA—Old Age Assistance
PA—Public Assistance
RO—Regional Office [of BPA or BFS]
SRS—Social and Rehabilitation Service
SSA—Social Security Administration
SSB—Social Security Board
STAS—State Technical Advisory Service

Mr. Jenkins [Republican from Ohio]. You think the Federal Government can do this job better than you can?

Mr. Tompkins [Massachusetts public welfare commissioner]. I do not say better; I think we can still do the job . . .

Mr. Jenkins. Massachusetts is a grand old State.

Mr. Tompkins. It bows to none.

Mr. Jenkins. I have heard that before. I am sorry to hear you say that she now bows to the Federal Government.

Mr. Tompkins. I do not think that, neither I nor any other resident of Massachusetts believes that Massachusetts is bowing to the Federal Government. We are recognizing rather that the limited revenues can be best helped by the . . . revenues that Congress has at its disposal.

Mr. Jenkins. Daniel Webster said, "Massachusetts, there she stands!" And we in the Midwest are sorry to hear that you are retreating.

Mr. Tompkins. I am not retreating.

—Hearings before the
House Ways and Means
Committee, 1949

Part I | The Federal Government as Grant Giver

1 | The Grant System

Federal grants to state and local governments have been growing rapidly in the United States. Congress enacted dozens of new grant-in-aid programs in the early 1960s, and the volume of federal aid in 1967, at $15.2 billion, was more than twice what it had been only six years before. Almost all state and local functions are supported by substantial aid.[1] And yet, although it steadily expands with use, the grant-in-aid system remains a subject of dispute. The central issue is "federal influence."

Critics of the grants say that state and local governments are withering under the impact of greater federal activity.[2] They cite the elaboration of conditions and the administrative supervision that accompany federal grants. Such conditions have become more numerous and detailed,[3] and in the 1960s they have been used as instruments of at least one major social change, racial integration. The argument is plausible, but not persuasive unless it can be shown that the conditions imposed by the federal government do cover a wide range of state and local government actions and are successfully enforced. Defenders of federal activity reply that, far from destroying state and local governments, federal aid is saving them from their own weaknesses, as the New Deal is said to have saved American capitalism in the 1930s. They point out that the scope of all governmental activity is expanding and that state and local governments are at least maintaining their share. They can cite the fact that state and local expenditures and employment have been rising much faster than federal expenditures and employment. (Between 1955 and 1965, federal expenditures, including those for defense, rose by 50 percent and civilian employment by 5 percent, while state and local expenditures rose by 115 percent and employment by 54 percent.)

Clearly, state and local governments are not withering away, and yet the trend seems to have been a flow of governmental power toward the center. Dollars spent and persons employed are imperfect indicators of the allocation of governmental functions. They do not answer the important question of how choices are made, social issues resolved, or major innovations in public policy sponsored. The growth of state and local expenditure and employment does not at all disprove the argument that those governments are being reduced to mere administrators of federally sponsored and federally directed programs rather than surviving as independent decisionmakers in a system where political functions are shared by different levels of government.

The debate between proponents of federal expansion and defenders of local autonomy is not new—it has a long and anguished history. For a hundred years after the founding of this country, the relation between the central government and the states was the nation's leading political question. It preoccupied the Supreme Court, inspired the greatest debates that took place in Congress, and in the end required a civil war to settle. The issue in the nineteenth century was a fundamental one: Shall there be a nation? What kind, if so? The federal-state relation arose repeatedly as a constitutional question, and responsibility for settlement therefore rested heavily on the Supreme Court, "arbiter of the federal system," and ultimately on the Union Army.

Today's issue is not the existence of a nation, but the best way of governing the one we have. For the most part answers are being worked out, not in august pronouncements of the Court and still less by armed force, but in more or less routine legislative acts and in the obscure daily performance of federal, state, and local bureaucracies.[4] If current debates over federalism do not have the apocalyptic character of their nineteenth-century predecessors, the questions they raise are important nonetheless. The grant system has become the dominant mode of conducting governmental activity at a time when such activity is expanding rapidly. It is therefore particularly urgent to ask how it functions and what results it produces. Does it lead to federal control at the state and local level, and, if so, just what actions are controlled and how? What are its implications for the structure of our institutions and the processes of our politics? How effective is it as a way of doing the things that governments seek to do? It is to these questions— and especially the question about federal control—that this book is addressed. My central purpose is to analyze the grant-in-aid system as an instrument of federal influence.

Characteristics of the Grant System

The origins of the grant system are variously traced—sometimes to the Smith-Lever Act of 1914, which authorized grants for agricultural extension, or to the Morrill Act of 1862, which authorized land grants for colleges, or even to the Northwest Ordinance of 1787, which included a promise of land grants for schools.[5] The federal highway act, passed in 1916, was the beginning of a large-scale program of assistance to the states that today accounts for the largest single share of grant expenditures. It was in the early 1920s that scholars first recognized the development of a "grant system," a regularized mode of conducting national business through the instrumentality of federal aid, and it was in the 1930s that federal grants grew to account for a significant share of federal expenditures and of state and local revenues.[6] Since then, grant programs have become so much more numerous and varied that it is appropriate to ask whether a grant system still exists.

By the mid-1960s, there were several hundred grant programs (problems of definition make an exact count difficult).[7] All of the federal executive departments and countless departmental subunits were engaged in administering them. They subsidized virtually all types of state and local activity, from planning and research to the building of public works to the provision of services. The immediate recipients might be state governments or local ones; the ultimate recipients might be consumers of government services (such as recipients of public assistance), suppliers of services to governments (such as construction companies), or state and local government personnel.

Just as the objects of grants are varied, so are the processes of grant giving. Some of the major differences are summarized in the following tabulation, with three parallel dimensions relating to the mode of allocating federal funds, the continuousness of the flow of funds, and the scope of distribution.*

Formula Grants	*Project Grants*
Statutory formula for allocation according to fixed objective criteria, e.g., area, population, per capita income	Allocation by administrative discretion according to subjective criteria ("merit" of application)
Flow of funds continuous; no fixed duration	Grant of limited duration
Universal (if unequal) distribution of funds	Selective distribution

Individually or together, the three dimensions form a continuum. Individual programs may fall at one end or the other or, if they combine features of both types, somewhere in the middle. Grants for those operations of governments that are universally and continuously performed, such as education and public assistance, tend to fall at the left of the table, whereas those for discontinuous activities, such as construction and development projects, tend to fall at the right. Grants that go to state governments tend to fall at the left, those to local governments at the right. (Grants to local governments are bound to be selective. Not *all* local governments are aided; if they were, it would be more logical and efficient to give grants through the states.) Yet despite these

---

* The terms "formula grants" and "project grants" are borrowed from official usage, but the characterizations are my own.

differences in process, federal grants are quite similar in form. Certain basic features are common to all, and it is these features that constitute the essential, identifying characteristics of the grant system.

All federal grants are given for a specified function. It would of course be possible for the federal government to collect and redistribute revenues to other governments without any stipulation for their use. It has often been argued in recent years that this should be done, but so far it has not. In practice, the giving of grants has been inseparable from the enunciation of federal purpose. Besides stating the function for which grants must be spent, the federal government specifies conditions that either elaborate the purpose or regulate the processes by which state and local governments accomplish the spending. In order to receive federal funds, state and local governments must submit "plans" for their use. Unless a federal administering agency approves these documents, and finds that the state or local government has satisfied certain conditions, funds are not granted. After this initial action takes place, unless the state or local government continues to satisfy federal conditions, funds may be withheld. Many variations of technique and detail may be found in the construction of grant formulas, in the content and specificity of federal conditions, in the organization of federal administering agencies, and in the strictness of the agencies' enforcement—but the framework itself has been quite stable and consistent.

In short, there *is* a grant system—a system by which the federal government seeks to influence the conduct of state and local governments in such a way as to promote the realization of its own goals. Fundamentally, federal influence is exercised in two ways. One is the act of grant giving itself, grant giving for a purpose. By offering money for the performance of a specified function, the federal government seeks to induce other governments to engage in that function, or if they are already engaged in it, to do more. The other way is through the conditions that accompany the grants. To the extent that participation in the grant program is elicited, and to the extent that the federal government is able to induce state and local governments to conform to the conditions it has laid down, federal goals are realized. To the extent that the federal government is able through these processes to alter conduct in ways of its own choosing, federal influence is exercised.

Consequences of the Grant System: Public Assistance in Massachusetts

From the large and growing family of grant programs, one middle-aged member has been singled out for analysis here. It is the public assistance program,* this nation's method for supporting persons who cannot support themselves, for which federal grants were authorized in the Social Security Act of 1935. I chose public assistance for three reasons. It is a major program, exceeded only by highway grants in the volume of annual federal expenditures. It is old enough to permit historical perspective. And it has involved all three levels of the federal system, thereby offering an opportunity to trace federal influence at both the state and the local levels.

Concentrating on one program, of course, precludes analysis of certain of the consequences of federal action. One of the questions most frequently asked about federal grants—how do they affect the allocation of state and local efforts *among* programs?—cannot be answered. On the other hand, concentrating on a single program permits detailed analysis of the full range of federal efforts to influence state and local conduct within that program. We can more clearly see the results of the setting of conditions as well as the giving of grants.

The choice of a single program also raises, as does any case study, the question of the extent to which findings are more gener-

---

* Throughout I use the term "public assistance" or "assistance." Popularly, the program is more often called "aid" or "relief" or, as of the 1960s, "welfare." I chose to conform to official terminology, which attaches broader meaning to the term "welfare." In federal usage, public assistance is a welfare program, but not the only one. In particular, federal organization and usage distinguish it from the child welfare program.

ally valid. Do conclusions about "federal influence" drawn from the public assistance program apply to other grant programs as well? One reply to this is to deny that it matters, on the ground that the case itself is of sufficient interest and importance to be worthy of study in its own right. Still, it is of interest here solely as an example of the grant system in action, and the question about the representativeness of the case therefore requires some sort of answer. In the absence of evidence from other programs (no other case studies exist), no answer can be conclusive. However, if it is true that grant programs constitute a system—that together they comprise a distinct mode of conducting federal affairs and that they have in common fundamental characteristics of form—then they also have common features as instruments of federal influence, and in a general way they can be expected to yield similar results. All operate within a common constitutional framework, the same federal system; all are enacted and financed by the same Congress; all of the federal administering agencies are responsible to the same President, and all confront essentially similar problems as a result of the size and diversity of the nation, the independent strength of state and local institutions, and the sensitivity of Congress to the needs of those institutions. In drawing my conclusions about federal influence, I have sought to emphasize factors that seem to be features of the grant system, rather than factors that seem to be unique to the case. Even so, the conclusions at best apply fully only to public assistance. They apply to other grant programs in varying degrees (depending in part on whether the programs are, like public assistance, of the "formula" rather than the "project" type). But I believe that they apply to all in some degree.

From the many possibilities, the public assistance experience of one state, Massachusetts, has been chosen for study. Given the aim of exploring the impact of federal action at other levels of the federal system, two choices were available to me: to analyze that impact in gross terms for the nation or in a variety of selected state settings, or to analyze it in more depth and detail for a single state. I chose the second alternative because it would facilitate the tracing of federal influence all the way to the bottom of the intergovernmental hierarchy, down to the behavior of the local worker; and because it would clarify not only the results of federal action, but also the processes of federal-state interaction by which the results were produced.

In theory, any state would have served the purpose: a federal grant program applies equally to all potentially eligible governments. The same offer of funds is made to all; the same conditions apply to all. The federal goals that are pursued in Massachusetts are the same as those pursued in Michigan, Minnesota, California, or Kentucky, and they are pursued with the same techniques. The characteristics of state and local political systems differ, however—and differ in such a way that federal goals are harder to realize in some states than in others. The conduct of state governments departs from the intended goals in varying degrees, and thus the extent to which the federal government seeks to exercise influence varies (as does the extent to which it succeeds). My purpose could best be served by the selection of a state in which governmental conduct had departed in significant respects from federal intentions. It could best be served, that is, by a case study marked by conflict as well as cooperation between the grant giver and the recipient, for situations of conflict are best suited to illuminate the possibilities and limits of federal influence in state and local affairs.

Massachusetts happened to suit this requirement very nicely. Indeed, few states could have suited it so well. It is not too much to say that federal involvement in the public assistance program in Massachusetts brought about a clash between two Americas, each with its own distinctive arrangement of public institutions, hierarchy of values, and mode of conducting public business. One, with its center of power in Washington, is bureaucratic and rationalistic. It values symmetry in the ordering of public institutions; universalism as the guiding principle of public programs (the development of abstract rules that apply equally to all people); efficiency in the conduct of public business; and professionalism in public personnel. The other America is traditional rather than rationalistic. It conducts public business in ways that vary from one locale to another, through institutions and processes that have developed largely through custom and habit and are nowhere highly systematic. It places little value on rules and abstract principles, and much on molding public action to suit particular persons and local circumstances. It places little or no value on professionalism in personnel, but much on identification with the local community. The second America by definition has no center of power, but its characteristic institutions, values, and methods were—as of 1935, when federal grants for public assistance began—exemplified in extreme form in Massachusetts' administration of assistance. Inevitably, federal activity in Massachusetts produced conflict as well as cooperation.

My analysis focuses on federal-state interaction. The core of the book, following a chapter that describes the formal structure of federal-state-local relations, is a series of five studies of the exercise of federal influence in the Massachusetts program. Each begins with a brief discussion of the content and formulation of a goal of the federal public assistance program, and then moves successively through descriptions of federal efforts to achieve the goal in Massachusetts, the state's response, and the consequences of federal-state interaction for the state. My concern in these chapters is much more with how federal policy gets carried out at the state and local levels than with how it gets formulated at the federal level, and much more with how state and local officials react to federal action than with how they themselves make and carry out policy. Hence these chapters (three to seven) do not at all constitute a full description of public assistance politics at either the federal level or in Massachusetts.[8] The book is mainly about *administrative* activity: the pursuit of federal objectives through the grant system is a task that falls to federal administrators; at the state level, conducting relations with the federal government is similarly a task that falls largely to administrators. (In a sense the book is not a single case study, but a collection of five cases from a single setting, assuming that a "case," or basic unit of observation, consists of a discrete sequence of federal-state interactions.) An analysis of federal influence (Chapter Eight) is derived from the five cases.

The actions described occurred between 1936, when federal grants for public assistance actually began, and 1967. For various reasons, mid-1967 proved to be a convenient stopping point. In Massachusetts, a radical change in the administrative structure occurred when the legislature enacted a bill providing for state administration, thus obliterating the last remnants of a system of local responsibility that arrived, literally, with the Pilgrims. On the federal level, the bureau that had administered public assistance grants since 1936, first (1936–1960) as the Bureau of Public Assistance and then (1961–1967) as the Bureau of Family Services, was dissolved and its personnel and functions were distributed among components of the newly created Social and Rehabilitation Service. This reorganization in turn symbolized a significant change in policy. An intensive effort in the early 1960s that connected the giving of social services to the poor with the giving of money came abruptly to an end. Although service giving continued to be stressed, it was now separated, at least on the federal organization chart, from the administration of money payments. Finally—and of more consequence for the purpose of the book—there were signs of major change in the character of federal-state relations. In the mid-1960s, the Johnson Administration began to formulate a doctrine of aid giving that permitted more discretion to state and local governments, in order to stimulate their "creativity." In the public assistance program, this contributed in 1968 to the promulgation of new federal policies and directives that were much more brief and general than what they replaced. For all of these reasons, 1936–1967 begins to seem a distinct era of federal-state relations in the public assistance program, whether viewed from the perspective of the federal government or from the perspective of Massachusetts.

Although this account is selective in terms of time (the "sample" covers thirty-one years), it is meant to be comprehensive in terms of events within that span, except insofar as selectivity is essential in order to produce a book of tolerable length. Not every event can be described, nor can every major event be described in detail, but no major events in the story of federal-Massachusetts relations have been omitted.

2 | The Sharing of the Assistance Function

One of the major issues that the grant system poses is whether federal aid should go to the states or to local governments. Since World War II many programs have bypassed the states, but these account for a small share of grant expenditures. The great portion of federal grants, about $9.8 billion of $11.1 billion as of 1965, is given to the states.

Congress has shown no consistent preference for state or local governments as grant recipients. When the issue comes up, it tends to split along partisan or ideological lines. In the 1960s, because Republican Party strength was concentrated in state governments and Democratic strength was concentrated in the cities, Republicans generally favored giving aid to the states, Democrats to localities. Sometimes the issue was a conservative-liberal one, as in the consideration of law-enforcement grants in 1968, when a coalition of Republicans and conservative Democrats amended the administration's bill to channel grants through the states. From the standpoint of federal administrators, both alternatives have advantages.

Giving aid through the states can enable the federal administration to take advantage of the states' formal authority over local governments. Because of the constitutional handicap that a federal system imposes, the federal government lacks authority to issue directives to other governments, state or local; but when it enters into a grant-giving relationship with the states, it is partly able to compensate for this deficiency. Insofar as the state can be induced to share federal values and objectives and act as the agent of the federal will, federal authority can be exercised over local governments by proxy. There is the further advantage that the states are the more inclusive governments, fewer in number. In any program the federal government can influence a wider range of activities by dealing with the states, and it can do so with less administrative inconvenience: doing business with fifty units is easier than it is with several hundred or thousand.

The argument for dealing directly with localities is that this method enhances federal control of the use of funds by avoiding dependence upon intermediary agencies, the states, which may not share federally defined purposes and may lack the administrative capacity to supervise local governments, especially big-city governments. Direct federal aid to localities may also be attractive to federal administrators because it means the proliferation of recipient agencies, and the more such agencies exist, the more widespread the pressure on congressmen to sustain the program. If he had only political interests to consider, as opposed to administrative convenience, the federal administrator would wish for a recipient agency in every congressional district, if not every county. From the standpoint of the President, if aid goes directly to local places, the federal government is more readily identifiable to the beneficiaries as the source of their benefactions, a consideration that assumed particular importance during the New Deal as a Democratic president sought to secure and reward the loyalty of city dwellers.[1]

How the choice is resolved for any given program is likely to depend on the nature of the program, the extent to which states may already be involved in it, and the particular objectives or values of the sponsors and prospective administrators of federal aid. The tendency has been to channel to the states funds for those activities that are universally engaged in, or in which state governments were already involved at the time the federal program got under way, such as highway construction, public assistance, and elementary and secondary education, although in education the federal administration has dealt with local districts as well as state governments. Aid has tended to go directly to local governments for new programs or those directed primarily to cities, such as public housing, urban renewal, and the antipoverty program.

At the time federal aid for public assistance began, aid giving to the states was the dominant form, firmly sanctioned by custom and (some would have argued) constitutional principle, although even in the 1930s experience with direct aid to localities was not unknown. Aid for highway construction and agricultural extension had been given directly to counties for brief periods, and some emergency relief funds in the form of loans had gone directly to cities.[2] Partly because of the strength of custom, the public assistance program was founded on the theory that the federal administration should have no relations with local governments, only with the states. This theory did not ignore the role of local governments in administration, but it rested on the assumption that state governments could be held responsible for their conduct. In more than a quarter of the states today, the public assistance program is carried out by counties—but from a purely formal standpoint, and to a great extent in practice as well, the federal administration has nothing to do with them. It does not send them directives, disburse money to them, or supervise their administrative conduct. Formally, it deals only with the states and is thus heavily dependent on state governments for the realization of its intentions.

More than custom led to reliance on the states, however. The choice also served objectives of policy and administration. By stimulating the exercise of state authority, the sponsors and first administrators of federal aid sought to expand the coverage of assistance programs, to enlarge the financing of them, and to improve administration by centralizing it at the state level. State participation in the assistance function had developed fitfully before this, and the Social Security Act was designed to accelerate and expand it throughout the nation.

The Evolution of Sharing

Poor relief in this country was originally a local function, an arrangement transplanted from England. States became involved gradually as they established institutions to house special classes of the poor—the insane, felons, the blind, the deaf, and so forth; after 1900, they created programs of financial aid for other special classes. Beginning in 1911 numerous states passed "mothers' aid" laws with which they authorized local governments to support, and sometimes themselves helped to support, mothers of young children whose husbands had died, deserted, or were disabled. In the 1920s, they began to enact similar laws for the benefit of the aged.

The federal government still took no part in caring for the poor, but as the social-work profession was formed it began to call for federal action. As early as 1901 a committee of the National Conference of Charities and Correction (later, the National Conference of Social Welfare) proposed the creation of a federal bureau of charities. Professor Sophonisba P. Breckinridge of the University of Chicago spoke for the profession early in 1927 in the very first issue of the *Social Service Review,* its scholarly journal:

the possibility suggests itself of developing on a national scale the services which have proven reasonably effective on a state-wide scale and which could be enormously stimulated and assisted by the service of a national authority . . . It is . . . clear that until . . . an agency exists equipped to stimulate, to inform, to direct, and to guide a national program on the basis of a national body of fact analyzed with a national purpose in view, the American public-welfare administration must remain chaotic, fragmentary, uneven, and inadequate, possessing neither of those features to which it is entitled by its public character, namely comprehensiveness and continuity. And nothing less than continuous, comprehensive, and progressive service in this field can be satisfactory to those who compose the professional group in social service.[3]

But for the Depression, the social-work profession might have had to wait a long time for federal action. The Depression greatly accelerated the development of welfare institutions at all levels of

government, while among the governments it accelerated centralization. State participation grew faster than before, and federal
participation now began.

The Depression exposed the political and fiscal limits of state
and local capacities. Although nearly all states had laws for aid to
mothers and the aged, these were not necessarily backed with state
funds, and they were not always mandatory for local governments. Only half of the counties in the country were giving mothers' aid as of 1934, and the number was actually declining. Even
where grants were given, the amounts were often tiny, and disparities among and within states were extreme. The average monthly
old-age assistance grant in 1934 ranged from $0.69 in North Da-
kota to $26.08 in Massachusetts; the average monthly mothers'
aid grant, from $8.81 in Louisiana to $51.83 in Massachusetts.
Administrative structures were just as varied and haphazard, for
state welfare agencies had developed unevenly. The lion's share
of the aid-giving function rested at the county level, with boards
of commissioners or judges; only twelve states had set up county
welfare agencies.[4]

The Social Security Act. Federal grants for support of the poor
were enacted in two steps: first a temporary law, the Federal
Emergency Relief Act of 1933, and then in 1935 a permanent
one, the Social Security Act, which authorized a mixture of programs including public assistance grants for three categories of
the poor—the aged, dependent children, and the blind. The act
was based on a report by a cabinet committee, the Committee on
Economic Security, which President Roosevelt appointed in 1934.
The Children's Bureau worked closely with the committee staff
and originated the proposal for aid to dependent children.[5]
Created in 1912 as part of the labor department, the bureau had
sought for some time to influence the evolution of state and local
welfare activities, in particular by advocating state and county
welfare departments staffed with trained workers.

As it emerged from the Committee on Economic Security, the
social security bill was intended to encourage what the professionals thought was progressive in state assistance administration and

to suppress what they thought was not. Above all, the authors sought to bring order out of the state and local chaos. Of course they wanted the act to bring about some measure of coordination and comprehensiveness on a national scale. They expected that all states would develop OAA (old-age assistance) and ADC (aid to dependent children) programs in response to federal grants; but, given the local basis of existing programs and the obstacles of custom and constitutional doctrine that lay in the way, they dared not hope for a truly national program. What they sought was reform at the state level through the use of national power. Most of the conditions for the receipt of federal aid were designed to encourage the development of state authority and to promote comprehensiveness and coordination within each state. In order to qualify for aid, a public assistance program had to be in effect throughout the state and be mandatory for local units. The state had to pay part of the costs and it had to establish a "single state agency," presumably a welfare department, to administer the program or supervise the local governments' administration.

Congress raised no objection to any of these conditions, though it did to some others that the professionals advocated. It was unwilling in 1935 (but agreed four years later) to authorize a requirement of merit systems, the professionals' device for improving the quality of state and local administration; and it would not give the authority for federal administrators to set standards for assistance payments. If the authors of the administration's bill had gone even further into structural matters and required the states to administer public assistance themselves, Congress might have reacted unfavorably and resisted so sweeping a disruption of familiar arrangements. So administration officials then and since have taken the position that a state can organize its assistance administration in its own way, as long as it exercises sufficient authority to meet federal requirements. It was clear from the start that federal power would be used to enhance state authority vis-à-vis local governments, but congressmen were not disturbed by that prospect, perhaps because most of their own districts are larger-than-local. Congressional debate over the Social Security Act concentrated on programs for unemployment and old-age insurance, which entailed radical changes in both the objects and the methods of federal action and were quite new even at the state level. By contrast, the public assistance titles simply subsidized programs that were already under way in most states and the technique, cash grants, was well established.

For federal administrative officials, the effort to bolster state welfare agencies involved more than a taste for order, rationality, and reform per se. It was also a matter of convenience. If the federal government was going to give assistance grants, other governments had to be responsible for receiving them and spending them in accordance with federal conditions. The fewer the number of recipient governments, the easier the job of administration. Giving grants directly to the country's more than two thousand counties would have been extremely inconvenient, even had it not been highly objectionable for other reasons, of which one was the poor reputation of county government. (Professor Breckinridge wrote that "the county is in the governmental system of the United States a retarded and retarding factor . . . the 'Dark Continent' in American public administration." [6] The states had to be the recipients, and as such they took on a new set of responsibilities. To meet these responsibilities, they either had to administer assistance themselves or to enlarge their exercise of authority over local governments.

The Federal-State Relationship

To qualify for federal grants, state governments had to submit plans for the approval of federal administrators. The Social Security Act stipulated certain elements of the plan as conditions for federal aid; if the plan satisfied these conditions, federal administrators had to approve it. (The conditions themselves will be described in the second part of this book.) Once the plan was approved, the federal government would pay a share of state expenditures—one half for OAA, one third for ADC. If the state should violate federal requirements, the administration might withhold payments after reasonable notice and an opportunity for review.

This form of grant giving followed a well-established pattern. Previous programs had called for submission of plans, set conditions for approval, and authorized the withholding of funds.[7] There was nothing new here unless it was the nature of the federal commitment of funds. Under the usual grant program, an appropriation determined by Congress was allocated among the states according to a statutory formula. In this case Congress supplied the statutory formula, but by promising to match whatever the states spent, in effect it was surrendering the power to determine the size of the appropriation. It put a ceiling on the amount it would match per individual recipient (half of thirty dollars was the initial maximum for an OAA recipient, for instance), but it had to provide matching funds for all recipients, however their numbers might rise or fall. If this departure from the usual pattern was significant, Congress failed to perceive it at the time.[8] The pattern of sharing in the assistance program, seeming to conform to familiar precedents, was not greatly debated in 1935.

To administer the program and others under the Social Security Act, Congress set up a three-man Social Security Board, after considering the alternative of assigning assistance programs to the Federal Emergency Relief Administration and other programs to the Labor Department. The Children's Bureau, having drafted the program for ADC, expected to administer it but lost out to the new board. The Board organized five service bureaus, of which the Bureau of Accounts and Audits and the Office of the General Counsel turned out to be the most important, and three operating bureaus, of which one—the Bureau of Public Assistance (BPA)—had responsibility for OAA and ADC.[9]

Since 1935 federal administrative procedures have been elaborated and administrative agencies have undergone numerous reorganizations and changes of title—the Social Security Board (SSB), which at first was independent, became part of the Federal Security Agency (FSA) in 1939 and then was turned into the

Social Security Administration in 1946; in 1961 the Bureau of Public Assistance became the Bureau of Family Services (BFS), and in 1963 a Welfare Administration was set up independently of the Social Security Administration; meanwhile, in 1953, the Federal Security Agency had become the Department of Health, Education, and Welfare (HEW).* But the essential forms and principles of the federal-state relation have endured throughout.

This relation revolves around the preparation and carrying out of the state plan. The plan is like a contract between the two governments: the state agrees to do what the plan says, and the federal government agrees to give grants as long as the state lives up to its plan or, more precisely, to those elements of its plan that come within the federal purview as defined by Congress. If the state plan does not meet federal requirements, then an issue of "conformity" is said to exist. This may result in the withholding of the entire grant.

In practice, a plan consists of all the state's laws and rules governing the particular category of public assistance; it is not a single, concise document that can easily be referred to. At first the Social Security Board issued few guidelines for what should be in a plan. The states had to discover what was expected of them on a case-by-case basis. As one critic put it, they had to "go fishing" for the limits of federal permissiveness.[10] In 1942 the BPA began a series of "state letters" embodying federal policy, and in 1945 it issued a *Handbook of Public Assistance Administration* in which policy statements were collected and organized. The handbook subsequently was kept up to date with periodic issu-

---

* Nor was this the end of the reorganization. In 1967 the Welfare Administration was merged with several other agencies to create the Social and Rehabilitation Service. Within it, an Assistance Payments Administration superseded the Bureau of Family Services as the administrator of public assistance. Because much of what follows consists of descriptions of events in a specific period of time, I have used organization titles appropriate to the context. But the reader should keep in mind that the BFS was really the BPA under another name, while the Welfare Administration was an offspring of the Social Security Administration, and the latter of the Social Security Board. Because the change of 1967 occurred after most of my research was completed, there are almost no references to the organizations created then. Where there is no specific context of time, I try to use a general term such as "the federal administrative agency" or "the federal administration."

ances of state letters and "handbook transmittals," an additional series created in 1963. The number of such communications to the states rose from zero, in the early years of the Board, to one hundred a year in the 1960s, about one every third working day, and the *Handbook* grew to a bulk of five inches.

When the federal administrative agency issues a new directive, states must respond with new plan material. Many of the provisions of a state plan—which is to say many of a state's public assistance policies and rules—originate in response to federal stimuli, but others may be developed by the state on its own initiative. These too must be submitted for federal approval and incorporation into the plan. Federal officials try to keep track of impending state actions in order to discourage any that would not be consistent with federal requirements. Review of the plan material is the federal administration's way of trying to obtain compliance in advance. It negotiates carefully the terms of the promise that the state makes in order to qualify for federal aid. In this way, federal requirements and state plan material are reconciled, thus rendering improbable the development of a conformity issue once approval of the plan material has been given.

Though it relies heavily on the advance negotiation of plan material, the federal administration naturally wants to find out whether the state is keeping its promises. It carries out *post hoc* reviews to verify that the state plan is actually meeting federal requirements, and that the state in general and with respect to particular acts is adhering to its plan. If a particular act does not meet federal requirements, then an issue of "matching" is said to arise; the federal penalty takes the form of "audit exceptions," the disallowance of matching funds for the particular expenditure. For example, if the federal administration finds that a state has aided an ADC child who is over the age limit set by federal law for the provision of aid, it will decline to share the cost of payments to that child. At what point the particular deviations become so numerous and serious as to raise the larger conformity question is a matter on which the federal administrative agency must use its judgment. Audit exceptions, unlike the withholding of the entire grant, are quite common, although the dollar volume of them, as of the 1960s, is not large.[11]

The main technique for the *post hoc* review was at first an audit of expenditures for each public assistance case. This technique created difficulties in federal-state relations because it resulted in a large volume of audit exceptions, and it caused tension within the federal administration because accountants rather than social workers were dominating supervision of the states. Social workers regarded the procedure as too negative—so much focused on fiscal regularity that social progress was slighted. In 1940 the universal fiscal audit was discontinued. Fiscal auditors, who currently operate out of the Audit Agency in HEW's Office of the Comptroller, continue to check a sample of cases, but the primary technique of supervision has become an administrative review that covers all aspects of state policy and administration. The administrative review suited the preferences of the social workers, who ran the BPA. In their hands it became a device for prodding the states to liberalize their programs as well as to abide by the canons of fiscal regularity and orderly administration. In addition to fiscal audits and the administrative review, there is a third supervisory technique, a personnel merit-system review, which is conducted by HEW's Division of State Merit Systems and is meant to assure that states are adhering to federal requirements in this area.[12]

In order to facilitate contact with the states, the Social Security Board created twelve regional offices, which have since been reduced to nine. A regional office is Washington headquarters in microcosm. It is headed by a director who oversees all HEW (formerly, SSB or FSA) activities in the region, and it contains representatives of the various bureaus and offices of the parent organization. The most important personnel with respect to public assistance administration are the regional representative and associate regional representatives of the bureau that administers public assistance (the BPA until 1961, then the BFS); the regional representative of the Division of State Merit Systems; the regional attorney, who represents the Office of the General Counsel; and the regional auditor. Normally, all communications between Washington and the states go through the regional office. Regional officials are the only federal officials that the state personnel see. The regional office interprets federal directives to state officials and advises them in the preparation of plan material. (This is officially called giving consultation or services, terminology that exemplifies the administrators' self-conscious professionalism and is incidentally a convenient euphemism to obscure the fact that the process may involve "exercising influence.") Although the bureau's central office at first maintained tight control over the approval of plan material, this function has steadily been delegated to regional offices. Regional personnel also conduct audits and administrative reviews. No matter what the precise division of formal authority, the central office has always been heavily dependent upon regional officials for information and appraisal of political realities and administrative performance. The character of federal relations with any state may be affected profoundly by the performance of regional office personnel, especially the representative of the bureau in charge of public assistance.

Assistance Administration in Massachusetts

The formal structure of federal-state relations can be thus described in general terms, but in practice the administration of federal aid has had to be adapted to the peculiarities of individual states. Intergovernmental problems arise and tension develops in varying degrees depending upon how closely the state measures up to the federal ideal. The pattern of state-local sharing has been especially important. Given the federal stress on the state-wide operation of programs and federal dependence on the exercise of state authority, relations have been most harmonious with states where a strong central authority already existed or could rapidly be developed in response to federal expectations.

In 1935 Massachusetts, at first glance, might have seemed such a state. It had been the first to set up a board of charities (in 1863), and one of the first to create a welfare department (in 1919). It was the first to give extensive consideration to old-age assistance (in 1910), one of the first to pass an OAA law that was state-wide in effect (in 1930), and the second to pass a mothers' aid law (in 1913). These events marked it as a progressive state, a leader in the field of social welfare, as did the quality of its welfare commissioners, who were professional men rather than political appointees.[13] All of this seemed to augur well.

On the other hand, although the state had long exercised supervisory functions, the supervision had not extended very far. Local units continued to make most of the important decisions about assistance administration. Furthermore, these local units were not counties, as in most other states (county government is very feeble in New England), but cities and towns—no fewer than 355 of them—making the Massachusetts system of assistance administration the most decentralized in the country. And though state supervision had a long history, the very length of that history threatened to be a handicap. Relationships with local governments had begun to be formed long before a federal role in assistance administration or a state role in the administration of federal aid had been dreamed of. Federal standards and expectations had played no part in shaping the conduct of the Massachusetts welfare agency; habits had been developed and state and local roles were defined in response to other influences. In other, less "progressive" states, where state supervision and administrative institutions had scarcely developed, radical changes stemmed from the Social Security Act. Welfare departments were set up for the first time and, being new, could readily adapt their behavior to federal expectations. In Massachusetts, arrangements of long standing were not easily changed, and, as it happened, they fell far short of the federal ideal. When federal administrators approached Massachusetts officials for the first time, they found them proud of the state's progressive reputation, satisfied with arrangements as they existed, and not in the least receptive to suggestions for reform.

Nor did it help the problem that, at almost the exact time federal aid began, the Massachusetts tradition of nonpolitical, professionally oriented welfare commissioners seemed to be coming to an end. The election of 1934 made James Michael Curley governor, and late in 1935 he appointed as welfare commissioner Walter V. McCarthy, who had headed Boston's welfare department when Curley was mayor. McCarthy did not get along with private-agency executives and other social-work professionals in the state. He would not talk to them, and they complained to the federal regional office.[14] Federal officials refused to be drawn into a private-agency assault upon McCarthy's administration. However they felt about the department's leadership (and they did not hold it in high regard either), they could do nothing to change it, had to work with it, and therefore sought to avoid giving gratuitous offense. Besides, they believed that the fundamental source of most problems in Massachusetts was the state's decentralized administrative structure. Commissioners might come and go, but the effects of the state's heritage of localism would endure, embedded as they were in institutional forms. Federal administrators would have been in a much stronger position had they been authorized by Congress to require full state administration. They believed from the very beginning that nothing less would solve their problems with Massachusetts and give the state agency the degree of authority that federal ideals and interests required it to have.

The Heritage of Localism. "The first axiom of Massachusetts public poor relief," Robert W. Kelso wrote in 1922, "is that the responsibility is local." [15] Each town should care for its own poor. This principle was embodied in the laws of the Massachusetts Bay Colony in 1639 and remained on the statute books until 1967, in the chapter on general relief: "Every town shall relieve and support all poor and indigent persons . . . whenever they stand in need thereof."

The state legislature asserted the local governments' obligation, and then local officials decided how that obligation should be met. Almost everywhere, decisions about helping the poor fell to boards of public welfare (called overseers of the poor before

1927). State law required the towns to establish such boards, and nearly all the cities did so too. In towns they were elected. The general governing body, the selectmen, might serve also as the board of public welfare, or a board might be elected independently. In cities, they were appointed by the mayor or manager or elected by the council.

Settlement laws expressed and perpetuated the extreme localism of assistance administration. For nearly three hundred years, until the last of them were repealed in 1963, these laws protected localities against having to support outsiders. The local government was obliged to help only those persons who had "settlement," which an individual might acquire by living in a city or town for five consecutive years without having received poor relief. To many local officials, the art of administration consisted in exploiting the settlement laws to the advantage of one's own place; Kelso called them "the commanding factor in the operations of selectmen and overseers of the poor." [16] After several centuries of legislative and judicial elaboration, they became enticing by their very intricacy. "It was kind of a game," one official recalled in 1965, referring to the zest and absorption with which some local administrators pursued the investigation of settlements. In each case, there was a chance that a thorough search and shrewd interpretation would result in putting responsibility for support on some other town. Litigation was frequent. During the Depression, the city of Lowell, for one, filed about seventy-five suits a year against other local governments in disputes over settlement.

The Beginnings of State Supervision, 1863–1935. It was the very rigidity of the principle of local responsibility that first drew the state government into poor relief. The essence of the Massachusetts law was that the town was responsible for its own poor and *only* its own. Those persons who were "unsettled"—for whom no city or town bore responsibility—became the responsibility of the state. Beginning as early as 1675, when the province legislature appropriated funds for refugees from King Philip's War, Massachusetts undertook to support those poor for whom the towns successfully denied responsibility. Eventually, in the nineteenth century, the state had so many unsettled poor in its care that it built four institutions to house them, and then, in order to supervise these and other charitable institutions, the legislature in 1863 created the Board of State Charities.

According to Kelso, Massachusetts' plan in 1863 was one of "centralizing policy and decentralizing administrative detail." [17] This was the arrangement that in fact developed in the succeeding century, but the reform itself did not go very far in that direction. The new board was supposed to reduce state costs by making the state institutions more efficient and by auditing claims made by local governments for support of the unsettled. For many years, it did little with respect to local administration except to supervise almshouses and collect statistics. It could not be expected to make policy until the legislature decided that the state government had a positive interest in the administration of poor relief.

This kind of interest began to develop in the twentieth century. In 1913 the legislature enacted a program under which the state would pay one third of the cost of support for mothers with dependent children under fourteen. It authorized the board of charity to supervise the local overseers' execution of the law, to inspect their records, to make rules "relative to notice," and to visit the homes of the families aided—powers that were passed on in 1919 to the board's successor, a department of public welfare. In 1930 the legislature again authorized help for a special class of poor, this time "deserving citizens" who were at least seventy years old. Again the state would pay a third of the cost, and again the state welfare agency was given supervisory power, this time in broader terms. It might make "such rules relative to notice and reimbursement and such other rules relating to . . . administration . . . as it deems necessary." [18] As of the mid-1930s then, on the eve of the Social Security Act, the state had a financial stake in three classes of cases—the unsettled poor, recipients of mothers' aid, and recipients of old-age assistance—and the stake was increasing rapidly because of the Depression.

Nonetheless, the state's authority to direct and supervise local welfare agencies was hardly being used. State rules were brief, general, and said little about determining eligibility and the amount of assistance. When local agencies aided a case for which, in their opinion, the state shared responsibility, they filed a claim for reimbursement. State workers investigated each of these cases and made their own judgments as to settlement status, eligibility, and need. They could not reverse the local decision, but they could decide whether to grant reimbursement. Intimidated by the long tradition of local autonomy, state welfare officials appeared to think that an aggressive assertion of their rule-making authority would be impracticable. At the same time, lacking confidence in local officials, they felt compelled to duplicate such of local action as was of financial interest to the state, a task that threatened to become impossible as the relief rolls grew.[19]

Extension of State Supervision, 1936–1966. In the three decades after 1935, the state expanded its role in the assistance program. Assistance laws were elaborated, state financial participation was increased, and the welfare department enlarged its rule-making authority and revised its methods of supervision.

The scope of state participation in assistance became broader as the legislature created new categories of assistance. In 1951 it authorized aid for poor persons who were disabled (DA). In 1960 it enacted a program of aid for the aged who were medically indigent (MAA); in 1966 this was superseded by a much broader program of assistance for the medically indigent ("Medicaid," or MA).* Extension of the categories led to a steady shrinking of the proportion of cases on general relief, a residual program in which the state did not participate. Finally, in 1963, the state began to share the costs even of general relief. Until then it had been responsible only for unsettled relief cases, but now it began to reimburse local governments for 20 percent of all general relief ex-

* As early as 1907 Massachusetts had enacted a program of aid for the blind, and after the Social Security Act was passed this benefited from federal grants. Technically, it is one of the public assistance categories, but in Massachusetts it has always been separated from the others in law and for purposes of administration. The Department of Public Welfare has had no responsibility for it, and so it is excluded from my account.

penditures. After 1963, therefore, no assistance cases remained in which the state did not have a financial interest.

While the legislature was enacting new programs of state aid, it was also revising older statutes in language that circumscribed local discretion. The state's OAA law, which began in 1930 as a mere 62 lines on the statute book, was eight times that long by the mid-1960s.[20] The ADC law, though less subject to amendment, approximately tripled in length.

Nor was the legislature's work confined to assertions of its own will; included in the large volume of new law were generous grants of authority to the state welfare department. With respect to ADC, the department was given, as of January 1, 1937, the power to make rules relative to reimbursement "and such other rules relating to administration [of ADC] as it deems necessary," language that already appeared in the OAA law. In 1941 the ADC law was further strengthened to empower the department to "adopt rules and regulations for . . . efficient administration" and to take "action as may be necessary or desirable for carrying out [the law's] purposes in conformity with all [federal grant-in-aid] requirements." [21] Similar language was added to the OAA title as well, along with the following very stringent stipulation:

[Local boards] shall be subject to the supervision of the department and shall comply with all rules and regulations adopted by the department . . . and no city or town shall receive reimbursement from the commonwealth under this chapter with respect to any case unless the department determines that the [standards of payment set forth in the law] have been complied with.[22]

In 1943 the legislature authorized the state department to approve local budgetary standards for OAA. In effect, this enabled the department to enforce its own standard:

no city or town shall receive reimbursement from the commonwealth under this chapter, or be entitled to participate in money received from the federal government . . . unless the department has approved its current budgetary standards and determined that the rules and regulations of said department in connection therewith have been complied with.[23]

The legislature was not quite so firm about the department's power over the ADC program, but a law passed in 1946 was perfectly explicit: The aid furnished "shall be in an amount to be determined in accordance with budgetary standards as approved by the department." [24]

These provisions, on top of the basic power to make all rules for OAA and ADC that were deemed necessary, would seem to provide an ample basis on which the department might act. Nevertheless, to observers in the 1930s and 1940s the department seemed timid, immobilized not so much by lack of authority as by lack of will and a fear of running into local resistance.[25] When the department did begin, in 1939, to strengthen control over local agencies, it acted in response to a highly critical report from a legislative commission, the contents of which influenced the department's organization and conduct of relations with local governments for years to come.

In 1937 the legislature set up a commission to study taxation and public expenditures. Because the assistance program accounted for a large and fast-growing share of expenditures (and perhaps also because would-be reformers of the welfare department seized upon the commission as a vehicle for realizing their ends), the commission singled out public assistance for special attention. A report on assistance—called the Haber Report after the research director, William Haber, a University of Michigan economics professor—was the first and most detailed of fourteen that the commission produced, and it went well beyond the matter of costs to cover the entire subject of administration. Like the Social Security Act itself, the Haber Report reflected prevailing professional conceptions of what assistance administration ought to be like—that is, centralized, professionalized, and uniform throughout the state. It recommended a number of major changes almost all of which would have enhanced the power and functions of the state.

The legislature almost completely rejected the Haber proposals, and the welfare department at first made only a defensive response. McCarthy was still commissioner, Curley having given way as governor in 1936 to a hand-picked successor under whom his department heads were secure. While conceding that changes must be made, McCarthy denied that the department had the power to make them.[26] However, the problem was soon taken out of his hands, for the election of 1938 brought a change of regime and of attitudes toward reform. Republican Leverett Saltonstall beat Curley in the contest for governor, and in 1939 he appointed a new welfare commissioner, a civic leader from Worcester, for the sole purpose of presiding over the reform of the department.[27]

In 1939 a system of rule making and supervision was laid down that was to last until 1968. In keeping with recommendations of the Haber Report, the department issued a manual of rules, policies, and procedures—tentatively, at first and then, in 1943, with instructions that local agencies should regard the manual as mandatory.[28] It incorporated detailed standards for determining need and assistance. Beginning in 1945, this manual was kept up to date with a series of "state letters," a procedure that paralleled the federal method for communicating with the states and, like it, though less dramatically, expanded with use. State letters to local agencies, which were issued at a rate of seven a year between 1945 and 1959, jumped to seventeen a year between 1960 and 1966. Meanwhile, in keeping with another recommendation of the Haber Report, the department stopped duplicating the local agencies' investigation of individual cases and instead developed a field staff to review decisions through a systematic sampling of local case records.

As field operations developed, so did the handling of appeals, which became one of the department's major supervisory techniques. A procedure for appeal by aggrieved applicants or recipients had been introduced into the OAA law in 1933, and in 1936, after passage of the Social Security Act, it was strengthened

and extended to ADC. Decisions of a state appeal board, later replaced by a departmental staff of appeals referees, were made
binding on local agencies. As of the mid-1960s, the department's
referees were hearing nearly two thousand appeals a year and
overturning the local decision in about 40 percent of them.[29]

Development of the state's rule-making and supervisory powers
after 1940 fulfilled the principle that, according to Kelso, had
been laid down for Massachusetts in 1863: centralization of policymaking, decentralization of administration. Local welfare
boards, which had long combined policymaking and administrative functions, were now confined to the administration of state-
prescribed laws and rules, except with respect to the ever-dimin-
ishing group of general relief cases. (Even after 1963, when state
aid for general relief began, local governments retained the power
to make rules for general relief.) This state-local division of functions, which seemed to Kelso to be highly desirable in the 1920s,
proved to be highly unstable after the 1930s. As the state expanded its policy- and rule-making role, it began to intervene in
administration too, both by trying to modify the principle of local
separatism and by circumscribing the exercise of particular administrative functions.

The Haber Report argued that the state could supervise better if
there were fewer local units. The remedy suggested by the report
and urged by the state welfare department for the next twenty-five
years was consolidation. Small towns should form welfare districts and hire staff members jointly. The legislature, in its sole response to the Haber Report, passed an authorizing act in 1938,
but although the law contained an incentive to consolidate—a
promise that the state would pay one third of administrative costs
in welfare districts—no consolidations took place. Not until the
1950s did districts actually begin to be formed, and then only because financial penalties against towns that failed to consolidate
were, in effect, combined with positive inducements. The legislature in 1950 required that all towns, no matter how small, hire a
staff member with civil service coverage. This imposed an addi-

tional expense on towns where administration had been performed by the elected board of public welfare for little or no pay. By entering into a welfare district, however, they might share this expense with other towns and with the state, which again offered to pay one third of the administrative costs of welfare districts. Still consolidations took place slowly. The state field staff coaxed and cajoled, and by 1966 the number of local administrative units had been reduced from more than 350 to 270, still much the highest number in the country.

As the state urged the smallest towns to stop administering welfare by themselves, it steadily imposed on all places new laws and rules circumscribing administrative conduct. Most of these covered personnel. In 1941 state law was amended to require that all local welfare workers come under the state's civil service system. Simultaneously, the state set up a welfare compensation board to determine salary schedules for local welfare employees. In 1949 the welfare department issued a handbook of administrative rules and procedures—comparable to the handbook of assistance policies issued in 1943—that prescribed caseload and supervisory standards and covered a wide range of other administrative matters. This was subsequently revised with periodic issuances of "administrators' letters." In 1960, the state also began sharing in administrative costs for OAA, ADC, and MAA (it had done so for DA since the program's beginning in 1951).

By the mid-1960s, then, local places had been compelled to give up or substantially compromise the power to decide what the qualifications of welfare administrators should be, how much they should be paid, and how many should be employed. Given these restrictions, along with state rules covering the substance of programs, there was almost nothing of importance that local boards of public welfare were free to decide for themselves. Except for their control over general relief (a small and declining fraction of the caseload) and their power to choose a local agency director if the incumbent should die, retire, or resign, all of their functions had been taken from them. Most important decisions were made by the state, and insofar as discretion remained at the local level, state action had assured that it would be in the hands of civil servants. The local boards had become an anachronism.

The Drive for State Administration. Despite the great enlargement of their power, state welfare officials in the 1960s remained dissatisfied with the system of state-supervised local administration. The persistence of a large number of local units, with very uneven caseloads, continued to pose problems. So did the lack of authority to appoint administrative personnel. Although local agency directors were formally obliged to follow rules issued by the state welfare commissioner (after approval by the department's fifteen-man advisory board, appointed by the governor, on which local directors were represented), they were not in fact the commissioner's organizational subordinates. There was a discontinuity in the chain of command. He did not appoint them; local welfare boards did, often in response to the wishes of mayors or city managers. His authority over them, therefore, was ambiguous. He felt it to be less effective (and therefore, if for no other reason, it *was* less effective) than was his authority with respect to subordinate officials in the state welfare department.

Many observers of the department in the mid-1960s, like those in the 1930s and 1940s, thought it weak, and the commissioner, Robert F. Ott, seemed to concede as much by his dissatisfaction with existing arrangements. Though the volume of rules issued by the state had been increasing, this was not necessarily a reliable sign of increased initiative. Most of those rules were made in response to federal changes. The department rarely did anything unless federal pressure provided the opportunity.

Less than intrepid in the making of rules, the department found enforcement difficult as well. When new programs got under way, there was often a lag in local response—inevitable, no doubt, in any new program, but state officials suspected that it resulted to some extent from negligence or a willful failure to comply. The launching of the MAA program in 1960, of a program for ADC-UP (aid to dependent children in families where the father was unemployed) in 1961, and of Medicaid in 1966 all stirred complaints from the state department that some local agencies were lagging in the execution of the program because they did not approve of its purpose or were opposed to increased welfare expenditures for any purpose. On a few occasions, local officials who disagreed with a particular state requirement defied the department openly, forcing it to obtain compliance through the process of appeals (which could be used only if the failure to comply adversely affected a recipient) or through withholding funds. Withholding was so drastic a sanction, however, that the department almost never used it. To obtain compliance, it relied on whatever devices of verbal persuasion its field staff had the patience, will, and wit to muster.

The large number of local agencies, the ambiguity of the state department's authority, the chronic difficulty of obtaining prompt and complete compliance, and the heavy investment of administrative effort in persuasion and negotiation all seemed to state officials to cry out for correction. The obvious solution lay in a system of state administration, and a campaign to establish it got under way in 1965.

The initiative for reform did not come from the department. Even had it been able to muster the administrative and political resources to lead such a campaign, doing so would have been inexpedient, for it might easily have permitted charges of "power grab." So the campaign was led by social welfare activists in Greater Boston, most of them associated with private agencies either as paid staff members or as the high-status civic leaders who serve on agency boards. The impetus came from United Community Services, Boston's federation of private agencies, and the Massachusetts Committee on Children and Youth, a research organization having public and private support. UCS and MCCY hired the National Study Service of New York to survey public assistance in Massachusetts. After several months of work, the study organization duly recommended state administration. Its "expert, impartial" report became the principal propaganda weapon of the proponents of reform.[30]

The reformers prepared a bill providing for the state's assumption of assistance costs and administration, introduced it in the 1966 session of the legislature, and lobbied hard for it with much support from the news media. They also had support from Governor John A. Volpe, who, as a Republican in a state where Republicans are the party of "good government," was relatively accessible to the reformers; he was, besides, interested in promoting the measure as a means to a popular end—"relieving the burden on the local property tax." The lieutenant-governor, Elliot L. Richardson, who was still more accessible to the reformers and thoroughly in sympathy with them, became a major advocate of the bill.

City politicians generally were silent or in favor of reform. State assumption of costs was highly attractive to them, for assistance costs in the cities were large and getting larger. Apart from that, the assistance function was threatening to become a severe liability as complaints about the program arose from diverse and unexpected sources, including the recipients. While the legislature was considering the bill, Boston suffered a slum riot that began with an ADC mothers' sit-in at a welfare office. Mayor John F. Collins, who had already endorsed state administration, suddenly showed fresh enthusiasm for the idea. Town politicians were more interested in retaining local administration. Selectmen were more strongly committed in principle to home rule, did not suffer as mayors did from a heavy tax burden for assistance or from so obvious a threat of political controversy, and in many cases received a small amount of compensation, perhaps a hundred dollars a year, for their service as welfare board members (a practice that dated from the time when they actually performed administration). Yet even they did not get much aroused about the issue. The only active, cohesive opposition came from the Public Welfare Administrators' Association.

The legislature, responsive both to the reformers' efforts and to the local politicians' desire to be rid of costs, passed the bill by large margins in the summer of 1967, and state administration went into effect on July 1, 1968.[31] Thirty-one years after federal aid had begun, Massachusetts now had a system that would suit federal ideals and interests.

The Federal Role. In the 1960s, federal officials wondered why the Social Security Board had approved the Massachusetts plan in the first place. "The mistake we made," one said—and others independently echoed the thought—"was in agreeing to this system in the first place." It is hard to see how the Board could have done otherwise, however. To have required a widespread consolidation of local units, let alone state administration, would have touched off a major controversy and might have delayed the provision of federal aid to Massachusetts, an intolerable result in the circumstances of the Depression and a rash political undertaking for a new agency.

Nor did federal officials later press for a system of state administration. This restraint in the face of the fragmented Massachusetts structure shows how strong their adherence was to the doctrine that the choice between state administration or state-supervised local administration should be a state's own. Once, late in 1938, BPA headquarters did recommend state administration for Massachusetts or, if that were not possible, formation of district units. The recommendation was contained in a memorandum for the regional representative, as one of several for him to use at his discretion in discussing with state welfare officials the content of state laws. He did not press it upon them, and he may never even have mentioned it.[32] In the late 1940s, when the state came under active federal pressure to accelerate consolidation of local units, the BPA was at pains to point out in communications with state officials that it was not attacking local administration as such.

Throughout the campaign for state administration in 1965–1967, federal regional officials maintained, in public, a discreet silence. Behind the scenes they did what they could to help, for example by giving information and advice to the National Study Service. (When the campaign ended successfully, the regional office reminded headquarters—in a bit of intrabureau boosterism—that "Region I will be [the] first region . . . to have all operations on a state-administered basis."[33]) But in general they stayed out of the newspapers and out of legislative hearing rooms or galleries. The continued to behave discreetly even after the federal welfare commissioner, in Boston for a professional meeting, made perfectly clear to the press that she favored state administration for Massachusetts. Yet, restrained as federal officials were during the actual campaign, the result was a victory for them quite as much as for the sponsoring groups.

A variety of forces had joined to bring about this shift of power from local governments to the state. State welfare officials, to serve the interest of their organization, sought enhanced authority. Pressure groups, notably recipients of old-age assistance, appealed to the state legislature for action because that was the most efficient way of attaining their objectives. Professional social workers, from their organizational base in private agencies, appealed for more state control because they expected it to serve such values as comprehensiveness and uniformity. Local politicians sought to shift costs to the state and, in so doing, could not avoid surrendering some control over program activity as well. (Both the Haber Report, in the late 1930s, and the adoption of state administration thirty years later came about as a result of a loose and rather improbable alliance between reformers and local or locally oriented politicians, the former to rationalize a disorderly, traditional administrative structure, the latter to unload a tax burden—interests that were different yet complementary.) Finally and—for the purposes of this book—most important, the role of the federal government itself was crucial. Each step of centralization after 1936 was taken with federal encouragement and approval, and some of the most important ones were taken in response to federal insistence. By a long series of actions, the federal administration had profoundly affected the interests that were at stake in the reform of 1967 and the distribution of power among the contestants. Just what the effects of federal action were will be shown in the next five chapters.

Part II | The Pursuit of Federal Goals

3 | Adequacy of Assistance

The federal government intends the dependent poor to receive an adequate amount of money. The Social Security Act, according to its preamble, is "to provide for the general welfare . . . by enabling the several States to make *more adequate* provision" for the aged, the blind, and dependent children.[1] In 1948 the Bureau of Public Assistance could define the goals of the federal program in two phrases: "adequacy of assistance" and "equitable administration."[2]

The federal government has sought to achieve adequacy primarily through the basic device of cash grants to the states. In addition, as a condition of aid, the Social Security Act has required that states share—to what extent, it does not say[3]—in the costs of assistance, which before the 1930s fell almost exclusively on local governments. In 1935 proponents of federal aid assumed that federal dollars would generate state dollars and that both, when added to local expenditures, would increase total expenditures for assistance and the size of individual payments.

Although these actions might contribute to adequacy, they could not assure that a federally approved standard of adequacy would be attained. Accordingly, in 1935 the administration asked Congress to include as a condition of grants that the states pay the poor "a reasonable subsistence compatible with decency and health." This would have given the federal administrators authority to set as a standard of adequacy the amount of such subsistence. Congress turned the administration down.

Virginians Harry F. Byrd in the Senate and Howard W. Smith in the House led the opposition. Appearing as a witness before the

43

Ways and Means Committee, Smith asked it to "report a bill that the states may participate in." He noted that if Virginia had to raise $15 per OAA recipient (enough exactly to match the proposed federal grant per recipient), the amount of its tax collections would have to be nearly doubled. He concluded: "My objection along that line would be answered by a provision in the bill which took away from some person in Washington the power to say when the State of Virginia could participate; in other words, for someone in Washington to say what was a reasonable and decent subsistence down in the Blue Ridge Mountains of Virginia." [4] As a member of the Finance Committee, which was considering the bill in the Senate, Byrd could challenge the administration directly. As hearings opened, he sought to get the administration witness—Edwin E. Witte, executive director of the Committee on Economic Security—to admit that the administration would have "dictatorial power" to withhold grants. Witte resisted, but when Senator Hugo Black of Alabama pursued the questioning in less polemical terms, he conceded Byrd's point:

> Senator Black. If . . . the State of Virginia should conclude to pay only $10 a month and the Federal Administrator concluded that that was not sufficient to give reasonable subsistence compatible with decency and health, then the Federal Administrator could in his discretion cut off the payments from the Federal Government to the State of Virginia.
> Mr. Witte. Yes, sir.
> Senator Black. That is correct?
> Mr. Witte. Yes, sir.

Witte interpreted Byrd's resistance as a manifestation of southern racism, and that is beyond doubt part of the truth—but after listening to Witte's testimony, representatives of all poor states must have thought it wise to oppose the administration's language. Witte ineptly illustrated the possible application of the law with the case of Nebraska:

The Administrator could conceivably refuse an allowance. What I mean is this: I want to illustrate that a little. In the State of Nebraska, because of the very bad conditions that have existed due to the drought, under a new law that was enacted in 1933 pensions had been paid of $2 a month in many of the counties. I think in a situation like that there would be a question whether the Federal Government should match that $2 by $1, and there might be a question whether that was complying with the law.[5]

The reasonable-subsistence standard was dropped, and on Byrd's initiative the language of the public assistance titles was amended to provide that federal aid was to enable each state to assist the needy "as far as practicable under the conditions in such State."

Congress' action meant that adequacy would remain only a vague objective; to make state programs more adequate, federal administrators would have to rely on techniques that were consistent with the interests of the states, including the poorest ones, and hence consistent with the preferences of a Congress so constituted as to embody state interests. In general, they would have to rely exclusively on positive inducements—cash grants that would serve Congress' interest in supplying benefits to states—rather than on the imposition of conditions that would compel state governments to tax and spend for the poor in federally stipulated amounts.

State decisions on payments to recipients could be influenced by manipulation of federal grant formulas. If adequacy of assistance had been the administrators' only goal, and if the President and Congress had shared an unqualified commitment to it, then these formulas could have been designed to maximize the states' incentive to increase assistance expenditures. This has not been done, and yet federal action with respect to the formulas has, on balance, promoted the objective of adequacy. Both Congress and the administration have acted as if that were an important goal.

The federal grant for each assistance category is based on the amount the state gives to a recipient. The federal government pays a percentage of the recipient's grant up to a maximum amount stipulated in the Social Security Act. For example, the original OAA formula provided that the federal matching share would be 50 percent, up to a maximum of $15. The ADC formula called for a matching share of one third, with a federal maximum of $6 for the first child and $4 for others in the same family.

Federal administrators, hoping to promote adequacy, have opposed the stipulation of a maximum. To them, the more a state gives a recipient, the more it should get from the federal government; but Congress has rejected this view. The position of administrators on the grant formulas, however, has not always been unambiguously liberal.

For one thing, they have been at least as much concerned with equity as with adequacy, equity both for states and for individuals within states, and the two goals are to some degree inconsistent. As early as 1939, administrators sought to persuade Congress to adopt a progressive grant formula, one that would benefit poor states more than wealthy ones so that the disparity in assistance payments between the two would be reduced. Congress, though it did not adopt the administration proposals, worked out its own version of a progressive formula, which it enacted in 1946. This was the device of two-step matching: the federal government would pay a high proportion of a specified initial share of the recipient's grant and a lower share of the remainder. For example, the OAA formula in 1946 was changed to call for payment of two thirds of the first $15 and one half of the amount over $15 up to the federal maximum of $22.50. This had an equalizing effect, as administrators wished—the poorest states, the ones with the lowest grants, would have their expenditures matched more liberally than the richest states would—but this formula would not promote adequacy. If a state acted rationally (to maximize the federal share of its expenditures), its grant per recipient would not exceed the amount of the first step in the two-step formula ($15 in the example).

Furthermore, it was the administrators' pursuit of equity that introduced perhaps the most anomalous element into a generally liberal statute. This was a provision, added to the Social Security Act in 1939, that required states, when determining the amount of a recipient's grant, to "take into account"—that is, subtract—any income or other resources that might be available to him. The provision was intended to establish as the fundamental principle of the act that assistance should be based on need. The administrators' commitment to this principle grew out of a characteristically professional striving for equity and objectivity—need was the standard that seemed best to suit this requirement—and also out of a political circumstance. The rise of the Townsend Movement in the 1930s, with its radical demand for a fixed pension for every elderly person, had a profound effect on the administrators' conception of public assistance policy. It was in reaction against the extravagance of the Townsendites that they became committed to a precise adjustment of assistance to income and resources. They drafted the amendment of 1939 and chose to submit it to congressional committees in executive session because they did not want to encourage a belief that the original law left any doubt that income must be deducted from grants.[6] Not until the 1960s did they retreat. With the Townsend Movement long dead, and the ADC rolls burgeoning, they began to look for ways of giving recipients an incentive to work. One way, and Congress agreed, was not to deduct all earnings from assistance checks. Since 1962 the Social Security Act has provided for recipients' retention of specified amounts of income.

Whereas administrators have not been unambiguously "liberal" in respect to grant formulas, neither has Congress been unambiguously "conservative." It has steadily liberalized the formulas for aid, both by increasing the federal share and raising the maximums, with the result that the federal government pays a far higher proportion of assistance costs in each category than it did in 1936. As of 1967, the matching formula in OAA provided that the federal government would pay 31/37 of the first $37 of state expenditure, plus a variable proportion (ranging from 50 to 65 percent, inversely correlated with state per capita income) of the remainder up to a federal maximum of $37.50. The ADC formula has similarly changed. Almost without exception, increases in the federal share—of which there were ten between 1935 and 1964—originated in the Senate. They certainly did not come from the White House. Presidents of otherwise divergent views have resisted liberalization of the federal formulas in the common belief that states are too much inclined to dip into the federal till. Administrators, though privately they might welcome Congress' action, therefore could not encourage it publicly.[7]

To achieve adequacy, administrators sought to enlarge not only the size of payments but also the scope of the programs, with respect both to classes of persons covered and to the types of support given them. One approach to greater coverage was to limit the states' freedom to restrict eligibility. Administrators persuaded Congress to enact, as conditions of federal aid, clauses limiting the length of state residence requirements and specifying that citizenship requirements should not be so strict as to exclude any citizen of the United States. Given Congress' reluctance to restrict state action, however, they had to rely mainly on other, more positive methods. The terms of federal incentives could be counted on to influence state action; states would probably choose to help those categories of persons whom the federal government would help them to help. Much depended, then, on the federal definition of the categories.

Congress adopted broad definitions for both OAA and ADC in 1935, and continued thereafter to broaden that for ADC (while expanding social security coverage for the elderly). It authorized federal OAA grants for needy persons of sixty-five years and over, a lower age limit than many states were using, and required states to adopt this standard beginning in 1940. For ADC, it began by offering grants for the support of children under sixteen, living with any of twelve classes of relatives, who were dependent because of a parent's death, continued absence from the home, or physical or mental incapacity. The age limit later was raised to eighteen and to twenty-one for those enrolled in school. In 1950 Congress authorized grants for the caretaker-relative and, in

1961, for children who were in foster homes. Also in 1961, in the most significant broadening of the original category, it authorized ADC for children who were dependent because of a parent's unemployment.

For federal administrators, liberalization of the original categories was a slow and unsatisfactory way to achieve adequacy. The Social Security Act had not long been in law before they began to be dissatisfied with the very concept of categorical aid, which was inconsistent with their belief that need ought to be the sole criterion of assistance. For a political reason—resistance of the aged—it was hard to attack the categorical principle; so administrators quickly resorted to the alternative of seeking congressional authorization for federal sharing of the costs of general assistance, the state-local program for supporting the residual group of poor. They got no response. Like the state legislatures before it, Congress preferred to single out for support those groups that seemed not to be at fault for their dependency—the very young, the very old, or the blind.

The administrators' desire, on one hand, to expand federal coverage and Congress' unwillingness, on the other, to accept general expansion resulted in a compromise—gradual expansion through the creation of new categories. In 1950 Congress enacted a program of aid for the poor who were permanently and totally disabled. This grew out of a major attempt by President Truman to liberalize the social insurance program by introducing coverage of disability. Congress, preferring to work through grants to the states, adopted a categorical assistance program instead. This program, along with enactment of ADC-UP in 1961, went far to satisfy the assistance administrators' desire to reach the residual group on general relief.

Other major expansions of the federal program covered medical care. At first, federal assistance grants were given only for cash payments to needy individuals, a definition constructed so narrowly as to discourage state and local maintenance of poorhouses or the giving of aid in kind. However, in order to encourage provision of medical care, Congress in the 1950s amended the

Social Security Act to authorize federal sharing in payments to doctors, hospitals, and other suppliers of such care. Soon the public assistance program became a vehicle for far-reaching extensions of the provision of medical care. In 1960 Congress created a new category, Medical Assistance to the Aged, for those over sixty-five who were not poor enough to be on OAA but too poor to pay medical bills. And five years later, what it did for the aged in 1960 Congress did for other categories of persons defined by the public assistance titles. That is, it authorized a program of aid for the medically indigent, popularly called Medicaid, covering all persons who might, if poor enough, be eligible for public assistance, as well as all children under twenty-one without regard to whether a parent was dead, absent, incapacitated, or unemployed. This program had the potentiality of reaching a huge share of the population. The medical-care amendments of the 1950s grew out of the initiative of federal assistance administrators, but the MAA and Medicaid programs, following the pattern of aid to the disabled, were a more or less accidental outcome of liberal campaigns to broaden the whole social insurance system.

As with grant formulas, then, so with program coverage: federal policy was pieced together through a compromise of the partly conflicting, partly consistent preferences of President, Congress, and bureaucracy. What resulted may not have been an "optimum" policy, if adequacy is regarded as the overriding goal, but it did tend to induce wider coverage. The extent to which federal action actually promoted adequacy had to depend on the response of the states. Because of the limits on its authority imposed by a federal system, the federal government had to pursue its objectives through the method of monetary incentives; whether it achieved those objectives depended fundamentally on the response to the incentives. Massachusetts, as it happened, was extremely responsive.

The State Response

First of all, states have had to decide whether to participate in the federal assistance programs. Given the offer of substantial grants and the lack, thanks to the Virginians in Congress, of major specific conditions touching the states' own level of taxation and expenditure, the probability of their participating was high. By the end of 1937 all but one (Virginia) were getting OAA grants, and it began to do so in 1938; all but ten were taking part in the ADC program, and all but one (Nevada) of those ten had begun to do so by the end of 1943. The subsequent creation of categorical programs also evoked nearly universal participation. States differed in the speed with which they responded, but most did respond eventually.[8]

The decision to participate, of course, is but one element of a state's response to an offer of public assistance grants. States must make for each program a wide range of decisions, including the fundamental ones of who shall be eligible and how large the payments shall be. The very existence of federal aid affects these decisions, but the precise impact of federal action is hard to predict and even to discern after participation in a state program has begun: it depends, as Senator Byrd wished, on the conditions in each state. State policy is a product of federal-state interaction, and that product, in view of the limits on the federal government's ability to define its own policy precisely and to impose that policy on other governments, is shaped by the nature of the institutions, processes, beliefs, values, and patterns of interaction that make up the state's own political system. States that of themselves are "progressive" or "welfare-oriented" or "liberal" are likely to respond to federal incentives quickly and with relatively liberal programs. Other states are likely to respond more slowly and with less generous programs. (This does not mean, though, that federal action magnifies or perpetuates differences among the states—just the reverse: in the absence of federal incentives, some states would not act at all, and others that might act independently become accustomed to waiting for federal action.)

What makes a state liberal is hard to say exactly, but comparative analyses of state welfare expenditures have indicated that certain socioeconomic characteristics—urbanization, industrialization, proportion of foreign stock, the level of per capita income—are very important.[9] Quite likely, it is not these factors per se but related characteristics of the political system that are crucial. Where the population is urbanized, political activity flourishes, facilitated by the ease of communication and organization. Both the politicians' promises and the constituents' demands increase in volume. Pressure groups are active (especially labor unions in an industrialized economy), and awareness of the possibilities of government action spreads among the populace. The presence of a high proportion of foreign stock is significant probably because it indicates the influence of cultures more tolerant than the native Protestant culture toward government activity on behalf of disadvantaged or dependent individuals.

By these theories, federal money would fall on fertile ground in Massachusetts, which to a marked degree has all of the socioeconomic characteristics associated with liberality. It has long been a heavily urbanized and industrialized state, with a high per capita income and a large proportion of foreign stock. Though Republicans regularly controlled the legislature until after World War II it has also been a state with a relatively high degree of party competition, another factor, that, according to political science theory, encourages liberality.[10]

Massachusetts has indeed been a liberal state. As of 1935, when federal aid became law, it had well-established mothers' aid and OAA laws, with average monthly payments in both programs that were the highest in the country. The mothers' aid law, although it did not actually use the term, left no doubt of the legislature's intent that aid should be adequate: "The aid furnished," it said, "shall be sufficient to enable [mothers] to bring up their children properly in their own homes." The OAA law was still more explicit. Section 1 began, "Adequate assistance to deserving citizens . . . seventy years of age or over . . . shall be granted." [11] (The history of OAA legislation in Massachusetts lends support to the theory that party competition is conducive to liberality. Proposals for old-age pensions in the state were made repeatedly after 1903 but did not win support from the Republican Party. In 1930, on the eve of a state election that the Democrats seemed likely to win, Republican leaders of the legislature changed positions and wrote an OAA bill themselves.[12])

Massachusetts qualified for OAA grants in March 1936 and for ADC grants six months later, and it has since been quick to respond, with qualifying legislation and other forms of plan material, to the creation of new federal categories or the broadening of old ones. The effect of federal action in the state has been to encourage further liberality, or adequacy, but it has done this in ways usually indirect and sometimes quite obscure.

Adequacy as Size of Payment

Federal aid appears not to have had much immediate and direct effect on the size of payments in Massachusetts. Precise comparisons of cash grants before and after the beginning of aid are impossible because of the lack of data for the years before it began (one readily discernible effect of federal participation was to improve and standardize the gathering and reporting of statistics). But if federal aid did have much effect, that effect should be evident in a series of years after 1935, for it would almost certainly have been gradual.[13] In fact, in the six years following the start of federal aid, average monthly OAA grants rose but slowly, and ADC grants actually tended to drop. They did not rise even when, after the Social Security Act amendments of 1939, the federal formula was liberalized to provide 50 percent matching, as in OAA.[14]

	OAA	*ADC*
1936	$24.85	$59.18
1937	27.14	60.12
1938	28.01	60.80
1939	28.43	59.72
1940	28.70	58.82
1941	29.06	57.17

In the same period, although federal and state assistance expenditures rose in Massachusetts, local expenditures fell, which suggests that federal aid was being used to cut the local share of payments to OAA and ADC recipients.[15]

Such figures show that federal aid had no substantial short-run impact on payments, but a more careful look suggests that indirectly, and over a somewhat longer period, federal action may have contributed importantly to increasing them. A large increase took place in the 1940s, along with fundamental changes in the processes by which payments were determined. The politics of public assistance budgets came alive in Massachusetts in the late 1930s, and federal action had something to do both with the way in which issues arose and the way in which they were settled.

Briefly, the main events were these: the rise of a powerful old-age lobby; enactment by the legislature of a minimum monthly standard of payment for OAA recipients; the state welfare department's proposal, in response, of a standard budget, by which grants would be determined for each recipient according to his need; the legislature's endorsement of the standard budget, which compelled local agencies to use it; and the legislature's decision, in 1948, that henceforth the standard budget should be automatically adjusted in relation to the cost of living. In most or all of these events, federal action probably had some effect, though the effects were invariably indirect and not always what federal administrators had intended.

The old-age lobby developed in the late 1930s, stimulated apparently by the Depression, action on behalf of the aged by both state and federal governments, and the example of political activity by the aged elsewhere in the country. It is hard to say at just what point the elderly poor in Massachusetts changed from a "potential group," a mass of unorganized people with some shared interests, into an "actual group," in which the shared interests became a basis for organized activity. At the time the state's OAA law was passed, in 1930, the aged were still unorganized and not especially active in agitating for it, though they were an identifiable constituent group to which politicians might appeal. By the late 1930s, they had an organization, the Senior Citizens and Associates of America, and a leader, Charles C. O'Donnell of Lynn,

who did their work at the state house and tutored them in exploiting the state welfare department's procedure for appealing local-
agency decisions. This activity reached a peak in the forties, and
though it later subsided, the lobby maintained a high level of demand. No session of the legislature went by without the submission of several bills.

In dealing with the legislature, this lobby had major assets. People over sixty-five represent a relatively large share of the state's
population (11 percent in 1960, compared with 9 percent for the
nation). They had their own committee, Old Age and Pensions,
which handles at least as much public assistance legislation as the
Committee on Public Welfare. They had the lobbying support of
labor, and often of local public assistance administrators.[16] Besides being more politically aware than other groups of recipients, they obviously were judged to be more deserving of support. Sympathy for them may have been especially strong in a
state where social values in general and politics in particular have
been especially subject to the influence of immigrant cultures,
especially that of the Irish. That the elderly poor deserve generous public support is a proposition with very strong moral as well
as political appeal to legislators whose Catholic upbringing has
imbued them with a strong sense of familial obligation to the
aged, and whose life experience includes observation of widespread poverty among the older generations of their own stock.
Not the least of their assets was O'Donnell himself. He was
stooped with age by the 1960s, but when he made his appeals for
a "crust of bread," they were delivered in a resounding voice and
with considerable flair.

Whatever the combination of reasons, political, moral, and personal, the legislature was highly responsive to the lobby's appeals.
Scarcely a year passed after 1936 without the passage of some
benefit for the aged. Through the legislature, the old-age lobby
had at least as much influence on Massachusetts public assistance
policy as any other organization in the state, including the welfare
department.

One of the lobby's earliest demands was for a statutory standard of payment. The original OAA law had set no standard except the vague one of adequacy. Despite numerous proposals for stipulating a monetary standard, the legislature in 1930 left to administrators—mainly local ones, over whom the state department exercised little authority at this time—the task of deciding what was adequate. As soon as federal aid began, the demand for such a standard was revived, for the federal matching formula provided a rationale. Inspired by the terms of the formula, a legislative commission in 1935 recommended that the legislature set a minimum payment of $30 per recipient per month, the maximum amount that the federal government would match. This was adopted in 1936 along with other changes that flowed from the Social Security Act.[17] When Congress in 1939 raised the federal matching maximum to $40, the Massachusetts legislature soon raised the state minimum accordingly.

These actions gave rise to federal-state tension as well as to intense controversy within the state. The legislature's setting of a statutory minimum was not the kind of response that federal administrators wished. The BPA had raised no objection to the legislature's setting of the $30 minimum in 1936, perhaps because the Bureau was new then and still working out its policies and testing its strength; but by 1939, having come to grips with the Townsend Movement, it knew what it did not want, and it did not want a minimum standard incorporated in the Massachusetts law. The granting of a fixed sum—a "pension" rather than an amount of assistance carefully adjusted to need—was precisely what the federal administration opposed. Over one hundred OAA bills were filed in the 1941 session of the Massachusetts legislature, nearly thirty of which called for a $40 minimum and limiting or prohibiting the deduction of income and other resources. As Welfare Commissioner Arthur G. Rotch routinely passed these proposals along for federal comment, it became clear that the BPA opposed all of them. Though Rotch agreed with the federal policy, he argued that the BPA had to accept a statutory standard because the Massachusetts legislature and others interested in old-age assistance were insisting that "some sum should be set down in the law." [18] The BPA finally agreed that a minimum would be acceptable as long as the law provided for the deduction of income. The BPA regional representative wrote that "it would not be possible for the Social Security Board to say that a [bill] is discriminatory and non-conformity legislation as long as the legislative figure is reasonably related to need, recipients are determined to be 'needy,' and all income and resources are taken into consideration in determining the amount of the grant." [19]

What came out of the legislature, at the end of a prolonged session in which OAA proposals were the major issue, was acceptable to the federal administration, for it did base assistance on need. But it was not acceptable to Governor Leverett Saltonstall, who objected to the inclusion of the $40 minimum even with a provision for deduction of income. Saltonstall twice vetoed the bill, accusing the legislature of raising expenditures without putting up the necessary revenue. The legislature, after repeated all-night sessions, twice passed the bill over his veto.[20]

The state welfare department had asked the legislature, in lieu of setting a minimum, to authorize it to enforce a state-wide standard budget, a set of uniform rules for determining need, resources, and amount of assistance. This was the approach to assistance payments favored by the federal administration and the social-work profession in general. The legislature did not agree to this in 1941, but two years later, following submission of a report on OAA grants by the department, it gave the department what it wanted—and inconsistently retained in the law the $40 minimum.[21] The department's newly acquired authority to enforce a standard budget did not extend to ADC, but the department also tried to get local agencies to use the budget for that category.

The effect of the department's budget rules was quickly apparent. Both OAA and ADC grants rose much faster between 1942 and 1947, the six years following issuance of the standard budget, than they did from 1936 to 1941, the six years following the start of federal aid, despite the fact that there were no increases in matching funds until 1946. These figures show the average monthly cash grant per case:

	OAA	*ADC*
1942	$32.19	$58.56
1943	35.87	67.39
1944	40.08	75.68
1945	42.85	80.75
1946	47.39	86.73
1947	51.61	97.90

Since OAA grants rose by 60 percent in these five years, the old-age lobby might have concluded that the department's judgment in budgetary matters could be trusted. Instead it continued to seek statutory safeguards, an effort that reached a climax in 1948 with the legislature's adoption of the cost-of-living formula. The OAA law was amended to provide that whenever the cost of living rose by 5 percent, using the standard budget of 1947 as a base, cash grants should rise by a like amount. (In 1965, the 5 percent was reduced to 3 percent.) The welfare department extended this procedure to ADC budgets so that, after 1948, in both categories grants rose automatically, independent of changes in the federal matching formula or the political temper of Massachusetts. Having committed itself to this principle, the legislature did not go through an annual debate over appropriations, a debate that in most other states has often ended in failure to appropriate the amount called for by application of the state welfare department's standard budget, and hence a failure to pay recipients 100 percent of need as determined by state administrators.[22] In Massachusetts, adoption of the cost-of-living formula kept the politics of public assistance budgets subdued.

The federal influence in all of these events is hard to state exactly, but if the Social Security Act had never been passed, assistance policy in Massachusetts would surely have evolved differently. Federal action stimulated the demands of the OAA lobby, shaped their content, and, by providing money, enabled the legislature to be more generous. Federal action, then, did promote adequacy of payments. At the same time, by its insistence on the strict application of a standard of need and the deduction of income from individual grants, the federal administration constrained the state government's generosity toward the aged. Although federal action stimulated demands from the OAA lobby and facilitated a response to them, the preoccupation with need placed controversial limitations on the nature of the response.*

Adequacy as Program Coverage

The federal effect on program coverage has been more direct and visible than that on size of payments. Because federal grants are offered for aid to certain categories of the poor, categories more inclusive than most states cover independently, the very act of accepting federal grants is often tantamount to an extension of coverage. This process of extension can be divided into two phases: the broadening of those categories (OAA and ADC) that already existed in most states when federal aid began and the creation of new categories (DA, MAA, and MA). In both, federal definitions of program scope were quickly reflected in Massachusetts policy.

* The conflict of 1941 over the legislature's enactment of a minimum standard of payment was the beginning, not the end, of this problem. Federal administrators continued to try to check the recurring tendency in the state to make gratuitous additions to OAA grants. Except for their efforts, OAA payments in Massachusetts might have gone higher still. The case of "free cash" illustrates the kind of issue that arose. In 1951 the legislature raised the monthly minimum for OAA payments to $75 (which, unlike earlier minimums, was not based on the federal matching formula—it was $25 more than the matching maximum then in effect). As a result, some recipients got more than they "needed," according to state budget standards. The excess of the statutory minimum over budgeted need was referred to as "free cash." The welfare department ruled that recipients who had medical expenses must use their free cash for that purpose. The public assistance program would pay for only those medical expenses in any month that exceeded the amount of free cash received in that month. In 1956 the legislature tried to supersede the department's rule with a law protecting the recipient's claim to the free cash, but Governor Christian A. Herter, acting on the recommendation of the welfare department, vetoed the bill. The department insisted on the free-cash rule, a state report explained, because the federal administration objected to provision of a grant that exceeded the standard of need. Mass., *Report Submitted by the Legislative Research Council Relative to Public Welfare and Old Age Assistance*, Feb. 11, 1957, House No. 3070, 69–76. This source describes as well a similar issue that arose when the federal administration complained that the Massachusetts standards of assistance failed to require the deduction of cash gifts, money that recipients got from friends, private social agencies, or relatives who were not legally liable for their support.

Broadening of the Original Categories. When federal aid began, the OAA program in Massachusetts was five years old, the ADC program, twenty-three. Caseloads in both had been rising steadily in the 1930s, but the rise became very much steeper after the start of federal grants in 1936. The following list of active cases shows what happened.[23]

	OAA	*ADC*
1930	—	2,795
1931	8,376	2,982
1932	16,802	3,379
1933	18,399	3,912
1934	20,320	4,123
1935	24,303	4,418
1936	45,276	5,082
1937	63,852	7,163
1938	73,772	9,282
1939	81,359	11,301 (est.)

The sharp increase after 1936 occurred because federal action had stimulated Massachusetts to broaden its standards of eligibility. In the OAA program, the link between federal stimulus and state response was plain. Before the Social Security Act was passed, state law set an age requirement of seventy and a residence requirement of twenty years. Reductions in both were being considered even before the act, and federal action precipitated the change. In 1936 the legislature reduced the age limit to sixty-five even though the Social Security Act would have permitted retention of the higher standard until 1940, and it reduced the residence requirement to conform to the maximum permitted by the act—five of the nine years preceding application, including the immediately preceding year. In the ADC program, the link between federal and state action was more subtle. The statutory changes in eligibility standards that flowed from provisions of federal law were minor. Before federal aid began, the Massachusetts law had applied to "all mothers and their dependent children under the age of sixteen." There was a residence requirement of three years. After the Social Security Act, the state statute was changed to embody federal definitions of eligibility. The list of possible caretakers was extended to include, besides the mother, eleven other classes of near relatives, but a requirement that the caretaker be "fit" and that home surroundings be such as to make for good character was not changed. A dependent child was defined as one "under the age of sixteen who has been deprived of parental support or care by reason of the death, continued absence from the home or physical or mental incapacity of a parent." The residence requirement was reduced from three years to one. It is hard to say just how important these changes were, but surely they were not important enough to account for the ensuing sharp rise in the caseload. The expanded definition of caretaker might have been crucial, except that the earlier law had not been interpreted strictly; aid had always gone to a few cases in which a relative other than the mother cared for the child. Besides, of the more than 2,000 new cases in 1937, only 438 were ones in which the caretaker relative was not the mother. The greatest portion of the increase occurred from including mothers who had not been included before.

Very probably, the sharp rise can be attributed to a relaxed interpretation of the fit-parent clause, a change that took place not in response to formal federal requirements, for none had been imposed, but in response to the opportunity to share the costs of ADC with the federal government. Unfit mothers, if excluded from ADC, either had to be not supported at all or had to be supported on general relief, the cost of which was borne exclusively by state and local governments. It appears that the state revised its concept of morality. Local administrators had set a pattern for this response. In the early thirties, in order to shift more of the cost of relief to the state, they began putting on mothers' aid persons who previously would have been regarded as unfit. In 1932 the state supervisor of mothers' aid reported: "Hitherto Mothers' Aid has been granted only to the best type of mothers, but recently . . . some local boards are extending [it] to any mother who may possibly come within the law. Fitness of the mother and her maintenance of good standards of home and child care must still be insisted upon." [24] Yet when the state faced a similar opportunity to shift costs, it made a similar response. New state rules issued on January 1, 1937, stipulated that women who had borne illegitimate children would no longer be barred from aid.[25] The consequences of broadening the interpretation of fitness (and acceptance of illegitimacy undoubtedly was not the only change) are suggested by the figures below, which give the proportion of widows in the ADC caseload for selected years. Begun as a program primarily for widows, mothers' aid was very gradually extended to others. As of 1935 the proportion of widows was about 70 percent and was falling at the rate of about 1 percent a year. By 1942 it was below 50 percent and by 1956 had fallen to 10 percent.[26]

1920	84.0%
1925	81.3
1930	75.8
1935	70.9
1936	68.3
1937	63.0
1938	56.2
1942	47.4
1948	32.6
1956	10.4

Eventually, a rise in the general incidence of broken families must have contributed to this trend, as did the provision of social security benefits to surviving dependents of deceased participants in that program. But it is clear that what set it off in the first place was a federally stimulated change in state assistance policy. ADC in Massachusetts began to be a program predominantly for the divorced and the deserted almost from the moment federal aid began.

Subsequent increases in the state's ADC caseload, which rose from 12,600 to 27,600 between 1956 and 1966, also resulted to some extent from federally inspired liberalizations of the category. Massachusetts responded promptly to federal increases in 1956 and 1965 in the age limit for dependent children and to the federal offer, first made in 1961, of aid to children who were dependent because of a parent's unemployment.[27] (Federal coverage, beginning in 1950, of the caretaker relative had no effect in Massachusetts because the state program already extended that far.)

Creation of New Categories. How quickly a state government responds to federal aid depends in part on whether the grant is for an activity in which it is already engaged. To the extent that a response entails new expenditures by the recipient government, the response is likely to be slow. To the extent that a response entails transfer of the costs of existing programs to the federal government, it is likely to be swift. A state in which there is a high level of government activity (a "liberal" state, in respect to public assistance) is likely to respond quickly to federal aid for two kinds of reasons. First, there is the political reason: whatever features of the state's politics account for the high level of government activity in the first place—say, much pressure-group activity or a competitive party system—will make it very sensitive to federal stimuli. Second, there is the economic reason: opportunities to transfer program costs will be greatest for those state governments whose program costs are already high.

The generally swift response to federal grants for OAA and ADC may be accounted for partly by the fact that state and local governments were already engaged in such programs. Although the federal grant programs required new expenditures by many states, they also enabled major transfers of existing costs. The situation was different with respect to the creation of the new categories, DA, MAA, and MA, but only in degree. Participation in these federal categories generally required of the recipient governments more new activity than had federal grants for OAA and ADC, but here again there were opportunities for transfers: the new programs were not altogether new. Disabled and medically indigent persons had to some extent been aided under general relief, and the traditional categorical programs had also been vehicles for providing medical assistance. In determining eligibility and assistance under these categories, states in varying degrees took medical needs into account.

Massachusetts, as a liberal state, responded promptly to all new federal programs, but to none more promptly than those for medical assistance. Provision of medical care, as much as any other aspect of its public assistance policy, distinguished Massachusetts from most other states. After the mid-1950s its rates of medical expenditure for public assistance recipients were among the highest in the nation.[28] This meant that it would be extremely sensitive to federal action in this field and would respond with alacrity to any offer of federal aid.

Like much else in the Massachusetts program, the origins of the state's medical-care policy can be traced to the demands of the old-age lobby. Before 1945 the provision of medical care had been left to the discretion of local agencies,[29] but in that year the legislature established a state policy with the following amendment to the OAA law: Old-age assistance shall "provide for adequate medical care for every recipient of assistance . . . and shall also include provision for the services of a physician of such recipient's choice, subject to such rules and regulations as shall be made by the department." [30] The state welfare department first responded to this by requiring local agencies to submit medical plans for its approval, a practice that still left much room for local variation. But several years later, in 1954, it issued a plan of its own, defining in liberal, comprehensive terms the care that must be provided and setting forth fee schedules it had negotiated with medical organizations. Federal action did not contribute to this development except by removing one obstacle to it. If the federal ban on payments other than to recipients of assistance had not been removed in 1950, the plan could not have been carried out, for it depended on the use of indirect or "vendor" payments.[31]

In the first full year following promulgation of the state plan, OAA medical vendor payments in Massachusetts amounted to over $23 million. In the year preceding enactment of the federal MAA program, they reached $40.5 million, approaching one half of the state's OAA expenditures of $96.4 million. The federal government contributed to these expenditures of course, but the federal matching maximum was such—or, to put it otherwise, the state's liberality was such—that Massachusetts was still spending far more for medical care in OAA than the federal government would participate in. This situation formed the background for the state's response to the MAA program, which gave Massachusetts an opportunity to transfer more than 15,000 OAA cases to the new category and thereby obtain from the federal government a higher share of the cost of supporting them, inasmuch as the grant formula in MAA (free of a matching maximum) was much more generous than in OAA. About $12 million a year in state and local costs could be transferred.

The state welfare department was in the greatest possible hurry to obtain federal funds under the new program. Commissioner Patrick A. Tompkins sent on enabling bill to the legislature through the governor in late September, a month after the federal act was passed, urging it to act "forthwith" if the state were "to receive Federal grants that are available beginning October 1 to the amount of almost $1,000,000 for the first month of operation." [32] By late November Massachusetts had enacted an MAA law, the second state in the country to do so; by December the department had submitted plan material to the BPA, although the bureau had not yet developed guidance; and by late March Tompkins had elicited approval of the state plan retroactive to October 1, the date the federal program went into effect. Speed, however, was attained at some cost: preparation and approval of the Massachusetts MAA plan had been so hasty that the contents continued for several years to be a source of difficulty in federal-state relations.

The state welfare department's response to the MAA law was so fast that a desire to economize may not alone explain it. Another explanation might be found in the nature of the department's role within the state's political system, certain features of which make the department highly sensitive to federally sponsored opportunities for action. The new federal offer of aid gave the department a rare and attractive opportunity to take the initiative in program expansion.

One of the effects of the combined aggressiveness of the old-age lobby and the legislature in Massachusetts was to put the state welfare department on the defensive (a situation reinforced by the inhibiting effect of the long tradition of local-agency independence). The department was in the embarrassing position of opposing legislation as often as proposing it. For years it struggled—unsuccessfully, as a glance at the OAA law will show—to protect its authority against a mass of statutory prescription. Federal action, insofar as it encouraged the old-age lobby to make demands but discouraged the department from yielding to demands that violated federal concepts of equity, tended to strengthen the pattern of legislative initiative and departmental resistance.

Governors, from whom the department had to draw political support, showed very little interest in it or its programs.[33] Like the department, they were on the defensive; it was they who had to put forth the revenue proposals to pay for the legislature's generosity to the aged. Saltonstall's fight with the legislature in 1941 shows how strongly he, for one, objected. To serve the governor's interests, the department had to prevent legislation more often than it had to promote it.[34] Against this background, Commissioner Tompkins' haste to get an MAA program under way becomes even more understandable. He wanted, as one source in the department suggested, "to make hay with the governor" by showing skill in obtaining federal money. At the same time, the department might for once cater to the legislature's abiding interest in providing benefits to the aged.

When the federal MA program was enacted in 1965, it too offered Massachusetts a chance to "save" money by transferring to the federal government a substantial amount of the cost of medical care already being supplied to public assistance recipients. Despite the benefits gained from MAA, Massachusetts was still, mainly because of the liberality of its medical programs, spending much more for assistance than the federal government would match. By participating in MA, the state would immediately receive an estimated $15.6 million a year more in federal money just for continuing its present level of medical assistance to the poor. There was never any doubt, therefore, that the state would participate. The only question was how far it should extend coverage. How should it define the medically indigent? Political party competition worked to produce a liberal definition.

The state welfare department, with the approval of Lieutenant-Governor Elliot Richardson, who had charge of welfare programs under the administration of Governor John Volpe, proposed to cover those people who, in addition to having specified levels of income and medical need, would be eligible under the established assistance categories. This was narrower coverage than the federal law authorized, for it would have excluded children in families that did not meet ADC eligibility standards. That is, it would have excluded, no matter what the family income, children in families where the father was present and employed. The administration proposed to defer coverage of such children until January 1, 1969.

This plan was submitted to the legislature in the summer of 1966, four months before an election in which Governor Volpe would be a candidate for re-election and Richardson a candidate for attorney-general. It might have been vulnerable to attack at any time in view of the liberality of the legislature and the high degree of party competition in the state, but coming from a Republican administration to a Democratic legislature shortly before a major election, it was especially so. Democratic legislative leaders said the proposal was "shockingly deficient," a "do-nothing Medicaid program," and called Richardson to account in public hearings. Senator Edward M. Kennedy, speaking at a fund-raising dinner for Democratic state senators, charged Volpe with "failing to take full advantage of the Federal programs enacted in Washington." [35] Giving in quickly, the governor announced that the administration would cover the additional children immediately. A program in any degree less liberal, even temporarily, than what the federal government would match had proved to be untenable.

The Consequences of Federal Financing

The Massachusetts public assistance program of the 1960s might or might not seem adequate, depending on the social and political perspectives of the viewer, but it was surely "more adequate" than when federal aid began, and federal aid plainly helped to make it so.[36] Assistance payments in general were higher and program coverage was broader than they would have been in the absence of federal action. On the other hand, the federal influence was so limited and indirect that it did not result in outcomes precisely of federal choosing. State decisions about size of payments and standards of eligibility, though subject to federal *influence,* were not subject to federal *control,* even insofar as control might be said to result from the attachment of conditions to grants that, in principle, the state might choose not to receive.

In the categories for which federal aid was first offered, cash payments were approximately tripled. The average cash grant per OAA case per month in 1936 was $24.85; in 1966 it was $80.39, and the average expenditure (cash grant plus vendor payments) was $93.55. The average cash grant per ADC case in 1936 was $59.18; in 1966 it was $172.45, and the average expenditure was $191.88. These were substantial increases, even allowing for a decline of about 50 percent in the value of the dollar. The more striking change in the state's program, however, and the one most clearly reflecting the impact of federal action, was the expansion of categories.

In 1936, when federal aid began, nearly two thirds of the cases in Massachusetts were being assisted under general relief; by

1966 this proportion had shrunk to 8 percent. Many factors accounted for the change, including the decline of unemployment and the increase of family disintegration as causes of dependency, but federal action, by stimulating the creation of new categories and broadening eligibility standards for old ones, was perhaps most important. These are the figures for the average number of cases per month, by category.[37]

	OAA	ADC	DA	MAA	GR	Total	GR as % of Total
1936	33,484	4,741	—	—	66,585	104,810	63.5%
1966	49,208	27,646	13,507	6,229	8,332	104,922	7.9

For recipients of public assistance, expansion of the categories meant that cash grants in general were larger. Over the course of half a century in Massachusetts, recipients were slowly shifted from a locally financed program conceived as a way of providing the barest subsistence to the poor to a series of programs with federal and state financial support and conceived as a way of providing "adequate" assistance. Whatever its precise effect on the size of payments within any given category, it is clear that, by stimulating enlargement of the categories, federal action did promote adequacy. The average monthly expenditure per case in 1966 as compared to 1936 was:

	OAA	ADC	DA	MAA	GR
1936	$24.85	$ 59.18	$ —	$ —	$26.37
1966	93.55	191.88	139.78	199.40	94.37

For state and local governments, expansion of the categories, combined with a rising standard of assistance payments, meant that their own expenditures rose even as federal expenditures and the federal *share* of expenditures rose. Under the stimulus of federal action, they carried out programs more generous than the independently financed program of general relief. The substitution of federal expenditures for local ones in Massachusetts, which took place to a slight extent immediately after the start of federal aid, did not last long. Whereas total expenditures by the cities and towns dropped after federal aid began, their expenditures for OAA and ADC rose. The following tabulation summarizes trends in intergovernmental expenditure for Massachusetts.

	Federal		*State*		*Cities and Towns*	
	Amount	*%*	*Amount*	*%*	*Amount*	*%*
1936	$ 4,967,943	14.8	$ 8,501,226	25.3	$20,117,083	59.9
1946	20,635,847	33.7	23,592,125	38.5	17,030,676	27.8
1956	47,581,642	37.0	50,287,024	39.2	30,621,722	23.8
1966	109,544,571	46.7	76,371,799	32.5	48,718,061	20.8

For federal administrators, federal grants are a means of access to state and local programs, and the steady substitution of federally aided programs for general relief thus meant more opportunities to influence state and local action. Whereas most state and local program activity in 1936 was beyond their reach, by 1966 very little was.

4 | Equity of Administration

If adequacy has been a first and fundamental goal of federal public assistance policy, its twin is equity. Federal administrators were determined that state programs should be fair. Equity, or fairness, might mean many things, but above all it was considered to mean uniformity: like cases must be treated alike.

The statutory basis for the requirement of uniformity is a provision in each of the public assistance titles of the Social Security Act that state plans must be "in effect in all political subdivisions of the State, and if administered by them, be mandatory upon them." This language was adopted in 1935 and has not been changed since.

Had Congress been willing to go so far, uniformity might have been required for the nation as a whole. By enacting detailed laws itself or giving federal administrators broad authority to make rules, Congress might have created through the medium of conditional grants a truly national assistance program. Inevitably, federal activity has had some equalizing effect on the states: programs spread as federal funds became available, and interstate differences in payment levels have diminished—diminished, but not disappeared, for Congress characteristically chose to preserve a large area of independence for state governments in matters of substance. The result is that federal administrators have had to seek standards of uniformity primarily *within* states rather than *among* them.

Federal administrators have sought uniformity in all aspects of state assistance programs. In their view, rules relating to the recruitment of social workers or to the determination of their salaries and travel allowances must be applied just as uniformly as those having to do directly with the treatment of recipients. Among all rules, however, the ones clearly most relevant to the realization of equity are those covering eligibility, need, and amount of assistance.

At first federal administrators concentrated on obtaining state-wide coverage, using the language of the Social Security Act to bring about the participation of all local units. The law was interpreted as requiring state-wide operation, but not necessarily uniformity. In the 1930s administrators did not attempt to require that standards of need and assistance be alike in all local units. They appear to have expected that the requirement of state-wide operation, combined with that of the state's sharing of assistance costs, would induce the states themselves to bring about uniformity; but by the 1940s it had become clear that this would not happen unless the requirements were amplified. Intrastate disparities in payments persisted, depending, federal administrators assumed, on the differing fiscal capacities of local governments. In states where local units could exercise discretion in raising their share of costs, such disparities were sure to develop.[1]

In 1946 the Social Security Board asked Congress to attack the problem of intrastate differences in payments by requiring states to adopt an equalizing formula for distributing assistance funds to local governments. Congress declined—what it would not do itself vis-à-vis state governments, it would not compel the states to do vis-à-vis their local governments [2]—but it did increase the federal matching share. On the strength of this change and its own authority, the Board began pressing the states to adopt state-wide standards of need and assistance. In the fall of 1946 the BPA called state commissioners to Washington to discuss program objectives.[3] They were told that they must develop state-wide budgets setting forth the consumption items (food, clothing, shelter, and such) to which recipients were entitled, definitions of whatever additional items were available, the dollar-and-cents amounts to be included in the budget for each item, and a uniform method for determining the recipients' resources. Three years later, in a second attempt to strengthen its statutory position, the Social Security Administration asked Congress to require state-wide standards of need and assistance. Congress would not do this either, but that did not alter the determination of the SSA, which by now was applying the requirement of state-wide operation as if it were a requirement of uniformity. Some states resisted, especially New York, whose welfare commissioner preferred to allow each county to set its own standards. But when that dispute was settled in 1951, the establishment of state-wide standards of need and assistance ceased to be a significant issue in federal-state relations. The states in general were conforming to federal policy.[4]

The requirement of state-wide operation helped to promote the achievement of adequacy. Sponsors and administrators of federal grants had from the start expected that this requirement would broaden coverage and raise grants (in conjunction with the requirement of state financial participation), especially in the poor localities. The possibility of using it for that purpose became even more apparent as time passed. Lacking the authority to set standards of assistance, federal administrators had no direct way of achieving adequacy. Instead they seized upon the partial solution of compelling states to set such standards on the ground that the principle of state-wide operation, reinterpreted to mean state-wide uniformity, required them. Thus the requirement of state-wide operation, which Congress had sanctioned with a statutory condition, was used as a means to the end of adequacy, which Congress had not so sanctioned. Indeed, the uniformity requirement gave federal administrators access to the entire range of state rules. In the course of insisting that rules be uniform, federal administrators could influence their content. A procedural requirement became a means for realizing substantive ends.

Equity, in the federal view, has aspects other than uniformity. Federal administrators have also sought to protect the dignity of recipients and to establish procedural safeguards for their benefit. Congress has shared this concern sufficiently to put a few such safeguards into law. The Social Security Act requires states to grant a fair hearing to any individual whose claim for assistance is denied or "not acted upon with reasonable promptness," terms added in 1950. Since 1939 the act has protected the anonymity of recipients by requiring states to "provide safeguards which restrict the use or disclosure of information concerning [them]." [5] It has always required that assistance payments to individuals be made directly so as to safeguard their independence.

These provisions have not gone as far as federal administrators would like. Many of them have been professional social workers, with the profession's commitment to "therapeutic" treatment of the poor. Had they been free to make federal policy by themselves, that policy surely would have gone farther toward preventing state and local efforts to impose upon the poor officially defined standards of right conduct. (Professional social workers generally call such efforts "punitive"; I will call them "moralistic.") Federal law, say, might have prohibited the states from imposing moralistic eligibility standards, or might have required that state plans include safeguards for the privacy of recipients. Congress, however, has been sympathetic to the moralistic practices of state and local governments. Its attitude has been expressed, for example, in action with respect to fathers who have deserted their families. In 1950 it enacted the so-called NOLEO amendment, which requires that state and local agencies notify law-enforcement officials when they give ADC to families that have been deserted. Federal administrators carried this out cautiously, for they preferred to concentrate on reconciling the family rather than punishing the father. And they did not share the belief of Congress that punitive action would cause fathers to increase support payments.

Lacking support from Congress, federal administrators have had, in attacking moralism in particular states, to rely upon their powers of persuasion and such fragments of authority as the Social Security Act supplied. They did not attempt a general attack until the 1960s, when the increasing visibility of welfare and civil rights issues moved them to do so. In 1961 the BPA announced that a state could not deny ADC to a child on the ground of an unsuitable home as long as the child remained in the home—this following a flagrant, well-publicized incident in Louisiana, where 23,000 children were removed from the ADC rolls in 1960 because their mothers had had an illegitimate child while receiving assistance.[6] And in 1966, after a wave of political activity associated with the antipoverty program—much of it expressed in vehement criticism of public assistance—the BFS issued a new directive requiring that state plans "include policies and procedures for determination of eligibility . . . that respect the rights of individuals . . . and not result in practices that violate the individual's privacy or personal dignity, or harass him, or violate his constitutional rights." [7] The directive said that states must especially guard against entering a home by force or without permission, making home visits outside of working hours, and searching the home for clues to possible deception.

Although technically it applied to state plans for all categories, implicitly this directive was also addressed to the treatment of ADC recipients. Manifestations of state and local moralism have been almost exclusively confined to this category, with its high incidence of desertion, divorce, and illegitimacy.

Equity in Massachusetts

As with adequacy, so with equity, or any other federal objective: the ability to realize the objective in any given state depends heavily on the state's political system.

To federal administrators, what seemed most relevant to their drive for intrastate uniformity was the locus of responsibility for administration. Uniformity seemed to depend primarily on whether the state administered assistance itself or left it up to local units. Publicly and officially, the federal administrators' position has been that state and local administration are both acceptable as long as federal standards are met, but in practice they have found that standards are more likely to be met if administration is performed by the state. Privately, therefore, they preferred that form.

Where administration is left to local agencies, as it was in Massachusetts until 1968, the degree of uniformity depends on the capacity of the state agency to supervise them effectively, and this in turn may depend on many factors, including the number and size of the local units, the degree of socioeconomic diversity within the state, the interest of the governor and legislature in assistance programs, the energy and competence of state administrators, the activity of state-wide pressure groups, and the state's traditional division of roles and powers in regard to its local governments.

Massachusetts was a special case because of the very great decentralization of its administrative structure. Once federal policy began to stress uniformity, Massachusetts with its myriad agencies became a chronic source of problems. No matter what the new federal or state rule, federal administrators always wondered whether all those agencies could be made to comply. Yet the problem may not have been so great as the numbers made it seem, or at least the number of local agencies may not have been a reliable index to the size of the uniformity problem in Massachusetts. It may plausibly be argued (though federal and state administrators would never have so argued, so intimidated were they by the numbers) that the very smallness of local units in Massachusetts rendered them vulnerable to state supervision. By contrast, where local units are large and have well-developed governments—such as the counties in California—it may be harder for a state agency to control them. Generally, it is the biggest local places that are freest of state supervision; in Massachusetts, Boston went almost completely unsupervised. Most of the agencies in Massachusetts were in small towns and consisted of only one or two employees. If the state could control their actions, it controlled the entire agency.

Whatever the plausibility of this argument, it would be relevant to the situation in Massachusetts only if the state welfare agency had enough capacity for supervision to take advantage of the local agencies' vulnerability, but that capacity was not very high. Most of the department's field staff had no special qualifications or training other than experience as local workers. They tended to function not as interpreters of state policy or supervisors of local administration, but as reviewers of routine entries in case records. Federal administrative reviews criticized their performance as too narrowly conceived, and local directors complained that they were ill-informed and their activities poorly coordinated. Local administrators, when charged with failure to conform to state policies, were likely to reply with a certain amount of pique that the state did not know what its policies were—that different field representatives and different district offices interpreted the policy manual in different ways.

The combination of a fragmented structure and a struggling but not very strong state agency meant that the Massachusetts situation was very likely to produce federal-state tensions, and it did, constantly. But the issues were not as grave as they might have been, given the characteristics of the structure, for there *were* important countervailing forces. The legislature in Massachusetts has long done much lawmaking for the cities and towns, despite their reputation for insularity and independence. The home-rule movement, which after the turn of the century left its mark on state constitutions throughout the nation, came last of all to New England. Massachusetts did not adopt a home-rule amendment until 1966. Neither in form nor in practice was the legislature restrained before then from making the most detailed decisions about seemingly local matters. Moreover, it is a legislature quite open to public pressure; [8] in the field of public assistance, as we have seen, it has been particularly responsive to the demands of the old-age lobby. This went far to overcome local separatism with respect to those matters in which the legislature showed an interest, among which was the crucial matter of a state standard budget.

If the fragmentation of its administrative structure made Massachusetts a likely source of uniformity problems, there was also reason to expect conflict with the federal administration over equity in its second sense: respect for individual rights.

It is hard to be sure what social or political circumstances lead one state to be more stringent than another in treatment of the poor, but one such factor may be ethnic prejudice. Punitive policies—and hence rights issues—are likely to develop where an ethnic group is discriminated against, especially if that group is disproportionately represented among the poor. The conflict with Louisiana in 1960–61 over the removal of 23,000 children from the rolls because their homes were judged unsuitable apparently fitted such a pattern: 95 percent of the children were Negroes. Massachusetts was less likely than most other states to pose issues of this kind. It has a relatively small Negro population and no significant history of discrimination against Negroes—quite the reverse. Its historically subject minority, the Irish, was running the state and many of its cities at the time the federal public assistance program began. The problem in Massachusetts arose from other sources.

Where there is a general tendency toward moralism in public affairs (where, that is, a tendency to put moral standards into law is characteristic of the local "culture"), such a tendency is likely to be manifested in the public assistance program. In Massachusetts, public policy has had a strongly puritanical case no matter whether Yankee Protestants or Irish Catholics were in charge of it, and public assistance laws are but one manifestation of this phenomenon. The OAA law until 1961 applied only to "deserving" persons and until 1968 asserted the obligation of children to support their parents. Over the objection of the welfare department, the legislature incorporated children's-responsibility provisions in the MAA law as well. This was not done from reluctance to spend public money for old people who were poor and sick—in MAA as in OAA, the legislature enacted standards of need and assistance that were relatively liberal—but in order to assert a moral principle. When the welfare commissioner protested the legislature's action to Senate President John E. Powers, Powers replied by citing the Fifth Commandment.[9] In ADC, aid was available only to mothers who were "fit" to bring up their children and who maintained homes "such as to make for good character." The values that suffused state law could be expected also to suffuse the attitudes and behavior of many public assistance employees.

Finally, another factor is the degree to which assistance administration is professionalized. The notion that the poor should not be discriminated against—should not be subject to undignified treatment because of their poverty or their "immorality," if and when the two coincide—is presumably much more prevalent among those who have received social-work training than among those who have not. In states where public assistance is professionalized—where policymaking is dominated by the administrative agency, and the administrative agency is dominated by trained social workers—policy and practices can be expected to conform to federal preferences. But this has not been the case in most states, and certainly not in Massachusetts, where a somewhat professionalized but also somewhat passive state department has shared policymaking functions with an aggressive legislature and, until 1968, shared administrative functions with a large number of almost completely unprofessionalized local agencies. Both policymaking and administration in Massachusetts have been open to the influence of nonprofessionals, and the more discretion rested with local agencies, the greater the nonprofessional influence was. It was at the local level that administrative officials themselves were least professionalized, and, perhaps more important, it was there that they were most exposed to the opinions of laymen: local directors bore responsibility directly to a citizen board and lacked the support for professional opinions that may be had from working in a large organization of fellow professionals. They worked in city or town halls, among local politicians and administrators of other functions, where they found little enthusiasm for the values of the social-work profession. As one local director explained to a university workshop:

I do think the feeling that people have towards assistance, especially general assistance and A.D.C. aggravates and complicates our problems . . .

When actually administering the program in the community where the recipients live among the non-recipients one gets to realize that the prevailing attitude in general is a

"Newburgh" attitude. This may be due in a large extent to the expanding of public welfare programs from year to year by substantial amendments to the Social Security Act. But it seems to be quite obvious that there is a wide gap between the thinking on the national level and the thinking of people in the communities and the neighborhoods . . .

The general public does not know what you are talking about when you talk about professional competence, and the need for better skills. *A good administrator* is one who can keep chiselers off the rolls—public welfare administration is as simple as that to them! [10]

Equity as Uniformity: Size of Payment

In 1935, the amount of aid given in Massachusetts varied greatly from place to place. The welfare department had developed a crude budget table for mothers' aid, but it was not binding. For OAA and mothers' aid, local agencies decided how much should be spent in each case, just as they did for general relief.

The first major limitation on local discretion came in 1936 when the legislature stipulated a $30 monthly minimum for OAA payments, a figure that was chosen because it was the maximum the federal government would match (it was raised to $40 after the matching maximum was similarly raised). The state department was hesitant to impose a standard budget, but in 1942 it did so, an action precipitated by the old-age lobby. This document contained detailed instructions for determining need, resources, and amount of assistance. The department did not say flatly that local agencies must follow this guide, but in 1943 the legislature required them to use it in OAA, and the department also sought to compel use of it in ADC. A state study in 1942 showed how much local budgeting practices had varied. City officials were likely to adapt payment to need according to a locally devised budget; rural agencies usually granted the minimum stipulated in the law (in effect, treating it as a maximum), with the result that rural grants were lower. Yet there were great differences among cities too; as of May 1941, the proportion of people receiving more than the statutory minimum of $30 a month ranged from less than 1 percent in one city to 57 percent in another.[11] Variations undoubtedly were even greater for ADC, for which no statutory minimum existed.

Federal administrative reviews show that the mandatory budget was a highly effective rule almost from the start. Conformance was achieved quickly in OAA, and after 1946, when the welfare department successfully sought a law that required the budget in ADC, federal reviews generally showed widespread conformance in all categories. They sometimes revealed a high incidence of error, apparently attributable to administrative inefficiency (such as failure to make prompt adjustments for cost-of-living increases) or the great complexity of budget rules, but no willful defiance of the standards. The budget was effective both because it had statutory sanction and because compliance was readily verifiable. To enforce it, state field representatives had only to check computations on budget sheets in case records, a method of supervision so convenient that their critics thought they relied on it excessively, at the sacrifice of other rules whose content was less specific.

With the law compelling use of a state budget, along with others making cost-of-living adjustments mandatory and stipulating the local share of costs, the Massachusetts legislature took away from local governments virtually all of their discretion with respect to assistance expenditures. Beginning in the 1940s, city and town governments had automatically to appropriate whatever was necessary to satisfy state laws and rules—much as Congress, under the terms of its promise to the states, had automatically to appropriate whatever was necessary to match state and local expenditures.[12] The federal role in this development was limited. The Massachusetts welfare department issued a standard budget several years before the federal administration began pressing states to do so. Yet had Massachusetts not acted when it did, federal requirements would have compelled it to act sooner or later,

and even as of 1942 the Massachusetts welfare department justified its budget rules to local agencies partly for the reason that
they conformed to federal expectations.

The effect of the state standard budget, and indirectly of the
federal requirement of uniformity, may be seen by comparing expenditure data for one of the federally aided categories and for
general relief, which until 1968 was not subject to state rules.[13]
The table below shows the grant per recipient per month for ADC
and for general relief in 1965 for the caseloads of five groups of
local places in Massachusetts, differentiated by size and social
class. My hypothesis was that urban places would be more liberal
than rural ones and that there would be a positive correlation between the status of the population (as measured by median family
income) and assistance grants.[14]

	ADC Grant Per Recipient Per Month	GR Grant Per Recipient Per Month
Rural towns	$40.16	$21.01
Urban lower-middle-class towns	40.93	24.79
Urban middle-class towns	40.53	25.79
Urban upper-middle-class towns	41.56	36.97
Cities	43.99	38.75

The next table compares ADC and general relief payments per
recipient per month for the 29 places (the "cities" in the preceding table) with 100 or more ADC cases as of July 1965.

	Range	Average Deviation	Standard Deviation
ADC	$35.93–51.86	$ 1.92	$ 2.76
GR	16.37–91.33	16.08	20.60

The data show far more variation for general relief than for ADC, both among the 29 cities considered individually and among the grouped cities and towns. (And what they show for ADC is greater than what actually existed.[15]) The hypotheses with respect to rural-urban and class differences were fully confirmed by the general relief data: urban payments were higher than rural ones, and there was a positive correlation between size of payment and status of the place. The rural-urban difference held for ADC too, but was much smaller. The class correlation did not hold. In sum, the state standard budget went far toward assuring uniformity of payment.

The standard budget cannot guarantee absolute uniformity, for it must permit the use of discretion in at least a few matters. As of 1965, the state allowed local agencies to add to the standard budget in three ways: by increasing rental allowances, either in individual cases or city-wide; by granting special needs, such as for "nursing or housekeeping services and . . . laundry, household chores, telephone, special diet, etc."; and by granting nonrecurring needs, which were special needs that did not persist, such as "expenses for moving, storage of furniture, replacement of household furnishings after a disaster, unusual household repairs, etc." [16] The figures above suggest that city agencies were more likely than those in the towns to add on to the basic budget with allowances for rent or special needs, but even where local agencies used their discretion to grant marginal extras, the extras were but a small fraction of total expenditures. Most assistance as of 1965 was being dispensed in conformance with the detailed specifications of the state standard budget.[17]

Equity as Uniformity: Determination of Eligibility in ADC

How much aid recipients shall receive is one major question of public assistance administration; the other is who shall receive it.

This particular decision is harder to supervise and control than decisions about budgets. Much depends on how the administering agency—the local agency, in the Massachusetts case, until 1968—treats an application for assistance. No matter what the rules say, it may discourage the making of written applications and may fail to record oral inquiries. If it fails to keep records of these matters, its actions are inaccessible to routine review. In addition, determination of eligibility entails a greater use of judgment than computation of a grant, especially in ADC. To determine the eligibility of an ADC applicant in Massachusetts, it has been necessary to ascertain not only the amount of the applicant's resources and the age of the dependent children, which are relatively simple matters, but to make a judgment about the incapacity of a parent (what constitutes incapacity?), about one's absence from the home (what constitutes desertion?), and, until 1962, about the fitness of the caretaker relative (who is a fit mother, and what is a suitable home?).[18] The possibilities for local deviation from state rules were so great that a uniformity issue was bound to arise.

It was, in fact, the very first issue to come up between the federal administration and Massachusetts. As of 1936, when Massachusetts submitted an ADC plan for approval by the Social Security Board, 119 towns had no cases at all, and 51 of these had not had one since the program began in 1913. Alerted by these facts, the Board challenged the welfare department to show that the ADC program was mandatory throughout the state. The Board's lawyers noted that local agencies had not been required to keep records of applications or to report rejected applications to the state.[19] Nor did the state provide for a hearing for persons whose applications had been denied, though an amendment pending before the legislature would satisfy this federal requirement. Negotiation on these points continued throughout much of 1936, delaying federal approval of the plan until September.

Between 1936, when federal aid was getting under way, and 1943, when the first binding manual of state policies and procedures was issued, the state considerably elaborated its policies on

ADC eligibility, but it continued to leave much to local discretion. With respect to the fit parent and suitable home requirements in ADC, the manual said:

> The intention is always to obtain the best possible sur-roundings for the child in the individual case rather than to pass judgment on the morals of the grantee-relative . . . The basis for the decision as to eligibility should be whether the grantee-relative is able to give the child reasonably good care in reasonably suitable home surroundings. In determin-ing fitness, past conditions are much less important than abil-ity and desire to learn.
>
> Because each situation differs, it is impossible and un-sound to set up an exact definition or standard of fitness and suitability, to be applied arbitrarily in all cases.

It then supplied guidance on such matters as the presence of a male boarder in the home, illegitimacy, and failure to pay bills. It was unlikely that such general rules would be applied by all local agencies in the same way—all the more so because these policies were quite different in spirit from what had preceded them. In the twenties and thirties the state had taken a stricter view of the fit-ness requirement, barring mothers' aid in cases of illegitimacy, where housing conditions fell short of the department's standards of propriety, or for other reasons. Local directors and workers need not have had long memories to recall the state's earlier posi-tion. This inconsistency of policies over time, as well as their gen-erality at any given time, made uniform compliance improbable.

The BPA spotted the problem quickly. In the 1940s administra-tive reviews reported that local agencies frequently denied the right to apply for ADC to women judged to be unfit, who were put on general relief instead; that in handling applications based on incapacity, some agencies required total incapacity while others did not; and that in cases of desertion, some required the mother to swear out a warrant against the absent father even though state rules did not call for this. By 1950 the regional office seemed ready to raise the administration of ADC eligibility as a major issue. The regional representative wrote Commissioner Tompkins that "the administration of the Aid to Dependent Children program . . . does not meet the purpose which the program was set up to achieve." Among several specific complaints, she declared that the state's willingness to permit local discretion in determining fitness "may be questioned as not consistent with the objectivity and uniformity required by the fair hearing and other provisions of the Massachusetts and Federal statutes." She urged the state to develop mandatory uniform criteria for determining fitness. "You will recognize the gravity of the situation," she concluded, "and will want to take steps immediately to correct the present practices." [20]

The welfare department did not respond to this demand. In late 1947, in a general progress report to the BPA, Commissioner Tompkins had acknowledged the reluctance of "a few local agencies to accept the broad definition of eligibility," but he denied that this was a major problem and said the state was working to eliminate it.[21] He probably sensed in 1950 that the federal position was not as strong as the tone of the regional representative's letter seems to suggest. There was nothing in federal law or BPA policies to prevent fit-parent or suitable-home provisions. Well over half of the states had them. The regional representative was limited to arguing that harsh local use of the fitness standard violated the principle of uniformity (agencies were not *equally* harsh), not a very secure basis from which to demand a change in state policy.

The weakness of the federal position may explain why, for the next ten years, the issue lay dormant; or it may be that the failure of the regional office to sustain its demand for corrective action was simply one example of a general phenomenon, the relaxing of federal surveillance as the program grew older. By the 1950s, the flow of federal funds was coming to be taken for granted on both sides. The Social Security Board had fought battles with various states, Massachusetts included, when federal standards were first promulgated. Settlements had been reached, state plans had been approved, and the program was becoming routine.

Another possibility is that Massachusetts was making enough progress in achieving uniformity to satisfy the regional office. Very probably, state supervision in the 1950s did tend to bring about increased consistency in the handling of ADC applications, but it is not likely that uniformity was achieved or that the regional office was satisfied. A few local agencies continued to resist state policy. One in the northeastern part of the state routinely refused ADC to women with illegitimate children. Another automatically removed from the rolls mothers who had remarried. The state could enforce its policy in these places only by stimulating appeals from aggrieved persons. That significant variations among local agencies persisted is suggested by a statistical analysis of ADC rates (children receiving ADC as a proportion of children under eighteen) as of 1960 in 29 cities, places with at least 100 ADC cases. Multiple regression analysis showed that three independent socioeconomic variables—percentage of women separated and divorced, percentage of families with incomes under $3,000, and percentage nonwhite of persons under eighteen—"explained" 62 percent of the variation in ADC rates; but this meant that a potentially significant amount of the variation, some portion of the "unexplained" 38 percent, might be the result of differences in the agency interpretation of eligibility rules, especially the fitness provision. From the multiple regression equation, it was possible to predict the rate for each city. That is, given its percentages of separated and divorced women, families with incomes under $3,000, and nonwhites under eighteen, one could say what its rate "ought" to have been. Deviation from the predicted rates ranged as of 1960 from 42.3 to —88.8 percent. The most extreme deviation occurred in the city in northeastern Massachusetts where ADC had been denied to mothers of illegitimate children.

The failure of the regional office to persist in its complaints seems to have been related to a change in the character of administrative reviews—evidence, perhaps, that federal surveillance was indeed becoming less acute as time passed. Reviews in Massachusetts between 1942 and 1950 were frequent and comprehensive. They covered every aspect of administration, often in a large number of local agencies, and yielded highly critical reports in great detail. Thereafter they were carried out intermittently and often covered only one program or one aspect of administration. In 1957, for example, the review in Massachusetts covered aid to the disabled in Boston. Not until 1960 did a review again entail a detailed, comprehensive survey of the ADC program, and then it revealed the persistence of problems that had agitated the regional office ten years earlier. Unlike the earlier federal criticism, this was followed by major changes in the state rules.

The review covered eighteen cities that together accounted for about two fifths of the state ADC caseload. It revealed, the regional representative's preliminary report to Washington said, "some very serious matters." One agency in the western part of the state was found to be withholding aid when a woman had an illegitimate child and to be requiring that clients' housing meet agency standards. In cases where such standards were not met, applicants were put on general relief. To the regional office, this seemed "obviously the local way of eliminating unmarried mothers, negroes and Puerto Ricans who have recently moved into that section." [22] Other practices cited included denying ADC to a mother who was employable or currently employed although earning so little as not to make her ineligible, and failure to act promptly on applications. The regional office discussed these findings with state officials in late 1960 and early 1961, and shortly thereafter the department revised its ADC policies. It repealed a rule that a woman must have been separated or deserted for at least six months in order to receive ADC, thereby making her eligible from the moment of separation, and repealed another that said ADC should not be granted unless need seemed likely to continue for at least three months. With respect to fitness of the parent and suitability of the home, the principal source of federal-state tension, the department adopted verbatim the language of

federal policy as newly framed after the controversy with Louisiana: aid should not be denied on grounds of unsuitability as
long as the child remained in the home. Nor was this all. In 1962,
in response to the department's assertion that the fit-parent and
suitable-home provisions of the ADC law were contrary to federal
requirements, the legislature repealed them altogether.

The department was quite willing to take these actions. There
were no lengthy federal-state negotiations, no hints that funds
might be withheld. The state's policies, after all, had always been
liberal, and most of its top officials shared the federal commitment to humane, "therapeutic" treatment of the poor. The only
issue was whether its policies were sufficiently precise and well
enough enforced to bring about local conformance. The federal
review in 1960 produced fresh evidence on this point that provided a stimulus to action. This was an example of how, from the
federal viewpoint, an administrative review ought to work. The
regional office exerted slight pressure on the basis of preliminary
findings, obtained a quick response, and by the time final findings
went to headquarters could already report improvements.

The repeal of the fitness law was similarly achieved with very
little federal pressure. The regional representative appears to
have wanted to use the federal directive of 1961 to compel a response from Massachusetts. Twice she wrote Washington, citing
the offending provisions of state law and the new directive and
asking for guidance—hoping, it would seem, to be told to press
the state for change. Twice the central office responded in noncommittal fashion.[23] But the state department was quite prepared to
act on its own. The directive from Washington on fitness and suitability, preserved in the commissioner's files, bears a simple penciled notation: "What do we need to do to comply?" [24] State
officials decided that they needed to amend the law, and a majority of the legislature acceded, responding to the claim that the
change was required by federal policy. There was strong opposition in the legislature, and one member subsequently tried to re-
store the fitness provision.

It is not clear why the department was so quick to respond to such slight federal pressure in 1960–61, whereas it had been unresponsive to the regional representative's strong language in 1950. But one likely explanation is that as time passed and state supervision grew, there was less hesitance about exercising authority.

The result of the various changes in 1961–62 was that local discretion in determining eligibility was almost completely eliminated. The effect can be seen in the movement of ADC rates. In agencies that had lower ADC rates in 1960 than they "should" have had, caseloads generally increased at a rapid rate in the next five years. Between 1960 and 1965, the city with the greatest deviation from the predicted rate in 1960 (—88.7 percent) had by far the biggest caseload increase in the state (226 percent compared to an average among cities of 90.5 percent). As of 1965, the amount of intercity variation in ADC rates explained by the three socioeconomic variables cited above had risen to 75 percent; the amount unexplained, and therefore possibly attributable to differences in agency discretion, had dropped from 38 to 25 percent.

Equity as Respect for Individual Rights

In Massachusetts, federal-state issues of uniformity have been very closely bound up with problems of recipients' rights. The regional representative's criticism in 1949–50 of the handling of ADC applications was addressed as much to the harshness of local attitudes as to a lack of uniformity, but the uniformity requirement, with at least some foundation in federal law, was relied upon in seeking correction. Not entirely, however: the regional representative charged that "the authoritative, punitive activity exercised by some local agencies" violated "the spirit of the principle of the right to a free-money payment as well as the right to the confidentiality of the relationship between client and agency." [25]

As an example of punitive activity, the review in 1949 noted:

The ———— agency [one of the biggest in the state] in its attempts to establish fitness of homes and parents . . . frequently uses methods which raise questions concerning the violation of its confidential relationship with clients. Such practices are the exposure of "moral" situations in the home to the police, discussions of such situations with persons who can give no useful information on the subject, and unnecessarily revealing its relationship with the client to school officials.

The review also cited the practice of at least two city agencies of requiring mothers to bring nonsupport action against putative and separated fathers. In general, it complained of "a need on the part of staff to 'supervise,' hold under 'surveillance' and emphasize the morals of the mother rather than the welfare of the child." [26] The corrective action sought from the state was clarification and stricter enforcement of its policy on fitness.

Ten years later, following the administrative review of 1960, the same federal complaints recurred, this time in more specific form. That review complained particularly about local-agency relations with police departments and courts. It found evidence throughout the state that policemen were being used to "watch" ADC mothers. "Some of this," the regional representative reported to Washington, "is in the guise of assisting in locating absent fathers but most of this results in a kind of 'community control' over ADC mothers." In one city, she reported, a mother who had a second illegitimate child while receiving ADC was forced to go to the district judge for some form of "directive action." This had "amounted to such drastic action as suspended sentences and short term jail sentences." None of the state's ADC changes in 1961 was addressed to these problems, however, and the final version of the federal review, though it reported these findings, did not stress them. [27] These matters were hard to handle because they involved the behavior of public agencies outside the state department's jurisdiction. In cities where harsh policies were in effect, the district judge or other law-enforcement officials might be the principal source of them, the local welfare department only a compliant partner.

The department had no clear rules governing local-agency relations with the police. To implement the NOLEO amendment, the policy manual provided that in cases of desertion the agency must notify the appropriate district court, and the mother must file a complaint against the father (the practice that, when used by a few local agencies before 1950 on their own initiative, had brought objections from the regional office). This rule said nothing at all about the police, but a later statement on relations with law-enforcement officials seemed to acknowledge that local agencies were working in conjunction with them. It said that welfare workers were not to exercise police powers; nor were police personnel working with the welfare department to get involved in welfare matters. Law-enforcement officials were expected to concern themselves primarily with helping to find and prosecute missing fathers. This constituted a mild injunction not to use the police for surveillance of recipients, and in effect acknowledged that they might be working closely with welfare departments for other purposes. In fact, a wide variety of local practices could be found in 1965–66. Even with respect to NOLEO procedures, on which the manual was perfectly explicit, some local agencies deviated —ironically, in the direction of greater leniency than the state permitted. Not all enforced the requirement of a formal complaint by the mother.[28] A few city welfare departments had police officers assigned on a full-time basis. Some, in uniform, merely stood inside welfare offices, to keep order (local officials said) or to intimidate applicants (their critics suspected). Other departments, as in Revere and Haverhill, had plain-clothes officers assigned to desks. Their principal job was to aid in the pursuit of deserting fathers, but they might also accompany workers on any investigation that could involve a violation of law, such as neglect of children or lewd and lascivious conduct. Fall River's arrangement for liaison with the police department was probably unique. Its welfare agency contained a former police officer who became a welfare worker, as does anyone, by passing the civil

service examination. He did not carry a caseload, but was assigned full-time to dealing with the police department.

In 1965–66 the regional office found an opportunity, not of its
own making, to intervene and compel enunciation of a new state
policy in regard to the police. The opportunity developed from
one incident in Massachusetts and the nearly simultaneous development of a new policy on individual rights by the BFS central
office.

Late in 1965 a lawyer in Springfield, a white man with a Negro
clientele and an interest in civil rights, wrote to the state welfare
commissioner complaining about the treatment of mothers of illegitimate children in the city. He charged that when an unwed
mother applied for aid, she was questioned in the welfare office by
two detectives. He said that they asked questions in the utmost
depth and detail about her sexual activity (lurid examples were
supplied), the answers to which might then be used to prosecute
her for lewd and lascivious conduct. The lawyer sent copies of his
letter to Secretary of Health, Education, and Welfare John W.
Gardner and U.S. Attorney General Nicholas Katzenbach, and
followed these up with the filing of a formal complaint of discrimination under Title VI of the Civil Rights Act of 1964.

Gardner's copy of the letter filtered down through the federal
bureaucracy for reply by the New England regional office of the
BFS. The reply could not have been more encouraging. It was
"more than pleasing," the regional representative wrote, to learn
that local residents were becoming aware of and aroused about
problems of welfare administration in Springfield.[29] A senior
member of the regional staff soon visited Springfield to talk with
the lawyer. Regional officials began meetings with state officials to
get them to investigate and correct the situation.

As usual, state officials did not condone the practices to which
federal officials objected, but they felt inhibited in taking corrective action (again it was the tradition of local independence).
The issue in Springfield was localized. It was not much publicized
outside the city, and there had been no similar complaints from
other places, although ADC recipients in Boston were beginning

to engage in protest activity. In these circumstances the state might well have dealt with the problem on a purely local basis, through efforts to influence the conduct of the Springfield agency alone. The appeal to the federal government, however, enlarged the issue. By identifying his appeal with what was then a major national issue—civil rights, treatment of the poor—the lawyer in Springfield was able to stimulate a federal response, and this response, translated into pressure on the state welfare department, brought about a change in state policy.

Aroused by the general agitation of rights issues, the BFS central office showed intense interest in the Springfield incident, which occurred almost exactly upon the appearance of the bureau's new rules on protection of rights. The Washington office followed events in the case with great care, used the regional staff to make a detailed investigation (contrary to the usual federal practice of communicating only with the state, and only about policy) and even declined at one point, in a rare rejection of a regional recommendation, to accept that office's view that the state response had been satisfactory and the issue had been settled. It was Washington that called for major revision, after a review of the Massachusetts policy manual. Nothing less would be accepted as a solution to the Springfield problem, which Washington officials expected to recur elsewhere in the state. In April, citing the newly issued bureau directive, the regional representative informed the state just what was expected of it:

> In view of the problems which you know exist in many places, we strongly recommend that you immediately initiate an evaluation and complete revision of all related policies to develop a unified and consistent standard for determination of eligibility in accord with the new Federal policies. Such a standard should specifically prohibit practices that violate privacy and dignity. It should define the term "law enforcement officer" wherever used, should state under what circumstances and how local welfare agencies may collaborate with the police, and should spell out what

police and other special investigatory activity is not permitted. It should clarify that no local policies and procedures more restrictive than the State plan are permissible.[30]

By the fall of 1966 the department had complied. Its new policy provided that police personnel must not be assigned to welfare agencies, must not be used for investigating cases, and must not be given any information about assistance recipients that did not relate to locating absent fathers. (Simultaneously, also in response to new federal directives, the department revised its rules on the collection of support payments from absent fathers, repealing the requirement that the mother swear out a warrant.)

Equity and State Administration

By 1967, on the eve of the adoption of state administration, it was hard to find a significant remaining area of local discretion except for the possibility of adding marginal items to the standard budget. The federal pursuit of equity had stimulated the development of state rules until, at least formally, there was almost no room left for the expression of distinctively local preferences or values.

Inevitably, the federal striving for equity amounted to an attack on localism, even if the effort did not go by that name. The only way to achieve state-wide uniformity was through the use of state authority. The only way to secure respect for the dignity of recipients was to suppress opportunities for expression of the interest in punishing "outsiders" or "undesirables" or the "unworthy" and in keeping taxes low. Although this interest was not exclusively or distinctively local, it could be given its most effective, structured expression at the local level. The attack on localism had made much headway by 1966, as the steady diminution of local discretion shows, but as long as vestiges of independence remained (in principle and to some extent in fact), they jeopardized the objective of equity. Some scraps of discretion survived, and some local directors might choose to use these scraps (or *not* use them in the question of paying for special needs) in ways not satisfactory to the professionals in the federal and state administrations. In any case, however they might use this discretion, local directors had to consider local mores and opinion, which were likely to prescribe the saving of tax money and the treatment of ADC cases such as to express the community's disapproval of family instability and immorality.

The drive for state administration was a logical climax to the long federal effort to achieve equity. One of the main arguments of the reformers was that local administration resulted in a lack of uniformity; yet their study report showed little evidence of differences in the application of the state standard budget. The report concluded that "much of the inequity and variation in treatment across the Commonwealth could not be measured in such tangible terms as amounts of money, but rather in the harder to define differences in the " 'spirit', the 'philosophy,' or the 'climate' which prevails around the giving of financial help." [31] From this statement, it may be seen what effects were anticipated from state administration by the sponsors, including federal administrators, who must be counted as tacit sponsors. The problem with local administration, as the report suggested and as Commissioner Ott reiterated before a legislative committee, was an intangible one, the "attitudes" of local administrators.[32] The problem lay not so much in the fact that these attitudes varied from one place to another as that in many places they were "wrong." The real trouble with local administration, in the reformers' view, rested in the failure of local administrators to share wholeheartedly the client-serving, therapeutic values espoused by the professionals in the federal and state administrations. The reformers assumed that this failure was to a considerable extent associated with the lack of professional training, but they assumed further that it was associated with localism per se. As long as agency directors shared the local ethos, felt closely bound to the community in which they worked, and bore responsibility, however tenuous, to local elected officials, some of them could be expected to exhibit the punitive attitudes to which the reformers objected. State administration, though it would not force incumbent local administrators out of jobs, was expected to reorient them, to subject them to a consistent set of expectations that specified client-serving behavior. Administrators must accept guidance from the top level of the state welfare department—and through it from the federal government—because there would be no other source of guidance.

5 | Efficiency of Administration

A third major objective of the federal government, more trouble-some in its relationship with Massachusetts than either adequacy or equity, was efficiency of administration. The original version of the Social Security Act authorized the Social Security Board to require such administrative methods as it found to be "necessary for the efficient operation" of the state plan. Here was a broad charter for intervention in state administration.

The requirement of efficiency could serve a wide variety of purposes depending on how federal administrators interpreted it. It could be used as a basis for prescribing fiscal controls and accounting procedures or, more broadly, for prescribing standards of staffing and organization. Federal administrators sought to do both, but they were especially concerned with staffing. Above all they wanted to eliminate politics in the selection of state and local personnel. If administrators were chosen impartially, according to objective standards of merit, they would be more likely to carry out programs impartially. The requirement of efficiency could be made to complement the requirement of equity.

Congress was wary of the federal administrators' interest in state personnel, so much so that in 1935 it removed from the administration's draft of the bill authority for the Social Security Board to require the establishment of merit systems. What the administration had sought to obtain explicitly, Congress explicitly denied. The Board's power to set standards of administrative efficiency was not to extend to methods for "selection, tenure of office and compensation of personnel."

In 1939, in the first major amendments to the act, the Board persuaded Congress to reverse itself. Since then federal administrators have been authorized to require of the states such methods of administration (including those relating to the establishment and maintenance of personnel standards on a merit basis) as would be "necessary for the proper and efficient operation" of the state plan.[1] (Note that "propriety" was now added to "efficiency" as a standard to be imposed upon the states.) This authority was limited only by a prohibition against action with respect to the selection, tenure of office, and compensation of any individual. In fact, this was how the Social Security Board has chosen to interpret the law in the first place. From the start of federal aid it had pressed the states to set hiring standards.[2] The amendments of 1939 simply strengthened its position.

Board Chairman Arthur J. Altmeyer told Congress that a merit system would mean less, not more, intervention in state affairs because, by making state administration more efficient, it would obviate the necessity for intervention. "We feel," he testified, "that the setting up of a merit system stabilizes and impersonalizes the relations between the Federal Government and the States." Both the Board and Congress had an interest in achieving stability. The Board had sought to withhold funds three times since 1935—in Ohio, Illinois, and Oklahoma. This was disruptive both to congressmen, who had to deal with aggrieved state officials, and to the Board, which had to deal with aggrieved congressmen. Experience with withholding had shown that it served no one's interests, least of all those of the Social Security Board. Altmeyer's distress with the experience was manifest:

That is an awful responsibility to place upon a Federal agency, to have it placed in a position where it has to watch the administration of a State system, which because of the absence of personnel standards and their proper application, reaches the point when it is necessary to withdraw grants . . . because of the acts of a few unfaithful public servants . . .

Now, the Board is criticized when it does not take action, and it is criticized when it does take action. If it does not take action the people say we are condoning extravagance and improper administration. When we do, then the gentlemen of the Congress come full force to the office of the Board and want to know why we have withdrawn the grants; and after we have withdrawn the grants, then the gentlemen of Congress, including a distinguished member of this committee, wants to know why we do not give them back the money lost during the period when, admittedly, they were not in compliance with the standards laid down in the Social Security Act.[3]

In those states where withholding had been tried or was contemplated, the Board thought that "incompetent and politically dominated personnel" were the source of the difficulty.[4] A merit-system requirement seemed the best way to solve the problem. In seeking to take state administrators out of politics, the Board was seeking to take itself out as well, for its withholding of funds had stirred up charges of partisanship. (In Ohio, the Board appeared to act in such a way as to penalize a governor who was an anti-New Deal Democrat.[5]) When Altmeyer spoke of "depersonalizing" federal-state relations, he meant that he wanted to "depoliticize" them. The Board's relations with the states would be smoother if administrators could deal with fellow administrators, free from the influence of politicians at any level.

Congress' approval of the merit-system requirement in 1939 gave the Social Security Board its principal means for the enforcement of the efficiency requirement, and action in 1946 provided another. The 1935 act had authorized so little federal participation in administrative expenditure for OAA, then the largest and most controversial category, that the Board lacked the financial leverage to gain access to state activities. Only 5 percent of federal OAA grants went for administration. In 1939 Altmeyer asked that the law be amended to authorize a 50 percent matching of OAA administrative expenses. Congress failed to act on the recommendation then—through an oversight, Altmeyer later testified—but it did respond when the request was renewed seven years later.

Efficiency in Massachusetts

The quest for efficient administration soon became a major source of conflict between the federal government and Massachusetts. The principal problem was not politics, although federal administrators occasionally uncovered evidence of favoritism in the appointment of local administrators. Instead it was the irrational quality of the state's localistic and decentralized administrative structure. The system of administration in Massachusetts was the very picture of asymmetry. In 1945, 6 percent of the 351 local units had two thirds of the public assistance caseload; about 130 of these units, in the opinion of the federal regional staff, were too small for administrative efficiency. Worker caseloads and supervisory ratios also varied widely throughout the state and even within the same agency. A regional official noted in 1946 that the size of worker caseloads in a given town might range from thirty to several hundred. Administrative costs per case were among the highest in the country, but within the state they showed the widest imaginable variations. Among personnel who were covered by civil service, job classifications often bore no relation to actual functions. "Social workers" did clerical work, "clerks" did social work, "supervisors" did social and clerical work. Records were often poorly kept. The state department had one of the largest field staffs in the country, but the supervision of local agencies was poor.[6] In the small towns administration was often informal and personalized, a responsibility of elected officials who had uncertain tenure and no specialized knowledge. A state report in 1942 conveyed the casual quality of small-town public service:

[One] chairman of a board of public welfare, a farmer in a rural community, said that he spent his evenings and spare time on 63 Old Age Assistance and 28 other cases, and received $550 per year. His wife did the clerical work at 35 cents per hour. In another rural place the selectman, the chairman of public welfare, had only 16 cases in the three categories and received almost the same salary, $540. Perhaps more common was the smaller salary of $100 per year received by the clerk of the public welfare board in another small community. Here there were 20 Old Age Assistance and 3 other cases. His wife, daughter and occasionally friends helped him by doing the clerical work without pay. In still another small town the selectman serving as chairman of public welfare received only $35 per year. He took care of 37 Old Age Assistance and 10 General Relief cases. He had done the work for eleven years for this small compensation and appeared to regard it as his civic duty. His wife helped him by doing clerical work and revisiting cases on a voluntary basis.[7]

It is hard to imagine a set of circumstances more thoroughly at odds with a professional administrator's concept of propriety and efficiency, and the federal administration was impatient to put things right—to render "orderly," "efficient," and "rational" what Massachusetts tradition had left in such untidy condition. After 1940 it relied mainly on the merit-system requirement. The issues that arose consequently were not resolved for a decade, and not fully resolved even then.

Application of the Merit-System Requirement

When the Social Security Board imposed a merit-system requirement, it anticipated problems in states where assistance was locally administered. Merit-system coverage was likely to be least extensive in these places, and the power of the state welfare agency to impose it would be most subject to challenge. Actually federal officials encountered few problems until they reached Massachusetts. At least, that is what they told the Massachusetts welfare commissioner, in a conference called to elicit from him a promise to conform.[8]

The problem was not that Massachusetts resisted merit-system coverage. Almost all public assistance employees of the state and those in the cities, except for agency directors, were already covered by the state's civil service system (which had been set up in 1884 to serve local governments as well as the state). State law required them to be covered. The only problem was in the towns, where coverage was optional and only a few had elected to bring their employees under the system. Now the Social Security Board said that they must. The state welfare commissioner, Arthur Rotch, did not object; nor did it appear likely that the legislature or local officials would. Town assistance employees could be expected to support the change as long as it would not jeopardize incumbents, who would gain from receiving tenure. The issue was not the substance of the new federal rule, but the timing and method of putting it into effect.

The Board issued its merit-system rules on November 1, 1939, and required state agencies to submit evidence of conformance by January 1. Full coverage did not actually have to be achieved by that time, but the state had to accept the standards and specify what it would do, and when, in order to achieve compliance. Rotch did not know how to respond. The normal method of compliance would be for him to submit to the legislature a bill making the necessary change in the civil service law. Another possibility, more troublesome but manifestly consistent with state law, would be to induce the towns to "volunteer" to come under civil service. In the closing months of 1939 neither of these steps could be taken. The legislature had adjourned and, because it was on a biennial schedule, would not convene again until 1941. Town meetings would not be held until March.

Federal officials argued that Rotch ought to create a merit system by administrative action. If necessary he could get the legislature to sanction his action later. This was the position taken by Jane M. Hoey, director of the Bureau of Public Assistance, and she was very firm about it. In her view, if Rotch did not take the action, Massachusetts would not be in conformity with federal requirements, and if he claimed that he lacked the authority to take it, this only confirmed Massachusetts' nonconformity because it showed that the state agency could not make rules that were binding on local agencies. (Thus it could not guarantee statewide operation of the state plan.) Miss Hoey stated her views in a telephone conversation with the Social Security Board's regional director in Boston, John Pearson. As the Washington office read the Massachusetts law, she told Pearson, there was nothing to prohibit Rotch from issuing merit-system rules himself. Admittedly, there was also not much to suggest that he could do it, and this was a flaw that the regional office and state officials ought to correct. The law should give the commissioner clear and broad rule-making authority. "I think we should have discussed this with the agency before this in order to have it strengthened by legislation," she told Pearson. On the other hand, there had been "pretty clear statements" from the legislature about "the desire to cooperate in any way necessary to get federal funds," and there had been no formal, successful challenges to the commissioner's rule-making power.[9]

Pearson responded with sympathy for Rotch's position. "There is a question," he told Miss Hoey, "from the standpoint of these two or three hundred towns that you want him to administer. He virtually takes over their welfare activities." Miss Hoey disagreed. The towns would retain power to appoint employees, and the state would simply serve them by setting up examination techniques. Pearson countered that Washington was expecting Rotch to act "in the face of a long-established civil service system." Over Pearson's objections, Miss Hoey urged him to suggest that Rotch make a trip to Washington. The problem might be settled by explaining to him what Washington wanted and persuading him to take the necessary steps. Otherwise, the Social Security Board would have to schedule a hearing, the formal stage preceding a finding of nonconformity and the withholding of funds.

Miss Hoey talked to Pearson on a Friday. The following Monday, Rotch met in Washington with Social Security Board officials. He asked them not to force him to extend the merit system on his own authority. He pointed out that only a very small proportion of the caseload was in the towns, and that as soon as the legislature reconvened it could be expected to act. If he went ahead by himself, there might be strong objections from local agencies, charges of "politics" from opposing party members in the legislature, and a challenge in court.

Federal officials professed sympathy with Rotch's problems, but they had their own to consider. Altmeyer said that the Social Security Board could not make an exception in Massachusetts without creating a dangerous precedent for the whole country. Rotch would have to take action right away, and if he doubted his authority to do so, "then," said Altmeyer, driving home Miss Hoey's point, "it raises the question of conformity with the Social Security Act, and I think we ought to schedule formal hearing and make our finding." Upon the suggestion of a hearing, Rotch yielded quickly: "If you tell me you can't do this thing [wait for the legislature to act], I have got to go back and do the thing the other way . . . I mean, I don't see the point to going through the formal hearing; I come down here to present the case and you tell me you can't do it, and that's that." [10]

Rotch signed a statement that he accepted the merit-system standards and would put them into effect. Federal officials in turn agreed to release the February grant to Massachusetts. (The date of the conference was January 23.) Afterward Rotch got a letter that might have been helpful had it only come sooner. It was from Congressman John W. McCormack, who wrote to say that, if he could be of help, Rotch should call on him. As a veteran member of the Ways and Means Committee, McCormack had been one of the most important supporters of the Social Security Act, and he had just become the Democratic majority leader. Hearing of the state's problem, he had written to Altmeyer asking for information. His letter was sent on January 26, and Altmeyer was able to assure him in reply that Massachusetts had accepted the Board's standards and that the Board had already approved the state's February grant. There was nothing for the congressman to be concerned about. [11]

As events proved, Rotch was right about the vulnerability of his position. His merit-system rules—which were issued in April 1940 after approval by the Social Security Board [12]—were tested in court and struck down. The state's Supreme Judicial Court held in 1942 that Rotch exceeded his authority in promulgating them, but by then the question was irrelevant. In 1941, at Rotch's request, the legislature extended the civil service system to all assistance employees, which legalized the effects of the commissioner's action, if not the action itself. In response to other bills submitted by Rotch under federal prodding, the legislature had also broadened the commissioner's authority: he could now make any rules for ADC and OAA "necessary or desirable for . . . conformity with all requirements governing the allowance of federal aid to the commonwealth." [13] Federal officials thus had achieved their immediate objective, extension of the merit system, and, incidentally, a more fundamental objective—the strengthening of the state agency's authority to carry out any federal requirement.

Nevertheless, the issue of civil service coverage was far from settled. A particular anomaly remained in the Massachusetts situation. The extension of civil service in 1940–41 had reached only local-agency staff members, and in many of the smallest towns there were no members to be reached. Administration was carried out by the elected members of local welfare boards, who were explicitly exempted from the extension of civil service. Before long, federal officials were beginning to wonder how they had let this happen. In the late 1940s, deciding that they could tolerate it no longer, they called for correction, and this touched off a major federal-state conflict.

The Exempt Administrators

BPA officials were well aware when the merit-system extension was effected in Massachusetts in 1940–41 that board members were exempted from it and that some of them were engaged in administration. Two categories of board members were involved.

Much the larger of the two consisted of the elected members in small towns, who worked without any staff. The other consisted of appointed members in a dozen or more cities, people who served simultaneously as board members and as agency directors. Federal merit-system standards provided that board members should be exempt, but this was predicated on the assumption that boards were policymaking bodies. The provision failed to anticipate that they might be administrators too.[14]

Federal administrators had ample opportunity in 1940 and 1941 to insist on a system of civil service that would reach even into the smallest towns. Their failure to do so has several possible explanations. One is that they did not realize how widespread the anomaly was in the state. The regional representative did not call it to Washington's attention—apparently he had not assembled data himself—and only in 1942 did the BPA's central office learn that in 131 towns, well over a third of all local units, elected officials were performing administration by themselves or with the help only of a clerk.[15] Another possibility is that the BPA's central office intended to force the change but, because of poor staff work or flaws in communication and organizational control, failed to convey its intention effectively to the regional office or, through it, to the state welfare department.[16] Federal officials in Washington, of course, had to deal with the problems of forty-seven states other than Massachusetts, so that competition for their attention was intense. Even with respect to Massachusetts alone, they had other problems to keep track of in 1940–41.[17] Still a third explanation is that federal officials chose to ignore the problem because it would be too difficult to deal with at the moment, both politically and administratively. To insist that very small towns with infinitesimal caseloads hire workers would have provoked intense resistance in Massachusetts and touched off a time-consuming dispute. Meanwhile, extension of the merit system, the primary federal objective, would have been delayed. This explanation is unlikely, however, if only because federal administrators did not face a choice between, on the one hand, approving a plan that fell far short of their requirements and, on the other, rejecting it and thereby cutting off federal aid. There was another way out, one not infrequently used in such situations.

In the approval of state plan material, federal administrators exercise a large amount of judgment. State laws and rules cannot, in the usual case, be expected to conform perfectly in letter and spirit to the federal intention, if only because that intention is quite likely to have been communicated to the states only in general terms. It is through the process of reviewing plans that federal officials decide precisely what it is they will require. Even if they begin this process with requirements fairly well defined, the question they must answer is not *whether* the state plan conforms to the requirements (the question is rarely so simple or clear-cut) but *how close* it comes. The presumption has to be in favor of the state or else the federal program would fail to function. Federal funds would be withheld more often than granted, and administrative operations would be fraught with uncertainty. Even in the face of plan material that falls short of their requirements, federal officials may grant formal approval but attach qualifications, or seek from state administrators quasi-formal statements that interpret and supplement the formal plan material so as to clarify the nature of the state's promise to conform.[18] When the Massachusetts merit-system extension was approved in 1940, federal administrators found that the state's rules were "substantially" in conformity with federal requirements—enough in conformity, that is, to warrant continuation of federal grants and yet not enough really to be satisfactory. One of the important deviations from federal standards was presumably the lack of workers in the small towns, but in 1940 federal administrators failed to seek any formal assurances from the state that the situation would be changed. They did urge the welfare department to impose standards of staffing and organization on local agencies and to make it "mandatory" that in each local unit there should be paid employees who would be subject to the state civil service system, but Massachusetts officials were not told—as they might have been—that such action was an essential condition for the continuation of federal aid.[19] It was this failure that subsequently made the problem such a difficult one for the federal administration to deal with.

When the issue surfaced again inside the BPA, it did so in response to inquiries from a new regional representative, Eleanore A. Schopke, who arrived in Boston in late 1944. In 1940–41, when federal consideration of the Massachusetts merit system was under way, she was the bureau's representative in the south central region and had no way of knowing what was going on in New England. Soon after arriving from Dallas, she discovered the anomaly of the exempt administrators and began to seek an explanation of it. In contrast to her predecessor, who had usually responded to regional peculiarities with tolerance, she was alert to uncover and correct deviations from federal rules, so much so that her arrival brought about an exchange of roles between the BPA's central office and its New England regional office. The central office had previously been more aggressive than the region in exacting conformance from the state, but thereafter it was the region that pressed for stronger action.[20] In July 1946 Miss Schopke recommended to the central office that any increase in the number of exempt administrators in Massachusetts be prohibited, and informed it that audit exceptions would probably to taken in existing cases. In other words, unless Washington objected, the regional office would not approve federal participation in the salaries of those administrators who were not covered by civil service.

Miss Schopke's questions spurred research into the history of the Massachusetts civil service law. After much analysis of the files, the BPA concluded that it never intended that anyone who was performing administrative duties should be exempt from civil service. "The Massachusetts law, as we understood it," one office memorandum said, "permits exceptions of individuals only in their role as board members," not in their role as administrators.[21] Several such memoranda showed that the exempt administrators represented a deviation from the federal *intention;* but before taking action against the state through audit exceptions, federal administrators wished to assure themselves that the prevailing practices deviated from the federal-state *understanding* reached in 1940. The evidence was against this. One memorandum conceded that "there may have been some misunderstanding of the state's objectives on our part," and that local agencies might not be aware that they were deviating because they had never been told by the state that they were.[22] The regional attorney concluded without hesitation that the board member-administrators were "in violation of the approved merit system," but he thought that the decision to take audit exceptions was "one for policy determination," that is, so difficult in the circumstances that it ought to be passed along to the Washington hierarchy.[23]

The problem of civil service coverage was not the only one in Massachusetts in the late 1940s. The state was coming to be viewed as a chronic delinquent in administrative matters. Classification and compensation plans for assistance employees, which were to have been prepared as part of the merit system, either did not exist or were not enforced. The state welfare department exercised no supervision over local administrative matters such as annual and sick leave, purchase and rent of office space and equipment, travel allowances, and telephone and postage expenses. Contrary to recommendations from the Social Security Board, the state did not share in local administrative expenses, and so it had never issued rules to govern them or conducted audits. Its supervision of local agencies was addressed only to the substance of the program, the determination of eligibility and the granting of assistance. Even in these matters federal auditors frequently found that local records were inadequate. Especially in those small towns where no worker was employed, records were likely to be missing or incomplete: a selectman might keep them, literally, in his pocket. Although all of these problems would sooner or later have caused trouble, it was the increase in 1946 in federal matching funds for administration that brought most of them sharply and suddenly to attention. Federal auditors began seeking out records that had been of little or no concern to them before. They wanted prompt and accurate reports of administrative costs, but the Massachusetts welfare department could not immediately say how much was being spent: it did not know, and it never had to find out before.

In mid-1947, at the request of Miss Schopke, BPA officials met in Washington to discuss "the whole of the Massachusetts situation," as one memorandum discreetly said.[24] Various sections of the BPA in addition to the regional office began to document the state's delinquencies. The climax of this effort was a long (ten single-spaced pages), formal submission to the social security commissioner early in 1948 detailing the problems of administration in Massachusetts and asking his guidance. This document identified problems of three kinds: participation by local board members in administration; operation of the merit system; and the state's failure to set standards for local administrative expenditures. At the root of the problems, the bureau argued, was the extremely decentralized system of administration:

> A basic problem in which many others have their roots is the use of 351 local jurisdictions to administer the program. The establishment of such an organization along traditional lines and the fact that it has been retained reflect the strength of the belief in local autonomy in the State, and the weakness of the concept in Massachusetts that public assistance is a state responsibility. While a fair degree of uniformity in regard to eligibility and amount of assistance has been achieved, the operation of all aspects of the programs for old-age assistance and aid to dependent children cannot be considered "proper and efficient." [25]

The result of the presentation to the comissioner was that Jane Hoey came to Boston, in April 1948, to tell Massachusetts officials what was wrong and what the Social Security Administration expected them to do about it.

An Issue of Conformity?

Massachusetts officials had ample ground for supposing that the federal administration was dissatisfied with the state agency's conduct. Critical letters and administrative reviews had been coming from the regional office for several years, and the latest review described problems that, according to Eleanore Schopke's covering letter, were "serious and urgent." [26] Still Miss Hoey's portentous visit came as a surprise. The gravity of the federal concern had not been appreciated, and for the next few months, as he came under increasing federal pressure, Commissioner Patrick Tompkins repeatedly complained that he had not been warned. He charged that federal officials were finding fault only because the increase in the federal share of administrative expenditures had given them the opportunity to do so. There was some truth in this, but some also in the barbed reply that Miss Schopke finally made:

> You may very well maintain that we are emphasizing the seriousness of the situation much more in 1948 that we did in 1946 or 1945 or 1944. This is true for two reasons: continued study of the situation brings to light more and more examples of serious deficiencies in personnel administration on a merit basis; it has always been the policy of the Social Security Administration to extend time and assistance in correcting weaknesses in the administration of the Public Assistance program if all concerned State officials are making every possible effort to correct them. [27]

The conference with Miss Hoey lasted a full day and was followed by a long letter in which she covered the entire range of complaints against the state, summing them up with the charge that it had failed to meet the responsibilities imposed under the Social Security Act. There were hints in both the conference and her letter that, if the state's response were not satisfactory, the BPA might raise an issue of conformity. [28]

Among the many complaints made by Miss Hoey, only one seemed to Commissioner Tompkins to pose special difficulty. This was the demand that the department bar elected welfare boards in the towns from administration and forced them to hire workers. In forwarding Miss Hoey's letter to Governor Robert Bradford,

Tompkins suggested that this would contravene "the constitutional form of government within the Commonwealth." He did not disagree with Miss Hoey's objective, but he did not believe he had authority to correct the situation. He urged that it be handled by new legislation to encourage or require the consolidation of small towns into welfare districts, an idea that had originated ten years before with the Haber Report. The proper vehicle for making such a proposal, Tompkins suggested, was the Recess Commission on Public Welfare Laws, whose establishment he had proposed to Bradford and the governor had proposed to the legislature in his inaugural address in 1947.[29] The commission had already begun its work. Tompkins also forwarded a copy of Miss Hoey's letter to Senator Ralph Mahar, the commission chairman, who came from a small town near the New Hampshire border.

In a reply to Miss Hoey in late June, Tompkins took the same position. He told her that a proposal by the Recess Commission would be "more desirable" and "potentially more successful" than any "fiat" from the commissioner. He also sought clarification of the federal position. If board members were to be precluded from taking part in administration, what would the penalty be for noncompliance? Would it be audit exceptions applied to the federal share of the board members' pay, or would it be withholding of the entire grant? [30] Miss Hoey rejected the view that Tompkins could not regulate the functions of board members, but if he thought he lacked such authority, then he should request enabling legislation. She did not respond directly to the question about the withholding of funds but said, "We have accepted your letter as a preliminary report [it had covered progress on many matters other than the problem of the elected officials] and have released grants for the first quarter of fiscal 1949." [31]

For the next two months, state officials and federal regional officials carried on discussions in Boston. Tompkins and Thomas J. Greehan, the state civil service director, maintained that they could not take corrective action independently and that the legislature would not be willing to act unless confronted with a clear threat of the withholding of funds.[32] The stakes were considerable. Local welfare board members were being threatened with a loss of authority and perhaps of pay that some received for administrative functions. Town governments were being threatened with the expense of hiring a worker or with a compromise of their autonomy by inclusion in a welfare district with one or more other towns. Repeatedly Tompkins asked regional officials if the Social Security Administration regarded the change as mandatory. If it did not, he declared, then no change could be expected.

Tompkins' tactic was one commonly used by state officials in negotiations with the federal administration. His predecessor, a more compliant man, did the same thing. In 1941, the regional representative had informed BPA headquarters that "Rotch repeatedly raises the question of what deviations must be corrected as over against what should be corrected, and the answer to these questions is not easily forthcoming. In some cases Mr. Rotch indicates that he will not propose a change unless he is told that it is mandatory." [33] The bureau assiduously avoided direct replies to all such questions. Its strategy was to get the greatest possible compliance from the state without withholding funds and without jeopardizing its own influence by making overt threats that could only result in congressional hostility or sacrifice of program goals. Thus it needed to maintain a degree of uncertainty among state officials. Federal officials sought objectives through negotiation; how long they might be willing to negotiate or what sanctions they might try to impose in case of failure was left to guesswork, and no amount of inquiry from state officials could elicit definite responses. Uncertainty and the time consumed by negotiations were severe enough costs to impose upon a state administrator that he would usually make concessions rather than suffer them indefinitely.

In this case, regional officials first said that Miss Hoey would provide clarification of federal intentions, but Tompkins found none in her letters. In the fall of 1948, notifying the central office once again that the state would not act unless forced to act, Miss Schopke wrote: "The regional director . . . thinks we just should no longer appease . . . he thinks we would be justified in raising [a conformity] question." She pointed out that there had been a long period of negotiation.[34] Still the central office said nothing. Again in December Miss Schopke notified Washington that there would be no progress until Miss Hoey definitely told Tompkins that there was a conformity issue.[35] She wrote to him two weeks later, in language that was firm but, as usual, left much to inference:

> Since you believe, as do the other gentlemen who have been associated with you in examining the statutes, that local boards of public welfare may legally operate the categorical programs and be exempt from civil service, we think it is imperative that you support legislative changes that will bring the Massachusetts plan into line with the requirements of the Social Security Act . . . We are reluctant to contemplate the possibility that the high standards of assistance for the needy in Massachusetts might be threatened by the loss of Federal financial participation.[36]

Preparation of a Bill

Miss Hoey's letter did little to improve Tompkins' position. The threat was still too vague to be interpreted as an ultimatum. How could the legislature be persuaded of the necessity to act? The answer, as Tompkins had anticipated, was to work through the medium of its own creature, the Recess Commission. On January 21, 1949, banner headlines appeared in the *Boston Traveler:* "BIG U.S. AID LOSS SEEN IN MASS." The Recess Commission had disclosed that $32 million in federal grants might be withheld.

Just how the commission happened to make this disclosure is not clear, but it was in the interest of both state and federal assistance officials that a "threat" should be publicized by an agency other than their own. Tompkins genuinely wanted to take action. The department had been committed for some time to the consolidation of rural units and would probably have sought this from the Recess Commission even in the absence of federal pressure. But he doubted his ability to get a change through the legislature and in any case preferred to expend federal influence for that purpose rather than his own or the governor's. For federal officials, the newspaper story meant that they might realize the benefits of the threat without incurring the responsibility of having issued it themselves. They did in fact deny responsibility for it in letters to members of Congress. When Senator Henry Cabot Lodge, among others, sent an inquiry to the Social Security Administration, Acting Administrator J. Donald Kingsley blandly observed, "The announcement in question appears to have been made by [a] special legislative recess commission," though he conceded that the problem "is one which we have notified the State Department of Public Welfare must be resolved at the earliest possible date." [37]

Early in March the Recess Commission issued a report repeating the threat ("the continuance of more than $32,000,000 in annual grants . . . is imperiled and jeopardized"), explaining the problem of the exempted board members and presenting recommendations, including a draft of legislation.[38] This bill did not get through the legislature. If Tompkins' contemporaneous interpretation is to be credited, the fault lay in large measure with the Social Security Administration, which failed, at a crucial and unanticipated moment in the legislative proceedings, to support him.

The moment came at a hearing of the public welfare committee. Federal officials were not there. They always prefer to speak indirectly, through the state agency, so it is their custom not to testify at public hearings of a state legislature.[39] On this occasion their influence was exercised by the wrong proxy. A witness for the Public Assistance Administrators' Association, an organization of local directors, read a letter from Commissioner Altmeyer to Congressman John F. Kennedy, a reply to an inquiry from Kennedy that had been stimulated by the association. The association's letter to Kennedy complained about a loss of home rule and asked about the extent of the Social Security Administration's authority.

It was addressed mainly to the question of administrative rules that were coming from the state—rules about size of staff, hours of work, sick leave, postage, supplies, travel, telephones, and so on, which the federal administration was compelling the state to issue. It did not raise the question of the exempt administrators, but ironically Altmeyer's reply to Kennedy did (on the assumption that this was what had stimulated the complaint) and was therefore relevant to the welfare committee's consideration of the Recess Commission's bill. Altmeyer's letter dealt in routine general terms with relations between the Social Security Administration and the state agencies. His comments on the Massachusetts situation conveyed none of the urgency of the representations that had been made to Tompkins for more than a year: there was no hint of a grave issue in federal-state relations, still less a suggestion that funds might be withheld. The letter closed with an assurance that "we have no intention of interfering with 'home rule' in Massachusetts." [40]

Tompkins was furious. He knew nothing of Altmeyer's letter until it was quoted at the hearing, where its effect was to undermine the department's position. Quick to put federal officials on the defensive, Tompkins charged Altmeyer with torpedoing the bill. "There was reasonably universal support of the principles contained in the report," he wrote. "The public hearing as a whole appeared to be winning substantial support . . . However, in the middle of the hearing, one witness produced a letter signed by you . . ." [41] To strengthen his own position, or perhaps to expose what he took to be federal duplicity, Tompkins reproduced the long series of warnings he had received from Miss Schopke and Miss Hoey and sent them to Kennedy, the welfare committee chairman, and the governor's office.

This incident well illustrates the limits and ambiguity of the federal administrators' position when a conflict occurs. They must exercise influence without seeming to. If they seem to exercise it, they become vulnerable to congressional intervention and probably also to general criticism: a large body of opinion holds that the federal government should not meddle in state and local affairs, and federal administrators naturally do not want to get caught doing so.

In addressing both state officials and congressmen, federal administrators are careful to justify their actions by reference to provisions of the Social Security Act: they are only doing what duty, as defined by Congress, compels them to do. In addressing state officials and even more in addressing Congress, they strive also to maintain the myth that the state agency alone is responsible for the rules it issues and other actions it takes. The legal structure of the federal-state relationship helps to support this myth: because federal rules and conditions have no effect until they have been converted into state rules, the federal will is embodied in state action, and the state incurs formal responsibility even for what has been imposed upon it as a condition of grants. State welfare officials, when compelled to do something bearing a political onus, seek to place responsibility on federal officials; federal officials adopt the disingenuous position that they are not to blame for laws and rules that come from the state. In practice, responsibility is hard to fix because it is shared: when the federal administration compels the state agency to issue a rule, but when the state agency drafts the rule and has some measure of discretion as to its content, both have, but can deny, responsibility for the consequences.

In the long conflict between the Social Security Administration and Massachusetts in the late 1940s, the SSA struggled to compel change in the state's administrative arrangements while avoiding the appearance of compulsion. Tompkins, in turn, sought to fix upon it the responsibility for all change, whether or not the state department shared the federal objectives or exercised significant discretion in achieving them. This game was at its liveliest in disputes over the state's promulgation of administrative rules, for these rules were more burdensome to local agencies than was the case with the legally more difficult change in board members' status; the former affected all local places in the state, the latter approximately one third of them. The BPA compelled the state to issue the rules and very much influenced their content. When the state agency at first responded with permissive and general rules that would have let local agencies operate much as they had been, the BPA commented that the agency was obliged to develop a state plan—a set of uniform, state-wide rules—and could not fulfill its responsibility by merely assembling a set of local plans.[42] When the rules were finally issued to local agencies in mid-1949, the state agency's letter of transmittal put the blame for them on the Social Security Administration. This touched off complaints by local administrators and taxpayers' groups to congressmen, especially from places where the new rules, which embodied caseload standards, would compel an increase in the number of workers. These complaints were passed along from congressional offices to the bureau, with requests for a reply. The bureau replied not only to them but to Tompkins, who got a lecture from Miss Hoey on the nature of the federal-state relationship:

> My immediate reason for communicating with you is my concern over an apparent misinterpretation of Federal requirements as stated in the material that has given rise to letters of protest from Fall River and Andover to Senator Lodge. The Senator has, in turn, forwarded the letters to us for explanation since they protest against Federal intervention in local administration, particularly in the increase in personnel they must employ and in the increased cost of operation. The Selectmen from Andover also object to the extensive amount of record keeping the instructions in your material entail and apparently consider them a federally imposed burden rather than a necessary adjunct to an efficiently administered program.
>
> When the first of these letters was received, we were at a loss to understand the allegations. However, when we reviewed your Handbook release . . . we were aware that certain sections of the material were written in such a manner as to imply that the specific provisions in the regulations were imposed by the Federal agency. This is inaccurate. The

requirement, in order to comply with the Social Security Act, is that the State establish and maintain methods of administration that are necessary for the proper and efficient operation of the plan. It follows that the detailed provisions of such standards must be determined by the State agency on a basis that is realistic within the State and will provide for efficient administration under State and Federal law.[43]

In the case of Altmeyer's letter, the federal agency's need to appear innocuous in the eyes of Congress had led it into trouble. The need to avoid the appearance of compulsion undermined the capacity to exercise compulsion, at least for the time being. The BPA now moved to recoup its position. The threat of denial of federal funds having been publicized, the bureau was heavily committed to obtaining favorable action from Massachusetts.

Once it became clear that the legislation would not pass in 1949, the bureau began to take measures better suited to emphasize the gravity of the situation. It started by sending Congressman Kennedy a letter that, by the urgency of its tone, "corrected" Altmeyer's. Its representations to officials in the state government also became more urgent, a change signified not just by what they said but to whom they said it. In 1948 negotiations had been carried on primarily by Miss Schopke and Commissioner Tompkins, with participation by BPA Director Hoey at critical moments. Now the BPA carried its case over Tompkins' head to Governor Paul A. Dever, and the rank of its own spokesmen was elevated accordingly. The federal position was enunciated by Miss Hoey, by the Social Security Administration's regional director, Lawrence J. Bresnahan, or by Commissioner Altmeyer.

In intermittent letters and meetings beginning in May 1949, they urged Dever to send a special message to the legislature backing the Recess Commission's bill. In December, on the eve of the legislative session, Bresnahan reminded Dever of "the necessity for action being taken at an early date" and, if this were not done, "the necessity for raising the question of conformity." [44] The federal resolve, by now quite firm, was further strengthened by the introduction in mid-1949 of a new and, in the circumstances, provocative issue. In a supplemental appropriation act, the legislature authorized the governor to appoint three deputy commissioners and a personnel supervisor in the welfare department without regard to civil service coverage. Miss Hoey reported to Bresnahan that, in Altmeyer's view, "this would be the straw that broke the camel's back . . . if these appointments were made it would result in a hearing." Bresnahan, however, was reluctant to convey this threat to Dever without being specifically assured of "the backing of the Washington office." "Otherwise," he pointed out to Miss Hoey, "anything I might say in the future would carry no weight." It was decided that Bresnahan would tell the governor that, if the appointments were purely political ones, the BPA would recommend a hearing in view of the entire situation in Massachusetts.[45]

Dever responded ambivalently to the federal representations. On one hand he professed agreement with federal objectives and a willingness to cooperate; on the other, he charged the federal administration with unfairness. Massachusetts administration . . . should not be impugned," he wrote, "because of any changed or newly discovered attitudes on the part of the Federal Security Agency" (a reference to the failure to pursue the issue in 1941).[46] And later, more insistently, he declared, "I . . . reject any wholesale indictment of our public welfare system on the ground of inefficiency. I am unable to accept any proposition that the administration of public welfare is necessarily and inevitably inefficient merely because it does not conform with rigid and arbitrary procedural rules." [47] The matter of the appointments was settled by his agreeing that the supervisor of personnel would be covered by civil service and that the other appointees, deputy commissioners, would not participate in the administration of federally aided activities. (Only one of the three was ever appointed.) On the issue of local boards, for a long time he avoided committing himself to sponsorship of a bill, and he never did send the legislature a special message, but in February the Recess Commission resubmitted its bill, presumably now with Dever's support. It remained to be seen, however, whether the bill would get through the legislature and, if so, in a form that the Social Security Administration would accept.

Passage of the Bill

Federal-state negotiations now entered their last phase, consideration of a bill, which would determine how far Massachusetts would go toward meeting federal desires. How much conformance federal officials could elicit from the state depended on their skill in negotiation, and this in turn depended heavily on the quality of information supplied by the regional office, whose members had to make estimates of the political situation in the state and of the administrative capacities of its welfare agency. Reported to Washington, along with the regional officials' own judgments, this information shaped the central office's definition of its negotiating position.

In January 1950, Miss Hoey wrote Tompkins that grants to Massachusetts were conditioned on the assumption that legislation would be secured in the coming session. It was "absolutely essential" that this be done.[48] Tompkins sent copies of her letter to the governor and to each member of the Recess Commission and the legislature's Committee on Public Welfare, but it gave them very little guidance as to what the federal administration expected the legislation to contain. It was an edict in regard to timing, not content. The question of content was being argued out within the BPA and between it and Tompkins.

Early in February, Miss Schopke sent Tompkins a copy of the Recess Commission's draft bill, marked with suggestions. Federal administrators had deleted a section that protected incumbent board member–administrators by allowing them to take noncompetitive civil service examinations, by which they might qualify for jobs merely through obtaining a passing grade. They strengthened other sections in order to give the state agency explicit authority to set staffing standards for local agencies and to compel consolidation of welfare agencies in small towns.[49] Shortly afterward Miss Schopke met with Tompkins to press for these changes and others that Washington now thought desirable: state participation in local administrative costs, a guarantee that all administrative units would have a full-time civil service employee (it had been noticed that the bill contained language authorizing part-time staff members), and a guarantee that henceforth the civil service division would certify eligible employees from district registers and then a state register so that localities could not confine hiring to their own residents. These conditions, though closely related to the federal goal of complete civil service coverage, were clearly separable from that goal. The first and third had been sought before without success, and Washington's urging of them now represented an effort to gain full advantage from the leverage already developed.

Washington's position, in the opinion of the regional office, seemed too ambitious; federal leverage was not that great. Tompkins told Miss Schopke that any amendment to make the bill stricter would jeopardize its passage. Specifically, important support might be lost from the Recess Commission chairman, Senator Mahar, who was fundamentally unsympathetic to the bill—he had complained publicly about "federal dictation" [50]—but who was willing to go along with the present version. The loss of Mahar's support, Tompkins said, would mean the loss of such Republican support as there was for the bill, and hence its defeat. (The Senate had a Republican majority.) After Tompkins said that he would not support amendments, Miss Schopke asked what he thought would happen if the Social Security Administration specified certain amendments as requirements. "He very flatly stated," Miss Schopke reported to Washington, "that it would mean the probable defeat of the legislation . . . opponents would in any event do their best to make it appear that Federal pressure was being used to alter the traditional Massachusetts pattern of local organization." Tompkins was not certain that the legislation would pass even in such a relatively weak form. The Selectmen's Association was objecting to federal interference. "Once you accept the King's shilling you are done," its counsel gloomily told the legislature, apparently stating a historical fact rather than a prediction, since the king's shilling had been accepted fifteen years before.[51]

Miss Schopke concurred in Tompkins' assessment of the legislative situation, and she asked the central office whether, in view of these circumstances, it still wanted to demand amendments. "If we do so," she warned, "we believe that you must recognize that such demands may jeopardize the passage of the legislation." The alternative, she suggested, was to seek informal assurances from the civil service division on crucial points.[52] Washington was reluctant to give in without getting legislative guarantees, "in light of our long experience with Massachusetts." Miss Hoey still urged as a minimal condition an amendment eliminating the reference to part-time employees, but on the whole she accepted Miss Schopke's alternative.[53]

Legislative consideration of the bill continued throughout the spring. Tompkins' reluctance to press for strengthening amendments meant that federal officials either would have to remain silent or make their own case before the legislature, in a setting uncongenial to them. In January, Tompkins had shrewdly invited them to make their own case: "I am confident," he wrote Miss Hoey, "that the Committee on Public Welfare, at the time that any public hearing is held . . . would welcome a personal appearance of either yourself . . . or Regional Staff members." [54]

It was a measure of the federal interest in the legislation that Bresnahan did make an appearance before the welfare committee [55]—and a sign of federal vulnerability in such situations that the statement he delivered was so innocuous. It contained no demands, no threat that funds would be withheld if satisfactory amendments were not made or even if the bill were not passed. First there was an assurance that the federal agency had no wish to interfere in business that was primarily the state's or to raise a question "concerning local administration as such." The concluding assertion was that "the state in the final analysis must be free to make its own decisions as to the administration of its own programs." In between these assurances were suggestions that the formation of districts be made mandatory, that open competitive examinations be required of all candidates for the new jobs, and that the use of district registers be required. Bresnahan argued that these changes would be "sound," could make future legislation unnecessary, and would avoid "possible difficulties" in holding to the federal standards.[56] This was language far more restrained than that used by Miss Hoey in internal bureau memoranda, and more restrained than that in preliminary drafts of Bresnahan's statement. One draft prepared in the regional office and submitted to the central office for review would have told the committee that the bill before it was "barely sufficient" to keep the federal administration from raising immediate questions . . . as to the efficient operation of the State plan." The draft contained strong hints that a conformity question would be raised if the legislation did not result in "efficient administration in small communities." [57] In deference to the reality of state power and to prevent charges of "dictation," this language was very much softened.

Far from adopting strengthening amendments, the Massachusetts legislature made the bill weaker. It did none of the things that Bresnahan had asked: it did not give the welfare department authority over districts; it left intact the guarantees for incumbents; it did not compel use of district registers. Bresnahan had not explicitly asked it to prohibit the use of part-time workers (Miss Hoey's "minimum demand"), and it did not do that either. What it did was to provide that the legislation should not take effect until 1952, and it eliminated language that had given the department a qualified power to effect combinations in special circumstances (though never without the consent of a participating town).

The regional office forwarded the legislature's bill to Washington with advice that it was the best that could be had, choosing to stress the fact that it would meet Miss Hoey's condition of "legislation at this session" and to ignore the fact that it would meet none of the substantive conditions the central office had tried to establish. The acting regional representative wrote: "If the determination is made that this legislation does not meet our requirements, and (as appears likely) no stronger bill were enacted, it would appear to us that we would have accomplished nothing . . . If the determination is made that this Bill docs meet the immediate requirement of 'legislation at this session,' it seems we would be able to carry on further negotiations in this area on a little bit firmer ground than heretofore." [58]

Washington accepted this view with great reluctance. An informal memorandum set forth this appraisal of the outcome:

Apparently this law presents us with the sort of dilemma we have been in for years in our negotiations with the Massachusetts agency. It is possible that efficient administration *could* be accomplished under the provisions of this bill. However, the bill does not of itself guarantee a major reform of local administration and from our knowledge of the nature of administration in the State over the past decade, it would not appear that we can expect substantial improvement on the basis of this legislation. [59]

This was more realistic than the argument that federal officials could now campaign for improvement on firmer ground. In fact the law had to be viewed as an unsatisfactory climax to a major federal effort to effect reform, and not as a basis for still another effort. In the campaign to secure change, the BPA had employed all of its resources short of the actual withholding of funds, and it would not be possible soon again to bring a like amount of pressure to bear on the Massachusetts agency.

The Consequences of Merit-System Extension

Beginning in the 1950s, federal complaints about inefficiency in Massachusetts diminished. It was still viewed as a problem state. The fact of administrative fragmentation was still frowned upon

—the existence of some three hundred administrative units was regarded by federal administrators as *prima facie* evidence that administration was neither proper nor efficient—but there were improvements in conformity to the state plan and in the conduct of local record keeping and reporting. The best evidence of this was a decrease in the volume of exceptions that federal auditors took in Massachusetts. The number of audit exceptions was high in comparison with other states, but by 1953 the regional auditor, in a memorandum to the regional director, reported: "The amount of exceptions which we are now taking . . . is much less than we used to take and reflect [*sic*] many improvements which have developed over the years since the program first started." [60]

There is no doubt that the extension of the merit system was one reason for this improvement, especially in those small towns where administration was previously performed by elected officials. And while extension of the merit system worked to improve administrative efficiency, it also had the effect of reducing the role of politics in job allocation, another important objective of federal policy. In the cities, where public assistance staffs (excepting directors) had been covered by civil service even before federal grants began, the principal effect of the federal requirement was to prevent an incoming mayor from appointing his own director. Previously directors might change as mayors changed, and job allocation was political in the sense that a mayor could reward a friend with an appointment. Now the directors stayed in office as mayors came and went. In many of the towns, the choice of assistance administrators had been political in another sense: that administrators, welfare boards or selectmen acting in that capacity, had been chosen through a competitive struggle for the popular vote. Now they had to be appointed through the civil service system. It was possible, of course, that in both cities and towns favoritism might survive the development and extension of the civil service system, depending on how manipulable that system might be. Welfare board members might seek on their own behalf or as agents of the mayor to place favored persons in jobs. Interviews with local directors in Massachusetts suggest that politics in this sense persisted through the 1940s and perhaps later in some local places. But by the 1960s it was a rare occurrence.[61]

At the local level, the reduction of politics in the allocation of administrative jobs reinforced the reduction of politics in another sense, as the process of making value judgments in public matters. Extension of the merit system, following upon federal participation in the public assistance program, coincided with the elaboration of state rules governing the program's substance, itself a response to federal action. Decisions about who should be aided and how much they should receive—which in the early 1930s had been matters for decision by local officials (typically, politically chosen local officials)—in the 1950s were largely made at the state level and were carried out by local officials who were no longer politically chosen.

Inevitably, the result was that local politicians—mayors and selectmen—began to lose interest in the assistance function. Upon taking office they soon discovered that they had very little control over it. Not only could they not decide which poor people in the community should get assistance; they could not even decide who should get the jobs in the assistance agency. This separation of the public assistance program from local politics helps to explain why, when state administration was proposed in the 1960s, most local politicians did not actively oppose it.[62]

6 | The Giving of Services

For the first twenty years, the purpose of the federal public assistance program was fairly simple and unambiguous. It was to give
money—"more adequate" amounts of money—to needy persons.
The Social Security Act said so in language that was terse and to
the point (for example, in Title IV as of 1951): "For the purpose
of enabling each State to furnish financial assistance, as far as
practicable under the conditions in such State, to needy dependent
children, there is hereby authorized to be appropriated . . . . ."
Federal administrators pursued the goal of adequacy, along with
the goals of equity and efficiency of administration, steadily and
with considerable commitment. They faced problems of technique (what administrative actions would achieve these goals)
and even more of politics (what Congress and the states would
agree to), but they suffered no self-doubt or division among themselves.

Beginning in the 1950s, this original purpose was expanded to
include another: helping recipients to become independent
through the giving of "social services." Congress incorporated
this enlarged purpose in the Social Security Act with amendments
in 1956 and 1962. By 1965, the act's purposive language was
quite long and complex (again, from Title IV):

> For the purpose of encouraging the care of dependent chil-
> dren in their own homes or in the homes of relatives by ena-
> bling each State to furnish financial assistance and rehabil-
> itation and other services, as far as practicable under the
> conditions in such State, to needy dependent children and the

parents or relatives with whom they are living to help maintain and strengthen family life and to help such parents or
relatives to attain or retain capability for the maximum self-
support and personal independence consistent with the
maintenance of continuing parental care and protection, there
is hereby authorized . . . . .

What service giving implies as a federal goal is hard to
specify. One federal pamphlet said that " 'providing services' . . . means, in a general way, helping people with their
problems." [1] It involved performance of social work for recipients, in addition to giving them financial assistance. If public
assistance had remained solely a state and local function, it might
never have been greatly influenced by the social-work profession,
and the goal of helping people with their problems might never
have been linked, at least on a nation-wide scale, to that of supporting the poor. But when the federal government entered the
field of public assistance, professional social workers entered the
federal administration, and from there they sought to impart their
values and purposes to assistance administration as a whole.

As early as 1943 the BPA told the states that they might claim
matching funds for the cost of providing services, but several
years passed before it sought to have the goal of service giving expressed in law. There were several reasons for its restraint, one of
which was its own ambivalence. At the outset the bureau showed
great sensitivity to the hazards of intervention in recipients' lives,
one indication being its insistence that money go directly to the recipient. In 1946 a BPA pamphlet set forth the rationale for nonin-
tervention, but in her foreword Director Hoey explained that the
author's position was not official and that "no single point of
view . . . exists among staff of the Bureau with regard to the
character of service in the administration of public assistance." [2]
Another factor restraining the Bureau was the lack of support
from private agencies, which enjoyed an advantageous division of
labor. Roughly speaking, public agencies gave money to several
million of the poor; private agencies performed the distinctively

professional function of casework for a much smaller clientele. Public agencies generally dealt with the most troubled people, those who were or were likely to become chronic dependents. Private agencies dealt selectively with those who were more self-sustaining and hence more promising as objects of casework. With their select, relatively responsive clientele, private agencies were able to attract trained workers and to give them light caseloads and the prestige that came with a monopoly of the casework function. Any expansion of public agencies into service giving would threaten the private agencies with a loss of monetary support and would result in the secularization of social services. The first proposals to Congress for explicit authority to match services, which the Social Security Administration advanced somewhat tentatively in 1949, met with resistance from Monsignor John O'Grady, secretary of the National Conference of Catholic Charities, and Congress itself was not eager to encourage the practice of social work with federal money.[3] Eventually these restraints gave way, and the BPA began to press more strongly for a statutory endorsement of service giving.

Success came in two stages. In 1956 Congress amended the Social Security Act to encourage states "to provide services to help needy individuals attain self-support or self-care." The amendments required states to describe in their plans the services they were giving, but did not require them to give any and offered no special monetary incentives to do so. Federal expenditure for service giving, though explicitly authorized, did not exceed the matching rate, 50 percent, for administrative activity in general. Six years later, the federal commitment was reaffirmed and supported with funds. In the Public Welfare Amendments of 1962, Congress required the states to give services in ADC and promised to pay 75 percent of the cost of service giving in all categories.[4]

The change in federal policy came about not so much through change within the BPA or Congress as through change in the assistance caseload. Contrary to an official prediction that the caseload would decline as the social security program spread,[5] it became clear by the mid-1950s that the assistance program, especially the politically vulnerable ADC portion of it, would persist and even grow. The bureau's response was to seize upon service giving as a solution. "Services" began to be presented to political leaders—and by them to the public—as a means to a widely shared goal: "rehabilitation of the poor," "an end to dependency," "restoration to self-support." Eisenhower embraced service giving as such in 1956, and so, with more rhetorical enthusiasm, did Kennedy in 1962.

Congress, also interested in being able to offer a solution to the dependency problem, now showed no objection to promoting services as long as this could be done in a way that was unambiguously beneficial to the states. Congress had steadily increased the federal contribution to state expenditures. This was usually done through a liberalization of the matching formula for assistance payments, but insofar as increasing aid to the states was for members of Congress an end in itself, increased matching of administrative costs was an equally satisfactory means to it. When, as in the grant system, federal aid to other governments is given conditionally, the devising of new conditions may be necessary in order to facilitate acts of new or increased aid giving. For members of Congress, motivated in part by an interest in the distribution of benefits to state and local constituencies, service giving may have seemed a convenient rationale for more aid giving quite apart from the desirable programmatic ends it allegedly would promote. The administration's bill in 1962 would have reduced grants to states that failed to give services, but Congress changed this so that the act would be all carrot and no stick.

Besides this support from politicians in 1962, federal administrators had support from the social-work profession outside the government. The Kennedy Administration enlisted representatives of private agencies and schools of social work to prepare a legislative program. Expansion of public agencies into service giving, though still objected to by some professional leaders in the private sector, increasingly appeared to others as an opportunity to be exploited. The result could be large public subsidies for professional activities, including graduate instruction in social work, and an increase in the demand for trained social workers that would redound to the benefit of the entire profession.[6]

The Kennedy Administration portrayed the amendments of 1962 as an important and highly promising innovation. The act contained many provisions to promote self-support. It authorized community work and training programs so that recipients might be prepared for jobs, and funds for the day care of children so that ADC mothers might work, but these and other measures received less stress than the promise of social services. "We believe," HEW Secretary Abraham Ribicoff testified, "that services represent the key to our efforts to help people become self-sufficient." [7]

The Federal Directive

The 1962 act said that if states gave services prescribed by the secretary of health, education, and welfare, the federal government would pay 75 percent of the costs. Before the Senate Finance Committee, Secretary Ribicoff had been able to define services in two sentences: "It refers to specific, long-term help which can be extended by properly trained workers through frequent home visits, guidance, counseling, and use of all available community resources in health, education, and welfare. It means bringing to bear on troubled families all the knowledge and skills which a community possesses." [8] But the Bureau of Family Services required 101 pages to explain what the states must do, and found the task quite difficult. State Letter 606, issued in November 1962 after months of preparation (work began long before the act was passed), was rewritten thirty-seven times.[9]

In principle, drafting this directive was no different from any other effort to define conditions for the receipt of funds. The problems and constraints were in general the same. On one hand, it was necessary to express conditions in terms sufficiently general and permissive to enable state and local governments to satisfy them. On the other, it was necessary to express at least some conditions in terms sufficiently specific to provide a basis for verifying compliance. In particular, directives must assure accountability for the expenditure of federal funds. The federal government exercises influence by giving money to induce the performance of a certain activity—activity X rather than (or more than) activity Y; if the federal intent is to be realized, and if principles of accountability are to be observed, X has to be defined in such terms that the federal administration can verify that federal money has gone for it and not Y or Z. In this case administrators had to develop a distinction between state and local administrative activity that involved giving prescribed services, which would be matched at 75 percent, and activity that did not involve giving services (or involved giving services that were *not* prescribed), which would continue to be matched at 50 percent.

What made drafting the service directive so difficult was the nature of the activity in question. For several reasons, service giving is hard to define in terms that can precisely and effectively guide state and local conduct. It is extremely decentralized, being a task principally for caseworkers, the lowest-ranking and most numerous class of employee excepting clerks and typists. It is also highly discretionary, in practice and according to social-work doctrine. The individual caseworker is presumed to use his judgment in adapting service to the individual needs of the client, always guided of course by professional principles and knowledge. Finally, service giving is not discrete; it is hard to distinguish from other types of activity that may be carried on by workers in association with it. (When a worker asks an ADC recipient the whereabouts of her husband, is the worker establishing the woman's eligibility to receive funds under the law—not necessarily a "service," but an activity incidental to the provision of monetary support—or is he taking a step to reunite the family, which, one would suppose, is a "service"?) A requirement to give services contrasts sharply in all these respects with a requirement, say, to establish a merit system covering assistance personnel.

The federal task was further complicated by doubts about the states' capabilities. Conformance would depend both on the state and local agencies' ability to give services themselves and on their ability to buy or beg them from other agencies. Federal policy to some extent relied on the latter approach. The 1962 amendments compelled child welfare and public assistance agencies to develop coordinated plans, and enabled assistance agencies to use federal funds in purchasing services from state health departments and vocational rehabilitation commissions, but there were difficulties in this approach. It was hard to get hitherto independent organizations to cooperate at any level of the federal system. In particular, state and local child welfare agencies, as clients of the Children's Bureau and as the elite of the welfare profession, had maintained a firm independence from the bigger, more plebeian public assistance agencies, and this independence could not quickly be overcome by federal directives—especially ones emanating from the BPA-turned-BFS, which bore most of the responsibility for putting the service amendments into effect. The problem faced by the BFS was not unusual. A federal agency administering grant programs often finds that, in order to attain its objectives at the state and local levels, it needs to influence organizations other than the immediate recipient of aid. Lacking a direct means of influence over other state and local agencies, the administering agency has to approach them indirectly, through pressures on its own client, or through trying to influence other federal grant-giving agencies. Inevitably, the federal agency is forced to work mainly through its own client; however imperfect its influence may be there, it has still less influence elsewhere. To carry out the service directives, then, the BFS had to rely primarily on assistance agencies.

The assistance agencies' ability to give services in turn depended on the existence of trained personnel, but as of 1960 only 1.2 percent of their caseworkers had master's degrees in social work. Thirty-three percent of all state and local employees lacked college degrees. In drafting the service directive, federal administrators had to decide whether to proceed on the congenial but impracticable assumption that only trained workers could give services or to define the service-giving function so as to bring it within range of the known or presumed capabilities of state and local staffs.

The administration dealt with its dilemmas in various ways. One was to define services primarily in terms of ends rather than means. In particular, prescribed services—those that states had to give in order to get the extra matching funds—were defined in terms of the problems to which service would be addressed.[10] Insofar as the BFS defined methods of service giving, it cast the definitions in general and even circular terms. "Community planning," one of five major methods identified, was defined as:

> activities of the staff of the agency in providing leadership and/or participating with other community agencies, organizations, and interested citizens in the development and/or extension of the broad range of resources and facilities to meet the social and economic needs of the community . . . Community planning includes all participation by agency staff in general community activities required by virtue of the position or office held.[11]

Accordingly, a local director who belongs to a service organization or gives a talk to a church club would be engaged in community planning. The directive said that the "basic method" of service giving was casework, and casework included "activities of the caseworker who carries primary and continuing responsibility for the case, and provides counseling and guidance or secures other services or facilities to meet the needs of individuals and families." Casework, in short, is what the caseworker does. The directive drew a distinction between basic casework service and skilled and intensive service, which the more troubled recipients would need. This was both an acknowledgment of the fact that most workers lacked the training to give skilled service and an implicit assertion that even the untrained could give basic casework service.

The BFS directive did stipulate a few conditions in highly specific terms, the most important of which were caseload, supervisory, and visiting standards. With respect to those cases requiring services, states had to maintain a standard of sixty cases per worker and five workers per supervisor, and had to make home visits at least once every three months. Though instrumental to the giving of services, these actions did not themselves constitute or guarantee service giving.

In order to make possible the immediate disbursal of the new funds without committing the federal administration to immediate and final approval of state plan material, the directive provided for phased compliance. A planning period was specified—September 1, 1962, to June 30, 1963—during which states could qualify for 75 percent matching funds with relative ease. After July 1, 1963, they had to promise to give the prescribed services. They could qualify for 75 percent matching for each category, provided they gave the services to all recipients in that category identified as needing them—all recipients, in other words, found to be afflicted with social problems. It was recognized that states might not be able to give all kinds of service (casework, community planning, and such) from the outset. Accordingly, they were supposed to engage in service giving progressively, beginning with whatever methods were feasible with existing resources but advancing to the full range of methods by July 1, 1967. Always they had to observe the principle of uniformity; whatever methods were used had to be used throughout the state.

Finally, the directive prescribed detailed rules for cost allocation. Cost allocation in public assistance had always required distinctions between costs of assistance and costs of administration and distinctions among categories. Now it became necessary further to distinguish between service giving and other kinds of administration while maintaining distinctions among categories. Several alternative allocation formulas were supplied, along with specific guides to differentiate between service giving and other administration. For example, the federal government would match at 75 percent (as service giving) "expenses of staff while attending in-service training sessions," but would match at only 50 percent "travel of personnel whose function is the recruitment and selection of personnel."

The Response in Massachusetts

With more federal matching money now available, states began to prepare plan material to qualify for it. In Massachusetts plan material before the adoption of state administration typically took the form of state letters and administrators' letters containing guidance for local administrators. State officials assimilated federal directives and then adapted and reinterpreted them in directives of their own. State policymaking for the giving of services was divided into two phases by the nature of the federal directive, which set different standards for the periods before and after July 1, 1963. The situation was further complicated in Massachusetts by a change of commissioners. Outgoing Governor Volpe removed Patrick Tompkins, who had been in office for seventeen years, late in 1962, so that most of the negotiating with the federal administration fell to his successor, Robert F. Ott. The phasing of federal policy and the change of commissioners meant that in Massachusetts there were two distinct sets of response, all the more distinct because the change of commissioners very much altered the quality of federal-state relations.

Service Policy: First Phase. The kind of response called for depended on the extent to which the state was already committed to service giving. Massachusetts was strongly committed by a directive (State Letter 69) issued to local agencies in 1954, which urged them to view ADC families "in terms of services needed" and outlined various requirements, including a quarterly visiting standard for ADC. This directive may have grown out of contemporaneous federal efforts—conferences, working papers, and the like—to stimulate attention to service giving in ADC.[12] The service amendments of 1956 had brought no further response. Massachusetts reacted then by citing policy already in effect.

The 1962 amendments, because they offered funds and imposed requirements, were a much more powerful stimulus to action, and Tompkins, as always when federal funds became available, was quick to act. It was not hard to anticipate federal policy, for the 1962 amendments were a long time in gestation. The administration sent a draft of its service directive to the states in January 1962, half a year before the law was enacted. It was no sooner in hand than Tompkins acted to put Massachusetts out front in the movement for service giving. He went to Washington in February to tell the House Ways and Means Committee that the program would undoubtedly help people to help themselves and that the states had been "crying" for federal leadership "in this entire field of intensive social services." [13] In March he notified local agencies that measures to emphasize social services should be anticipated, and on July 2 he issued a state letter putting new policies for ADC into effect as of July 1. (This was the date named by both the House and Senate bills for the availability of new federal funds; before enactment, however, it was changed to September 1.) Tompkins followed this up with a letter to administrators on August 27 setting forth procedures for claiming the new funds and a state letter on August 28 calling for the inauguration of social services for aged and disabled recipients as of September 1. [14]

His first service directive, of July 2, received prompt approval from the BFS for incorporation into the state plan, but the next, those of August 27 and 28, did not. In the interim the amendments had been enacted, and the bureau declined to approve subsequent plan material on services—or Tompkins' claim for 75 percent matching funds—until its own service directive had been issued in final form. (This did not occur until November 30, although technically the new funds were available on September 1; the BFS therefore had to approve claims retroactively.) Unwilling to be denied, Tompkins flew to Washington in mid-October, went straight to the bureau chief, Kathryn D. Goodwin, and got her consent to claim the 75 percent rate for the quarter September 1–December 30, 1962.[15] This was where matters stood when Ott's appointment was announced.

Service Policy: Second Phase. The next few months, as Massachusetts sought to its perfect plan material by the July 1 deadline, were trying for the new commissioner. Federal regional officials, who normally would have helped with state planning, were preoccupied with a congressionally inspired review of ADC eligibility. In February the New England regional representative notified state commissioners that his office would be unable to consult with them about services until May 1. In Massachusetts Ott was new not only to his job but to the public assistance program, having come to the commissionership by way of the child welfare division of the state department. And he was heir to an unhappy legacy in federal-state relations.

It is often argued that a shared professionalism among federal and state officials produces consensus and cooperation in the administration of grant programs. This may be true as a general rule—it is what federal public assistance officials strive for—but deviations may occur because of differing degrees of identification with the profession, or different interpretations of what professionalism requires, or conflicts of role and personality that prove more powerful than professional attachments. As of the early 1960s, relations between Massachusetts assistance officials and federal regional officials were almost completely severed. Tompkins as commissioner ignored the regional office as much as he could; when an opportunity to get more funds made intergovernmental business unavoidable, he carried it on with Washington instead. The department did not submit draft policies to the regional office for comment; several times it rebuffed requests for information or meetings; its offices were not freely open to federal officials; and it had not resolved numerous issues between the two governments that resulted from state failures to meet plan requirements. This situation developed despite the presumed bonds of professionalism. Tompkins had gone to a graduate school of social work (though he did not get a master's degree), had spent all his life in private and public welfare work, and shared the profession's general commitment to liberal grants, a service-oriented program, and formal qualifications for workers. For the most part, the federal-state tensions had sources other than differences of belief. Regional officials tried Tompkins' patience; he was a brusque man who found it hard to participate in the time-consuming diplomatic processes that characterize intergovermental business in a federal system. In his view, regional officials were parrots, mere mouthpieces for Washington.[16] He preferred to save time by talking directly to the central office. Regional officials also limited his independence; he was a strong-willed man who liked to do things by himself, and they made constant demands on him for cooperation in matters large and small. They also failed to satisfy his expectations of loyalty. In Tompkins' opinion, the regional office should act as a partisan of the state in relations with Washington, but in his experience it did just the opposite. All of these sources of tension may have been aggravated by personality differences. Tompkins was a bluff, bold product of Boston's immigrant neighborhoods, the typical Irish Catholic "man of big family and proud of it." Throughout his tenure the federal regional representative was Protestant, midwestern, and, like many BPA personnel, a spinster. They did not get along.

About the time Tompkins was replaced as commissioner, the regional representative retired and things got off to a fresh start. Ott was a man of modest demeanor and unswerving professional orthodoxy who decided right away that relations with the regional office must be improved. Massachusetts began to bring policy into line with federal expectations and to seek regional office guidance, with the result that regional officials began to act on behalf of the state. With their new access to policymaking, they acquired a stake in the central office's approval of state policies. Throughout the difficult negotiations over services that began in 1963, regional officials interpreted the Massachusetts department's actions sympathetically and pressed the central office for prompt, favorable responses.

There were many problems in these negotiations. It was not clear that Massachusetts had qualified for 75 percent matching funds even for the period between January 1 and June 30, 1963. Tompkins' direct appeal to Miss Goodwin had bypassed the central office staff as well as the regional office, which led to confusion. Though Miss Goodwin approved one quarterly claim for 75 percent matching funds, the bureau staff had never formally approved the plan material on which this claim was based—and, having been bypassed, was presumably in no hurry to do so. The state's cost allocation plan posed difficulties and so, above all else, did the effort to apply federal caseload and supervisory standards to the decentralized administrative system in Massachusetts. Caseloads in the state as of June 30, 1963, ranged from one to 371, and 189 agencies had no supervisors at all because they had only one social-work employee, a director-worker who performed all the work by himself. In struggling with the service directive, one of his first tasks in office, Ott confirmed his view that state administration must be adopted.[17] Federal policy, predicated on the existence of rationalized administrative structures, was impossible to carry out where such a structure did not exist.

Slowly the troubles were worked out. With the help of regional officials and, at one point, a consultant from Washington, Massachusetts drafted and redrafted its plans. Its service directives set the caseload, supervisory, and visiting standards required by the federal administration. Tompkins' July 1962 directive on ADC services had exceeded these standards, but Ott modified it in recognition of the fact that the state would not be able to enforce standards more stringent than federal ones.[18] Approvals from Washington trickled in, and by the beginning of 1965 Massachusetts had qualified for 75 percent matching in ADC and in the adult categories, OAA and DA. The effects on federal grants to the state are shown in the following table. The federal share of administrative costs (which here include costs of services) rose from 49.5 percent in 1962 to 56.2 percent in 1965.[19]

	All Categories		ADC	
1962	$ 6.6 million	49.5%	$1.9 million	49.6%
1965	$10.2 million	56.2%	$4.6 million	61.6%

Effects of the Service Policy

One way to measure the impact of the new policy, if the estimates of the Kennedy Administration were to be taken at face value, would be by the rise in the number of persons rehabilitated. Mercifully, administrators did not attempt to measure performance in these terms. But it can be inferred from caseload data that the volume of "rehabilitation" was insignificant. The average monthly ADC caseload rose steadily in Massachusetts, as in the nation as a whole, after the service policy went into effect in July 1963.

1963	20,273
1964	23,151
1965	25,228
1966	27,646
1967	33,092

It may be unfair to look for a reduction in the caseload. Perhaps the administration's claims for its proposals should be accepted for what they surely were—devices of political persuasion and not serious predictions. But then what effects of the service amendments can we look for?

One highly predictable result would seem to be a decline in caseload and supervisory ratios, given the imposition of federal standards. In Massachusetts these standards were somewhat more stringent than what state policy had previously called for (though the federal distinction between service and nonservice cases made comparison difficult). In any case, the state's earlier standards had not been enforced. In enforcing rules, the state in practice (though not in principle) consistently drew a distinction between those that were federally imposed and those that were its own. It enforced the federal ones more strictly because the fact of their origin and the associated threat of federal sanctions were available as a means of influencing local agencies.

After 1963 the number of workers and supervisors in Massachusetts increased sharply, but the rise in the number of workers was offset by a corresponding rise in the number of cases. The total number of cases per local worker did not drop substantially, as the following figures show.[20]

	Average Monthly Cases	Caseworkers	Caseload Ratio
1960	113,851	1,037	109.7
1961	116,463	1,102	105.7
1962	113,908	1,067	106.7
1963	118,074	1,122	105.2
1964	122,630	1,187	103.3
1965	128,202	1,224	104.8

This does not mean, however, that the federal standards had no effect. Closer analysis shows that they altered caseload ratios within and among the categories. The federal standard of sixty cases per worker applied only to problem cases, those defined as objects of service giving, as was true also of the quarterly visiting standard. In Massachusetts 85–90 percent of the ADC cases, but only 20–40 percent of other cases, were so classified. The remaining, nonservice, cases had to be visited only once a year, and workers might carry up to one hundred and eighty of them. To facilitate conformance with federal standards, the state required the largest local departments to "segregate" their caseloads—that is, divide them into family cases (ADC recipients) and adult cases (OAA, DA, and MAA)—and assign workers exclusively to one or the other type of case. In effect, workers were shifted from the adult categories, which were relatively problem-free, to ADC, and within all categories their workload was redefined so as to compel or encourage concentration on problem cases. The following figures on cases per local worker indicate what happened.[21]

	OAA	DA	MAA	ADC
1960	152.5	98.6	—	62.7
1961	147.4	99.2	232.0	64.4
1962	150.9	93.5	129.7	69.0
1963	153.0	100.0	132.0	60.0
1964	184.1	108.7	127.2	51.5
1965	188.2	104.0	131.4	53.4
1966	151.0		—	57.0
1967	164.8		—	58.8

Note: This tabulation should not be taken to indicate that workers were assigned exclusively to one category. That was not true in the usual case before 1963, and thereafter it was true only with respect to ADC. These figures were arrived at by prorating the categories among workers.

These changes might or might not have facilitated service giving. The redistribution of cases was at best only instrumental to the provision of services. Whether they were in fact provided depended on what the worker did with the cases he had.

Service Giving Before and After the 1962 Amendments. If only professional social workers could give services, and if professionals are persons with graduate training in social work, then very few services could be given in Massachusetts. In 1960 only 2.6 percent of the public assistance caseworkers in the state had two or more years of graduate study in social work, and well over half lacked a bachelor's degree. However, on the assumption of the BFS that untrained workers could perform basic casework service, Massachusetts and other states could still be expected to do what the federal directive asked of them.

By the broadest definition of services—helping people with their problems in ways other than financial—Massachusetts workers not only could give such help; they had been doing it for years. Especially in small towns, where workers were less harried than in cities, they had often gone to great lengths to help in emergencies or to give continuing aid to persons in need of it. There was the worker in a Boston suburb with an aged, nearly blind client who probably should have been in a nursing home but did not want to go; the worker stopped by once a week and helped the woman clean her apartment. ("She likes her," the local director explained.) Or the director in one small town who, unable to find an emergency foster home for a child, took the child into her own home for several weeks. However, because of the lack of case recording, no one could say to what extent or in what circumstances help had been given. In 1954, when the state department issued its first service directive, it hired a professional social worker to study records and report on the giving of services before and after the directive. The second, post-directive phase of the research was never completed, and the first phase yielded inconclusive results because the records were so uninformative. Lacking both the professional's vocabulary and his self-conscious sense of expertise, the Massachusetts worker has recorded little about clients and still less about himself. Information about clients typically has been confined to more or less objective facts (marital and employment history, ages and names of children, physical and mental defects, condition of housing). Unlike the professional, the worker does not "diagnose" the case; he merely describes it. But he does not describe his own activity with respect to it. The record is primarily a history of changes in eligibility status, payments, residence, and the like, and not of the worker's handling of the case.

Though not professionally trained themselves, workers in the mid-1960s generally shared the professional commitment to service giving. When asked if the federal-state emphasis on services was desirable, they seemed to regard the question as uninteresting or foolish because susceptible to only one answer. "How can you not want to help?" one worker asked in return. "You go into these homes and see all these awful problems. It's just natural to want to do something about them." "Helping people with their problems" seemed to satisfy a natural impulse and also to be consistent with the cultural values of both the local community and the larger society.[22]

In view of the workers' commitment to service giving, they might have been expected to regard the 1962 amendments as a welcome improvement in federal policies. The purpose of the act was to enable them to do what they said they wanted to do. The new federal policies were designed to increase, through reduction and reallocation of caseloads, the time available for giving services.

Oddly, workers did not experience the change as an improvement, although it would perhaps be more accurate to say that they did not experience much change. When asked about the effect of the 1962 amendments, some workers did not know what to answer because the title of the legislation was unfamiliar to them. However, all were aware of an increased stress on services even if they did not associate it with a particular act or directive. They saw the shift toward service giving as a long-term development rather than as the product of any one piece of legislation, and they associated it with a parallel trend toward more lenient eligibility standards and larger grants. In their view, it was part of a gradual liberalization of the entire program. What was promoted by federal officials in 1962 as a dramatic overhauling of the assistance program did not appear so dramatic from the perspective of the local worker.

Insofar as they experienced change after 1962 in their workloads, most workers regarded the change as unfavorable, or at least not conducive to the giving of services. Most reported that they did not have more time for service giving. In the summer of 1968, a year after the federally designated "progression period" had come to an end, a state-wide sample of 140 veteran workers (those hired in 1963 or before) were asked to name the single most important change in their workload in the preceding five years. Nearly half (66) of them answered "increase in paperwork." Only 26 listed "decrease in caseload" or "increase in service giving," and these were disproportionately concentrated in a single agency. Twenty-four cited "increase in caseload" as the single most important change. A large majority (92) said that the time available to devote to services had actually decreased since 1963.[23]

One reason that workers did not feel less burdened by caseloads is that caseloads had not declined. Only 10 of the 140 veteran workers questioned in 1968 said that their caseloads had decreased within the three preceding years, whereas 103 said they had increased. Moreover, among a total of 265 workers questioned (veterans and nonveterans) in eleven agencies, caseloads almost without exception exceeded federal standards, often by large amounts. The steady increase in the number of recipients, combined with worker turnover, meant that at any given time incumbent workers were likely to have very much larger caseloads than the standards prescribed. Authorizations of new workers' jobs lagged behind growth in the number of recipients, and workers could not always be found to fill even those jobs that had been authorized.

Nor did the reallocation of cases seem to produce the desired effect. For ADC workers, the effect of having a low caseload (in relation to adult-category workers) inevitably tended to be offset by more problem cases. There is some evidence from experience in Massachusetts that the burden of such a caseload affects the worker's morale and heightens his sense of frustration.[24] Adult-category workers, with numerically larger caseloads but fewer cases formally designated for receipt of service, seem not to have perceived a low volume of "service cases" as an advantage. In practice, workers did not consistently distinguish between service and nonservice cases. When I asked them to state how many of each they had, workers often were unable to answer either because they did not remember or because they did not find the question meaningful. Although the act of formal classification had to be performed for purposes of record keeping, many workers ceased to make use of the distinction in the actual conduct of their work. "All my cases need service," was a frequent response. "They wouldn't be on welfare if they didn't."

The principal change that most workers did perceive in their workload—an increase in paperwork—contributed to what was in their opinion the most important obstacle to the giving of services. Close to half of the average worker's time apparently is spent on paperwork.[25] Most workers felt that if they did not have to meet this and other competing demands on their time, service giving could be performed much more effectively. Asked to assess the relative importance of various obstacles to service giving, such as "recipients' resistance to intervention in their lives," "shortage of help from other agencies," and "the difficulty of changing human behavior," workers named far more frequently than any other, "lack of time for casework (because of excessive caseloads, paperwork, etc.)." [26] If the workers' statements can be taken at face value, the federal government should have sought to facilitate service giving by reducing paperwork as well as the size of caseloads.[27] Enunciation of the federal requirements for service giving, however, had the inescapable effect of increasing paperwork.

In the grant system, the imposition of any federal requirement generates paperwork for administrative personnel in the recipient governments. From the federal perspective, full reports and records are essential, inasmuch as opportunities for the direct observation of state and local conduct are limited by the nature of the constitutional system. Federal administrators depend heavily upon written records to see that funds are spent as federal laws and rules require. From the perspective of recipient governments, demonstrating that federal requirements have been fulfilled—or, to put it otherwise, assuring that the agency will qualify for federal funds—becomes for each state or local administrator a task of high priority. State and local personnel must make reports to the federal administration with evidence that requirements have been fulfilled, and they must create within their own agencies records that will satisfy federal auditors and reviewers. Where this burden falls depends heavily upon whose function the federal requirement is addressed to; in the case of service giving, it fell principally on caseworkers, who were the givers of service. The discretionary nature of service giving made the burden all the greater, for it is an activity inherently difficult to report succinctly through the entering of symbols on standard forms. It required preparation of a narrative in each case record, an extremely time-consuming chore, especially for workers who, lacking much formal education, frequently lacked the case with words that such education tends to develop.

Although workers did not distinguish sharply between paperwork associated with service giving and other paperwork, and although paperwork was a major complaint long before 1962, the *increase* that workers complained of in the 1960s apparently flowed primarily from the federal service directives. To meet federal standards, Massachusetts imposed a number of new recording requirements.[28] It may be that the workers' appraisal of the demands of paperwork should not be taken at face value. Workers may tend to exaggerate the time paperwork requires and the obstacle to other achievements it represents because it is an obstacle that can be blamed on tangible but remote others ("they," higher-ranking officials, are always piling on more paperwork). It is, therefore, at least theoretically remediable, raising no doubts about the workers' own competence or about the essential feasibility of the social-work enterprise. Although paperwork is undoubtedly an obstacle to service giving, it may also be a refuge from it. But if so, then real increases in paperwork have the effect of increasing the opportunities to take refuge. In general the grant system tends to induce and to legitimize a preoccupation with paperwork, for that is the activity through which the state or local employee can most easily fulfill the function of showing that federal requirements have been met. It is, in other words, the activity through which he can best fulfill the element of his function that derives distinctively from the grant system.

In random interviews in 1965–66, as my research for this book was beginning, some workers asserted that paperwork had increased so much that the giving of services was actually decreasing. To find out how extensive a belief this was, in 1968 I asked local directors to characterize the service-giving activity of their agencies since 1962. Of 174 who responded to the question, only

39 said that they were giving fewer services than before. On the other hand, still fewer (36) said that they gave more services than before. The largest number (61) responded that they gave the same services but kept fuller records. The question, with responses, is as follows.[29]

Since 1962 the federal and state governments have placed increased stress on giving services. Which of the following statements best describes what your agency has done since then?

We give more services than we did before.	36	20.7%
We give services just as we always did, but now we record them more fully.	61	35.1
There has been no change at all. We give services and record them just as we always did.	38	21.8
We give fewer services than before. Paperwork has grown so fast that we have less time to give services than we used to.	39	22.4

What local directors think may not be conclusive evidence in this matter, but in the absence of full and comparable case records, both before and after 1962, it is probably the best evidence obtainable. It strongly suggests that local workers did change their behavior after 1962 in response to federal directives, but the change was not in their behavior toward recipients; it was in what they wrote down about their behavior toward recipients.

Federal Enforcement

To keep track of service giving, the federal administration relied on reporting requirements and administrative reviews. In 1964 the BFS began asking the states for annual progress reports, for which it supplied a lengthy standard form. At about the same time it instituted semiannual statistical reports that could provide a basis for accounting to Congress and the public on the volume of service giving. But these methods were no substitute for reviews by the bureau's own staff.

The BFS conducted a nation-wide review of service giving in 1966. Federal officials prepared for each state an "agency profile," an all-inclusive survey of administrative structure, staffing, program goals, and plans for services. Subsequently they conducted a field survey, drawing on case records and interviews in a sample of local agencies (or state subunits). Because the progression period was still under way, states were not expected to be complying fully with federal service standards. The BFS sought only to learn how they were getting along in putting service plans into effect.

The agency profile for Massachusetts reported major progress since 1962 in the organization and distribution of policy material (a new manual was being issued), simplification of standards of assistance, and liberalization of certain state laws and policies. On the other hand, federal officials noted that many provisions of law and policy were "inconsistent with the department's social service program goals," such as residence requirements in all programs except MAA and relative-responsibility provisions in OAA, MAA, and DA.[30] Federal administrators were using the service requirement, like the uniformity requirement, as a means of access to the entire range of state action. Addressing themselves to services, they interpreted the term broadly in order to move toward a generally more liberal program.

The review of local-agency activity was less a progress report than a current description of service giving. From the federal point of view, whether change had occurred since 1962 was, technically, irrelevant. The important question was the extent to which standards were then being met. In Massachusetts the review covered four local agencies of varying size. Findings were mixed. The agencies were providing numerous social services, but there were deficiencies in case descriptions, more than half of which were incomplete, and in treatment plans. Though federal standards required that there be a plan for each case, such plans were often not recorded and, when recorded, were incomplete. The review reported that "caseworkers frequently operated according to a plan which was not written and covered only the current visit" —hardly a plan at all. Reviewers found that workers shared the federal services goals; yet there was disquieting evidence that local agencies acted as if their strategy were not to maximize services, but to maximize the federal proportion of expenditures. One agency had been classifying every adult case for receipt of services whether or not social studies revealed that services were needed. Operating on the same principle, but drawing a different inference from it, two other agencies were underclassifying cases for service because they doubted that they could meet federal caseload and visiting standards. That did not necessarily mean that workers failed to give services where needed. The federal reviewers found that, in practice, workers did not distinguish sharply between service giving in "defined" cases (those classified for receipt of services) and others. "They referred to the additional work involved in defined service cases because of visiting and recording requirements, rather than to services to help clients in the defined problem areas." The same was true of the state department's newly designated social-service specialists, who "appeared to be concerned with the counting and reporting of services rather than with the provision of services." It seemed that state workers too, in response to the combination of federal rules and monetary incentives, behaved as if their objective were to satisfy the rules (and thereby secure federal funds for their organization) rather than to attain the program goals.[31]

As for community planning—along with casework, a service required even during the progression period—the review reported much local activity that fitted the federal definition. "Community planning activities of the Director of the ———Welfare Department included interpreting program through speeches to community groups and membership on the community council . . . The Director of the———Welfare Department was an officer of more than 15 community groups and committees . . . The Director of the————Welfare Department had been a leader in community activities for almost 30 years." There was no evidence that local directors who engaged in community activity were doing so in response to guidance from the state. They had been giving talks to community groups and serving on community councils long before that became a federal requirement for the receipt of funds, and there was no evidence that imposition of the requirement made the slightest difference in their behavior.

In the spring of 1967, as the progression period neared its end, federal officials took another look at state activity. The central office asked regional officials to supply information on each state. In Massachusetts there was a flurry of concern about caseload and supervisory standards, for a few local governments had flatly refused to concede that the federal and state governments could tell them how many workers they must employ. After long negotiations, threats by the state to withhold funds, and letters from Commissioner Ott warning local officials (mayors, councillors, selectmen) that if they failed to authorize the necessary jobs they would jeopardize federal grants for the whole state, they yielded.[32]

Also in the spring, the BFS issued a short statement of standards for the continuation of 75 percent matching. (By now, nearly all states had qualified for the extra funds in ADC, and most had in the adult categories.) The standards were so vague and permissive that it would have been hard for states not to meet them, and it was equally hard for regional officials to enforce them. States had to complete their classification of cases and give the full scope of services to those needing them, but this requirement would be met if "all such cases have been assigned to staff for the provision of the services and service plans are being implemented for all cases." In other words, each case would have to be assigned to a worker, and the worker would have to be performing casework. Though the formal progression period had passed, the concept of progression still infused federal criteria. The states must develop methods by which service giving would be reviewed and improved. Even caseload and supervisory standards, the one seemingly specific requirement in the original directive, now proved impossible to enforce. States would not be considered as failing to comply as long as the necessary jobs had been authorized and recruitment attempts were under way.[33]

In Massachusetts, the July deadline passed without any reduction in federal aid.

Service Giving as an Example of Federal Influence

How much influence the federal government exercises through the grant system depends very much on the nature of the conduct it tries to influence. Service giving is an example of the kind of conduct that is hard for the federal administration to reach: decentralized, discretionary, consisting of complex, recurrent (yet incompletely routinized) interactions between thousands of caseworkers and millions of clients—interactions that are not susceptible to brief and objective description and hence not readily susceptible to administrative review. This is the kind of behavior that is hard to subject to administrative control in any institutional setting; the grant system, with its intergovernmental divisions of authority and method of control-through-conditions, simply magnifies the difficulties.

Attempting to adapt to the difficulties of control, the federal administration sought to realize its goal of service giving through the stipulation of a few highly specific conditions—caseload and visiting standards. But here again the result was to reveal the limits of its influence. The fact is that caseload standards were not met, at least in Massachusetts, and it was not feasible for the federal administration to insist that they be met: this assumed a very great capacity to manipulate or rapidly adapt to the volume of cases. Conformance depended on a rapidly changing situation that was largely beyond the control of state and local agencies (indeed, they had surrendered control largely in response to the long-standing federal insistence that all persons who apply and are eligible for assistance should receive it promptly). The fact that failure to meet federal standards resulted not from any willful defiance of federal requirements but largely from the force of circumstances made it very difficult for the federal administration to deal with.

Although the effort to encourage service giving illustrates problems associated with realizing certain kinds of federal intentions, it also illustrates with exceptional clarity a problem that is associated with the pursuit through the grant system of any federal goal: the production, as an unintended consequence of federal action, of state and local behavior that is directed toward increasing federal funds rather than toward attaining federally prescribed programmatic ends. The phenomenon of goal displacement in organizational behavior is a common one, by no means uniquely a product of the grant system. However, by elevating the receipt of federal funds into the motivating principle of action, the grant system as a mode of governmental conduct encourages the phenomenon. State and local agencies are led to act *as if* they value certain ends in order to enhance their organizational resources, whether or not they actually do value them. The principal result of the service directives in Massachusetts appears to have been to stimulate a large volume of goal-displacing behavior, manifested in acts of purely formal compliance with federal directives the sole purpose of which was to create evidence of compliance.

The limits on the federal ability directly to influence the behavior of recipient agencies indicate the great importance of indirect influence, through the indoctrination of state and local administrators so that their values and program objectives will be the same as those of federal administrators. Again, the case of service giving illustrates the nature of the problem. Even if the federal administration had succeeded in greatly increasing the volume of service giving in Massachusetts, that would not have necessarily led to the fulfillment of federal goals. There remained the problem of whether the manner of service giving met federal preferences. Did it conform to professional criteria? The consultant who studied case records for the state department in 1954 reported a "lack of knowledge or conception by the workers of what *service* is." [34] Massachusetts workers did not conceive of their function as a "professional service" that entailed treatment of a social problem. Rather, their actions were intuitive responses to the personal needs or social deviations of individual recipients. In conversation with one another or with an academic observer, workers talked about particular cases rather than about service giving as a function, recipients as a group, or classes of social problems. Unlike the professional, they were not greatly concerned about maintaining social distance from recipients. The worker might conceive of the home visit as a "chat between friends" rather than as a consultation between expert adviser and client. Thus the possibility arose that acts of service giving would depend on the nature of personal relations between worker and recipient rather than on the "objective need" of the recipient.

The only way, then, that service giving could be made to conform to federal preferences was by the professionalization of state and local personnel, an undertaking for which the federal administration had already shown intense concern.

7 | Professionalization of Personnel

An effort to professionalize state and local personnel is characteristic of many grant programs. Federal administrators, usually professionals themselves, wish their counterparts at other levels of government to be professionals as well. Accordingly, they seek to influence the selection and training of state and local employees.

"Professionalism" in the context of the federal public assistance program implies possession of those skills and attitudes characteristic of both the professional public administrator and the professional social worker. State and local personnel are expected to value and to implement those principles that are generally regarded as proper to administrative conduct, such as impartiality in dealing with clients, clarity in the enunciation of policies, and thoroughness and accuracy in record keeping. They are also expected to have the humane attitudes toward the poor characteristic of the social-work profession rather than the punitive attitudes that the profession attributes to laymen, and those who deal with clients are expected to be skilled in the treatment of personal and social "problems."

The federal assistance administrators' effort to professionalize their state and local counterparts has always been conditioned by distrust in Congress. In 1935 the House Ways and Means Committee removed a merit-system requirement from the social security bill for fear it would be used to make the states hire professional social workers. Representative Fred M. Vinson of Kentucky insisted that "No damned social workers are going to come into my State to tell our people whom they shall hire." [1] Four years

158

later, when the Social Security Board appealed again for the requirement, Congressman McCormack of Massachusetts reminded Commissioner Altmeyer that "Congress has not, let us say, an antifeeling, but they have a feeling of hesitancy, if not opposition—and I am one of them—toward these fine people who are the social workers of the country." McCormack believed that assistance "should be handled by people of local ability who have knowledge of local conditions and the background and surroundings of the people." Altmeyer sought to reassure Congress by pointing out that in states already having merit systems, the proportion of professionally trained workers was less than 5 percent.[2]

Notwithstanding objections from the Ways and Means Committee (the Senate's contrary views prevailed in conference), Congress in 1939 gave the Social Security Board authority to set personnel standards, perhaps because it was sympathetic to some degree of professionalism in the performance of public administration (on the assumption that it would lead to "efficiency") if not in the performance of social work. Even before this was done, the Board was demanding—on the basis of its authority to require efficient administration—that state plans include minimum standards for education, training, and experience. When the amendment was passed, the Board's power over these matters was much strengthened.

Since that time maintenance and improvement of personnel standards have been a major preoccupation of federal assistance administrators. The effort to professionalize state and local personnel may have been greater in public assistance than in other grant programs, for the gap in professional attainment among governments has been especially wide. A federal survey in 1950 showed that 57 percent of federal assistance employees had two or more years of graduate study in a school of social work, whereas only 4 percent of state and local employees did. Only 1 percent of federal employees lacked bachelor's degrees, whereas 40 percent of state and local employees did. Another survey ten years later showed that the educational levels of state and local employees had not increased significantly, although, because the educational level of federal employees had fallen, the intergovernmental gap had narrowed slightly.[3]

Following adoption of the merit-system amendment in 1939, the Social Security Board issued "Standards for a Merit System of Personnel Administration," a distinct body of rules that required, among other things, the establishment of classification and compensation plans and open competitive examinations. In these matters as in most others, the Board's rules were concerned more with method than with content. The Board required that a merit system be set up, but the precise content of the rules remained largely within the discretion of the states. Whether the federal administration's objective of greater professionalism would in fact be achieved depended heavily on circumstances in each state.

Professionalism in Massachusetts

The Massachusetts case is a good illustration of the problems that federal administrators might face. Extension of the state's civil service system to all assistance personnel, though achieved between 1940 and 1950 at the expense of great federal effort, did not go far toward enhancing professional quality. For reasons rooted deep in the social structure and political institutions of the state, its civil service system was not well suited to that purpose.

Professionalism is manifested in the possession of certain skills and attitudes but, because these are difficult to measure, a readily measurable surrogate—"amount of formal education"—is often resorted to as an indicator of the degree of professionalism. By this measure, public assistance employees in Massachusetts have been extremely "unprofessional." As of 1960, 42.7 percent of them, the highest percentage in the nation, had no college education at all. Professionalism was not an objective of the state's personnel policy. In 1935, as Congress was passing the Social Security Act—and for much the same reason: to provide security to the poor—the Massachusetts legislature was amending the civil service law to prohibit the imposition of any educational requirements.[4]

Although the civil service system posed one obstacle to professionalism, the extreme localism of the administrative structure posed another. Localism, as Congressman McCormack's remarks suggest, may be conceived of as one alternative to professionalism; they represent competing conceptions of the proper criteria of public employment. According to the localistic conception, the special qualification of the public administrator lies in his knowledge of and attachment to the particular community in which he functions; according to the professional conception, it lies in the possession of more universalized skills and attitudes associated with the occupational function. The system of city and town administration in Massachusetts contributed to the development and maintenance of the localistic conception. Most administrators had long careers in the same city or town, and the localized character of the job was one of its main attractions. The federal personnel survey of 1960 showed that Massachusetts employees were much more likely to remain in the same agency than those in other states. "Median years of social welfare experience with present agency" for employees in Massachusetts was 13.5, compared with 6.6 years in all states and 11.5 years in the second-ranking state, Oklahoma. Attachment to place may also help to explain why turnover among public assistance personnel in Massachusetts has been almost the lowest in the nation—9.5 separations per 100 employees in 1959, compared to a national rate of 21.

The state welfare department was more professionalized than the local staffs. The commissioners either had social-work training themselves (like Tompkins and Ott) or were members of a civic elite sympathetic to the social-work profession (like Rotch). The rest of the state staff was generally better educated than local personnel, though it was by no means completely professionalized. In 1960, 45 percent of the department's field representatives lacked college degrees, whereas 63 percent of the local workers, 68 percent of the local supervisors, and 77 percent of the local directors lacked them.

From the start of federal aid, officials urged the state department to raise personnel standards. The department did not actively resist, but it could not pursue the objective of greater professionalism without meeting resistance from local employees and from the legislature and the Division of Civil Service, both of which traditionally protected the interests of public employees and neither of which wanted public employment to become exclusive.[5] In the face of this resistance, the department tended to be unresponsive to federal pressure. Between 1940 and 1950, as federal merit-system standards were applied to Massachusetts, conflicts broke out repeatedly. The efforts of regional officials to bring about change were hampered not only by resistance within the state, but by a lack of detailed federal requirements that might, with Washington's backing, be insisted upon.

These conflicts were never really settled, and for more than a decade after 1950 they lay dormant. Though the Massachusetts system of recruiting and promoting personnel departed radically from the federal ideal, not until 1964 was it directly and fundamentally challenged. Then, in the wake of the 1962 amendments, the federal administration for the first time specified educational standards for state and local workers. The principal requirement was that caseworkers and casework supervisors appointed after October 1, 1965, have bachelor's degrees. This touched off intense controversy in Massachusetts, where it necessitated modification of the thirty-year-old law against all educational requirements.

The Aftermath of the Merit-System Extension, 1940–1950

In the decade after the merit-system requirement was applied to Massachusetts, problems arose constantly in the state's response to it. Perhaps the most vexing of them grew out of the requirement of a state-wide salary schedule, the "welfare compensation plan." Getting 351 cities and towns quite varied in size and social structure to abide by such a schedule took far more effort than the state's civil service division was willing to invest. Nor did the division satisfy the federal demand for a classification plan. These two matters were the subject of intensive negotiations for much of the decade, and a recurrent source of friction well into the 1960s. (The city of Cambridge, for one, refused to conform to the compensation plan.)

Troublesome as these issues were, they need not have stood in the way of the federal desire for better-qualified personnel. The compensation plan in particular was a response as much to the federal desire for equity as to the desire for professionalism. The intention was to secure equal pay for equal work, and the BPA objected quite as much to local deviations in excess of the salary schedule, which might have attracted high-quality personnel in particular places, as to local failures to meet the schedule. But there were issues that touched more directly on the problem of quality, issues having to do with the conduct of examinations and the setting of entrance requirements.

Integrity of Examinations. The first of these issues developed out of the examinations that were given in 1940 to candidates for positions newly covered by civil service. In some ways, it set the pattern for later ones.

Soon after Commissioner Rotch set up a merit system in 1940, civil service examinations were administered to incumbents and other applicants. Even before the results became known, the Massachusetts Association of Relief Officers prepared a bill that would have nullified them by automatically extending civil service coverage to incumbents. Meanwhile, the welfare department filed a bill to validate the commissioner's action and the examinations given under it.

Faced with these alternatives, the legislature temporized. It did not want to act without knowing the results of the examinations. If the proportion of incumbents failing was low—on the order of 10 to 15 percent—the legislature's civil service committee was prepared to act favorably on the department's bill, but if, as was rumored, the percentage of failures was much higher, the committee wanted to take steps to protect the threatened incumbents.

In March 1941, Civil Service Director Ulysses J. Lupien reported to Commissioner Rotch that 70 incumbents out of 255, or 27.5 percent, had failed. Sensitive to the interests of local employees, and even more to the desires of the legislature's committee on civil service, Lupien urged consideration of a blanketing-in provision. His would have been less generous than the Relief Officers': he proposed to cover incumbents as of July 1, 1935, the date of the Social Security Act, rather than those as of April 1940, the date Rotch's merit system went into effect. This would have lowered the percentage of disqualified incumbents from 27.5 to 15. Lupien asked Rotch to recommend this to the Social Security Board, and Rotch obliged. He sent a copy of Lupien's letter to the BPA regional representative, adding his own endorsement: "In view of the fact that the [civil service] committee and many of the legislators are quite concerned about this whole matter, I recommend that the Social Security Board give its approval." [6]

When the Relief Officers' bill began to circulate in the fall of 1940, federal officials in the region and in Washington agreed that it was completely unacceptable. The regional attorney argued in a memorandum to the central office that it would constitute a "clear violation" of Board standards; the general counsel and Jane Hoey concurred; and the regional representative informed Rotch that if the blanketing-in provision were passed, it would "raise a question of Plan conformity." [7] Now, faced with a recommendation from Lupien and Rotch and a recalcitrant legislature, regional officials began to waver. As they analyzed the situation, relying heavily upon the opinions of Lupien and Rotch, it would be best to accept a blanketing-in provision. It had become clear that a bill validating the commissioner's action was essential if merit system coverage were to stand. The action was being challenged in the courts and Rotch was almost certain to lose. Through negotiations with state civil service and welfare officials, the regional office had succeeded in adding several provisions to the department's bill, including one for the welfare compensation plan, which were very important in the federal view. To the regional office, it appeared that the choice was between accepting a bill that was on the whole essential to federal purposes, although it would be flawed by a blanketing-in provision, and adamant opposition to the provision at the possible cost of losing the whole bill. [8]

Despite the regional office's preference for compromise, the central office stood firm. The legislature's civil service committee made two trips to Washington to talk with Board officials and found that they could not be made to yield. In June 1941, the department's bill, with several federally inspired provisions and without the blanketing-in, was passed.

Even then it was not clear that federal objectives had been secured, for the process of hearing appeals from the examinations had not been completed. One of the distinguishing features of the Massachusetts civil service system is the frequency with which examination results are overturned on appeal.[9] The legislature might not have yielded to the Social Security Board were it not for this possibility of protecting incumbents. Through appeals the number of failures was eventually reduced from 70 to 50. The Board's Washington office prodded the regional office to keep track of appeal results and to make sure that incumbents who failed were actually compelled to give up their jobs. Not until June 1942 was it satisfied on this point.[10]

The struggle over examination results ended with a federal victory, but the circumstances of the struggle illustrated the obstacles that federal officials would face in their effort to improve the quality of state and local personnel: a legislature sensitive to the interests of job seekers, a civil service agency sensitive to the desires of the legislature, and a public welfare agency formally committed to higher personnel standards but unwilling or unable to challenge the civil service division or the legislature. This pattern persisted for a long time, a source of frustration to federal officials whose doctrine was that a "single state agency," the welfare department, should be responsible for meeting federal standards.

Local Registers. A second issue that developed in the early 1940s concerned the territorial units from which local employees should be recruited. The Massachusetts practice before 1940 represented an extreme of localism. The civil service division announced job openings for a specific place, and only residents of that place were admitted to the examination. This was in conflict with Social Security Board policy, which prohibited such residence requirements. The Board wanted examinations to be open to all residents of the state and the list of eligibles to be a single state-wide list.

For two years, regional officials negotiated with state officials in an effort to reconcile Massachusetts practice with federal preferences. They succeeded in getting the civil service division to substitute district examinations for local ones (a district was one of the administrative areas defined by the state welfare department to facilitate supervision of local agencies—there were seven as of 1941); but they failed to get provisions for use of state-wide examinations and registers incorporated in the civil service law. Instead, the legislature merely provided that if the list of eligibles were exhausted for any city or town, the civil service director "might" certify eligibles from a district list.

Federal policy in this matter was not very exacting. Although it prohibited local-residence requirements in the conduct of examinations, it did not prohibit the preferential hiring of local residents. The federal objective was to open up examinations to all competitors and, hopefully, if no local residents were on the register, to compel hiring from a district or state list. In practice, many Massachusetts communities continued to hire only their own residents. Those that wanted to hire from a district list could do so—such a list was available to them—but the civil service division did not compel them to.

Provisional Appointments. A third issue concerned the making of provisional appointments—appointees who had not passed a civil service exam—when no list of eligibles was available. Federal policy permitted such appointments but specified that these appointees must meet the same qualifications as others, that the same individual should not receive successive appointments, and that provisionals be terminated after six months. In 1941 the Massachusetts legislature stipulated that assistance employees appointed provisionally must meet minimum qualifications, a measure that was federally inspired. But issues arose in the next decade over whether this law was being observed and over the volume and duration of provisional appointments.

Federal merit-system audits in the mid-1940s showed that well over half of the new appointments were provisional. Examinations were given infrequently (as of the 1960s, social-worker examinations were still given only once a year), with the result that registers were exhausted much of the time. There were numerous cases in which provisional appointments extended far beyond six months and appointees did not meet qualifications.

This situation was one of several that contributed to federal dissatisfaction with Massachusetts and to the intensive effort to bring about improvement in 1948–50. The regional office also dealt with it separately, by taking audit exceptions for the salaries of provisionals who had served more than six months. When this was first done—with respect to junior clerk-typists, junior clerk-stenographers, and junior clerks in Waltham and Springfield—Commissioner Tompkins protested that the regional office was acting arbitrarily. He charged the regional representative, Eleanore Schopke, with impugning the integrity of the civil service division. "It is quite clear to me," he wrote, ". . . that neither chicanery nor connivance is employed for purposes of disposition of the available eligibles in order to continue favorite provisionals in specifically designated positions either in State government or local government." In response to her request for information, Tompkins declared that "the State Division of Civil Service, acting in its broad, general administrative areas, does not necessarily have to explain to any other branch of government its priority of selections for Civil Service Examinations." [11]

The subsequent exchange between the regional office and Tompkins shows federal-state relations at a point of maximum stress. Miss Schopke declined to rebut his allegations but called attention to "one statement . . . with which we are in disagreement":

You state that you believe no exceptions should be taken unless ". . . there is specific evidence that can be produced by your auditors that positive effort to violate and actual violation of the mandate of the Civil Service Commission took place." On the contrary, we believe that audit exceptions must be taken unless we find that every reasonable effort has been made by the State to meet our Merit System Standards within the requirements of the Civil Service Law. In the absence of sufficient evidence, exceptions have been taken.

Tompkins replied that there was "more than *sufficient evidence*" that " 'every reasonable effort has been made by the State' to meet *your* Merit System Standards." And he added:

We, too, are desirous to make final determinations and particularly with respect to principles of relationships existing between the Federal jurisdiction of government and the local jurisdiction of government, including the State. If it is to be the continuing principle of the Federal Security Agency to challenge either by implication or directly the good faith and legal administrative action of this Department, the State Division of Civil Service, and local appointing authorities, insofar as compliance with the Merit System Plan provisions of the Commonwealth are concerned . . . it would appear that this principle of relationship needs serious review at a higher echelon level than that of the Regional Office insofar as operating policy with respect to the Merit System Plan is concerned.[12]

In keeping with his threat, Tompkins appealed over the head of the regional representative to the deputy commissioner of social security in an effort to get the audit exceptions reversed.

Tompkins had the last word in this exchange with Miss Schopke, but there is no evidence that she changed her mind about the audit exceptions. The retention of provisional appointees for more than six months continued to be a subject of frequent, though less angry, negotiation between federal and state officials. In the 1960s it was still the most important single source of audit exceptions.

Educational Qualifications. Finally, there was the issue of job qualifications. If the federal administration could impose a high standard, its basic objective of high-quality personnel could be realized, and other issues over the civil service system would diminish in importance.

Admission to the civil service in Massachusetts is not achieved, as for federal service, by an examination that tests general knowledge or the ability to reason. Instead, there are as many examinations as there are job classifications, each designed to test knowledge of the particular body of law or set of facts pertinent to the particular job. This has meant that the content of examinations could be prepared for through cram courses or employment experience that provided exposure to the subject matter. Promotions generally have been based on competitive examinations, but great weight is given to seniority. With respect to assistance personnel, in 1940 federal officials found that jobholders frequently entered welfare offices as clerks, acquired sufficient knowledge to pass an examination for worker, and might then move through the ranks to supervisor or even director. The examination for worker stressed factual knowledge of welfare laws such as a clerk could be expected to require.*

Federal officials hoped to reform this system through raising the formal qualifications for workers. The Social Security Board had no specific requirement on this point; it merely said that job specifications for all classes should be "suitable for performance of the duties of the position." Regional officials hoped that, through on-the-scene influence, they might elevate Massachusetts standards. In order to comply with merit-system standards Massachusetts had to have a classification plan that would contain descriptions and minimal qualifications for each job. A federal consultant came from Washington to help in preparing this plan. In cooperation with the state welfare department, the consultant drew up

---

* Here, for example, are questions that were used in the late 1930s:

A woman with dependent children can be assisted under the A.D.C. law even if she is not a widow. True or False.

The Pondville Hospital is under the State Department of (1) Mental Health, (2) Public Health, (3) Correction, (4) Education, (5) Public Welfare.

The records of births and deaths in a community is usually referred to as————.

standards for the category of social worker that excluded clerks. To be eligible, a candidate must have done casework or completed four years of college or some combination of the two.

The new standard did not last long. It was drawn up in 1942, and in 1943 Civil Service Director Lupien proposed to change it so that anyone with six years of clerical experience might qualify. Lupien had never agreed that the new standard was desirable. Anything that restricted entrance to the civil service made the division's job of recruitment more difficult, not to mention aggravating its relations with the legislature. He asked Rotch to inquire if a change would mean the withholding of federal funds. Rotch did so, apologetically, telling the regional representative that he was prepared to urge that the standard be maintained.[13]

Rotch's question—he actually asked the regional office how far standards might be lowered without jeopardizing grants—was not of the kind that would elicit a candid reply from the Social Security Board. All the Board would say was that it did not consider "six years of any and all types of clerical experience" as suitable qualifying experience for the class of social worker.[14] Lupien found this answer hard to interpret; his successor in 1945, Thomas J. Greehan, noticed that it contained possibilities. Since the Board would not accept "any and all types" of clerical experience, Greehan proposed giving credit for only one type of clerical experience, that obtained from work "directly related to social casework." When regional officials objected to his admitting clerks to workers' examinations, he explained that he would not admit those "who have been filing or merely answering the telephone." He would admit only those who had "actually determined eligibility and need, made recommendations, and rendered other services." Regional officials yielded, with much reluctance. They regarded the change as a deviation from Board standards, but they rationalized it on the ground that the Board permitted standards to be relaxed during the war. Inevitably, the federal concession proved impossible to retract even after the end of the war. By 1948 regional officials were mainly concerned with getting the civil service director to abide by his agreement to distinguish among the various clerk-candidates according to their experience. Personnel reviews convinced them that no clerk was barred from the workers' examination who had served six years in any welfare agency.

This did not mean that federal pressure produced no change at all in standards of entrance. Partly as a result of prodding and suggestion from regional officials and "technical assistance" in the form of sample questions, the examinations for social worker changed fundamentally between 1940 and 1960. They ceased to depend on detailed knowledge of state law and began to depend on knowledge of the received wisdom of the social-work profession.*

Whatever the effect of these examinations on the process of selection, by the criterion of formal education Massachusetts workers continued to be extremely unprofessionalized. A federal survey in 1962 showed that 30.6 percent of the caseworkers hired in the previous year had no college education whatever, a higher percentage than in any other state except Arkansas.[15]

* The following examples are drawn from an examination in 1962:

The case worker's frame of mind at the time of the initial interview must be such that he approaches the client with the attitude that:

(1) care should be taken in handling the interview since most people applying for aid are emotionally unstable persons;

(2) if sympathy is shown it will cause the client to be too dependent on the interviewer and thus cause him to lose his interviewing initiative;

(3) the client is an emotionally healthy person and should be treated as such until proven otherwise;

(4) care should be taken to detect the slightest signs of fraud, since most persons applying for aid are inherently dishonest.

The marks by which a particular professional service is distinguished from other professional services are its field, its objectives, its vocational resources and its characteristic methods of work. Which one of the following five phrases best distinguishes the equipment of the social case worker from that of the lawyer, doctor, teacher or nurse?

(1) A more complete knowledge of the interrelationship of local, state and federal government units;

(2) Knowledge of symptoms and causes in deviations of individual human behavior from accepted standards;

(3) Ability to impart knowledge to others because of more adequate education and broader experience;

(4) Capacity to understand and accept the importance of cultural differences;

(5) The ability to use scientific method and carefully control experiments.

The College-Degree Requirement

The federal effort at professionalization intensified as the stress on services increased. On the assumption that ability to rehabilitate the poor could be acquired through training, and only in that way, federal administrators coupled measures for service giving with measures to raise educational levels. One approach was to finance attendance at schools of social work. Another was to require the states to conduct in-service training programs. A third, adopted in the fall of 1964, was to stipulate formal educational requirements—the college degree for newly hired caseworkers and casework supervisors.

The Massachusetts Response. Even before the degree requirement was imposed, the Massachusetts welfare department had responded to the rising federal pressure for improvements in personnel. In 1962 Commissioner Tompkins persuaded the civil service division to adopt standards for the caseworker category that in effect required a college education. Still, such a requirement was not explicit, and it did not stand in the way of promotions for all those who had obtained workers' jobs under the previous standard. Thus the requirement of a degree for both workers and supervisors had a major impact on Massachusetts.

The federal directive was neither unwelcome nor surprising to Commissioner Ott. He had taken office with two basic aims: to shift assistance administration from local governments to the state and to raise the educational level of workers. To achieve the first goal, he looked for help mainly to private or quasi-public organizations in Massachusetts; to achieve the second, he looked to the federal government. He knew that he would not be able to act ununless federal officials "forced" him to.[16]

Ott had made clear in conversations with the federal welfare commissioner, Ellen Winston, and with BFS officials that he would be receptive to an educational requirement. Soon after taking office Dr. Winston—she preferred to be called "doctor," as the holder of a Ph.D. degree in sociology—had sent BFS teams to gather suggestions from state commissioners for program improvement. When the New England team visited Ott, in the spring of 1964, he stressed the importance of an educational standard for workers. He did not at the time recommend one for supervisors, but he was not displeased to find in November that the federal directive included that too.

Soon after the directive arrived, Ott requested a meeting with regional officials to discuss the contents and the Massachusetts response. In reply, the regional representative, Neil P. Fallon, identified for discussion four actions that seemed necessary for implementing the new requirements:

1. Revision of the Personnel Law to permit educational requirements for any appointment, promotion or temporary transfer to positions in the grant-in-aided agencies subject to Federal standards for a merit system of personnel administration.

2. Revision of the Personnel Law to eliminate initial certification on a town residence basis. We recommend that certification be on a statewide basis.

3. Establishment of minimum qualification requirements for the designated State and local positions . . .

4. Require the Director of Civil Service to certify that provisional appointees, persons promoted and temporary transfers meet the minimum qualification requirements. Revision of the law governing the promotion system may be needed to make these changes effective.[17]

Within limits, regional officials can interpret the central office's directives to fit the special circumstances of each state. Depending on their own predilections, their interpretations may be strict in order to eliminate peculiarities or lenient in order to adapt to them. At least since the late 1940s, the New England office had tended toward strict interpretation. In this particular case the directive opened up for regional officials an opportunity to effect changes that they very much wanted but that could not be achieved without active support both within the state and from Washington. Their interpretation went beyond what was explicitly called for. The directive applied only to public welfare, but the regional office was asking for a bill that would authorize educational requirements for all federally aided positions. No new requirements were imposed with respect to residence (though old ones were reiterated), and none with respect to coverage of provisional and temporary appointees. Actions 2 and 4 in the regional office list were added in an effort to cure long-standing problems in Massachusetts; though the directive did not require this, it provided an occasion for doing so.

Meeting early in December with Ott and his staff, regional officials found them receptive to the federal position, although concerned about probable opposition from the civil service division and the legislature, especially to action that would jeopardize the promotional chances of incumbent workers. It was agreed that the state department would draft "the best possible bill" for submission to the legislature.[18] By late January this was done, and Ott sent the draft to Governor Volpe, saying it was "a matter of fair import that all federal funds will be withdrawn from all public assistance programs in this Commonwealth unless there is a compliance with the prescribed requirements." Because it was prepared in cooperation with regional officials, the bill met their specifications.[19]

Gathering Support. Once the bill was drafted, the initiative for action belonged to Ott. The legislature had to be induced to act quickly, for the Welfare Administration's deadline for compliance was July 1. The regional office might help by supplying information and affirmations of federal intentions (or, more likely, by urging the central office to supply them), but a combination of constitutional tradition, political expediency, and the established protocol of federal-state relations prevented it from taking a leading part in the ensuing campaign. Ott sought help from two sources: the governor's office and civic and professional organizations that could lobby for his bill.

He needed support from the governor if only to have the bill put before the legislature. After the legislative session begins, only the governor may freely introduce bills; those from other sources require a suspension of the rules. Beyond that formality, of course, the bill would benefit from Volpe's active endorsement. The situation was auspicious, not so much because of Volpe's interest in welfare programs as because of his willingness to give free rein to the concern of Lieutenant-Governor Elliot Richardson. Proponents of the bill could not have wanted a better ally at the top of the executive branch. A former assistant secretary of health, education, and welfare (in the Eisenhower Administration), Richardson had an understanding with Volpe that he would have charge of such fields in their administration of the state government. Before taking office in January, he had been given a day-long briefing at the HEW regional office. When Ott's letter finally came to Volpe's attention (it was lost for nearly three weeks in the governor's office, and anxiety mounted among its backers), he referred it to Richardson. Wholly sympathetic with the federal directive, Richardson incorporated Ott's recommendations in a special health and welfare message to the legislature, which Volpe delivered on April 1.

Lobbying support was also readily available, for there were many professional and civic groups with an interest in civil service reform. These included the League of Women Voters, the Citizens for Advancement of the Public Service, the Massachusetts Public Health Association, the Massachusetts Committee on Children and Youth, the eastern Massachusetts chapter of the National Association of Social Workers (NASW), and the United Community Services of Metropolitan Boston. Several of these groups had already been trying to get the legislature to permit imposition of educational requirements, and they were planning to try again in 1965. Naturally they were pleased to have the federal government as an ally, even if its interest was limited to those programs in which it had a financial stake. (One of the reasons the welfare department drafted the bill so as to cover other than welfare personnel was to increase the range of support for it.) Soon after sending his draft bill to Governor Volpe, Ott called together representatives of these organizations and of the schools of social work in Greater Boston to alert them to the opportunity for action. This *ad hoc* group—with the associate regional representative of the BFS participating in the role of "consultant" [20]—continued to function in a loose fashion, but most of the planning and much of the telephoning, letter writing, and actual buttonholing of legislators was done by the executive director of the NASW chapter, Beverly Fliegel, with help from a member of the staff of the Committee on Children and Youth.[21]

Once alerted, supporters of reform were quick to take action. Lobbying began as early as March 15, when Mrs. Fliegel spotted Representative Royal Bolling, the House chairman of the civil service committee, in the Golden Dome, a restaurant next to the State House which is the scene of much politicking, and proceeded to tell him why he ought to support Ott's forthcoming bill. Although legislators were naturally the object of much lobbying, so, less predictably, was the Welfare Administration in Washington. One of the first acts of the *ad hoc* group was to write Dr. Winston to thank her for the directive, assure her that the NASW and other organizations were working hard for the necessary legislation, and urge her to stand firm against compromise. Richardson was also in touch with the Welfare Administration, and for a similar purpose. In a phone conversation with Deputy Commissioner Joseph Meyers in early March and in a telegram to Dr. Winston three weeks later, he sought clarification of their position. To some extent, Richardson's inquiries were a probing of the federal intent; the degree to which the Volpe administration should commit itself to legislation might depend on the firmness of the backing it could expect from Washington. But they were also, like the *ad hoc* group's letter, meant to encourage a firm stand and to draw the Welfare Administration into making such a stand in public. Richardson used Dr. Winston's reply to his telegram in the public hearing on Ott's bill.

Without Dr. Winston's saying anything in public, the Welfare Administration's influence had long since been put on the line by its friends in Massachusetts. Although the federal administration was reluctant to threaten withholding, and although the state agency, with its obligation to interpret the federal position with reasonable fidelity, could not say that such a threat had been made, private groups allied with the state agency were under no such constraint. They were free, with its tacit encouragement, to attribute any words they liked to federal sources, and hence to make it appear that the state was seriously threatened with the loss of funds. The most effective ally of the state agency in this respect was Boston's largest daily newspaper, the *Globe*, whose evening edition on February 15 bore the following headline over its lead story: "State May Lose Millions in U.S. Welfare Funds." Without quoting any federal officials or documents, the *Globe* reported that funds might be withheld unless the state complied with the educational-requirement directive, the existence of which had not been publicized before. The sources identified by reporter Jean Dietz were the February bulletin of the League of Women Voters, which "predicted" the possible loss of funds, and Richardson, who "confirmed" it. Actually, Mrs. Dietz had first been alerted to the matter, quite confidentially, by Commissioner Ott himself, and it is perhaps no accident that the story appeared at the time Ott was waiting for the governor's reply to his letter of late January. The story was the first, and probably the most important, of many in the *Globe* which aided the reformers, along with repeated editorials exhorting and chastising the legislature. Federal officials thought so highly of the *Globe*'s help that when the struggle was over, and a satisfactory bill had been passed, Dr. Winston sent Mrs. Dietz a thank-you letter for her support and the "sympathetic way" in which she had "presented the facts in the situation to the reading public." [22]

The Opposition. Ott and the regional officials presumed that they would encounter opposition from the civil service division and the legislature, which had more than once in recent years rejected bills that would have repealed the general prohibition against educational requirements. These expectations were confirmed in an executive session with the legislature's Committee on

Civil Service in early March. Civil Service Director W. Henry Finnegan, a crusty and tendentious man, charged that the federal directive violated the Constitution, states' rights, and the laws of Massachusetts, that it discriminated against the unfortunate, and that it misused the taxpayers' dollars. Committee members, though more restrained, were deeply concerned about protecting incumbent workers' chances for promotion. Federal officials came away discouraged by the meeting and uneasy about a suggestion from Finnegan that legislators go to Washington to talk to administrators and Congressman McCormack. Finnegan had already called one of McCormack's staff members.

From now on, both sides were preoccupied with what McCormack would do. With nearly forty years of service in Congress he was Speaker of the House and, if he became interested in the issue, the Welfare Administration might think it prudent to give ground. On the assumption that he disagreed with the principle of educational requirements, proponents of the bill did not expect to get his support, but they hoped at least to dissuade him from helping their opponents. In mid-April the Reverend Joseph W. Alves, president of the NASW chapter, wrote to McCormack that "a few persons" were resisting the directive and might "seek Congressional help in forcing the Department of Health, Education, and Welfare to compromise their position." Alves said that if this happened it would be "devastating" to Massachusetts. "I felt it important to alert you to this issue and to the appreciation of local groups for the HEW directive. It would be most reassuring to know that there will not be support from your Office for efforts to weaken the Federal Directive. With that assurance those of us working for excellence in public service in Massachusetts can concentrate on enacting the needed legislation locally." [23] McCormack's reply, a copy of which he sent to HEW Secretary Anthony J. Celebrezze, was not reassuring at all. He wrote:

> . . . I am frank in stating it is pretty hard for me to reconcile myself with the opinion that a person who did not go to college and who is eminently qualified simply through self

education and experience should be denied appointment to
the position mentioned in your letter. For example, if one
had to be a graduate of college to be a Member of Congress,
I could not have been a Member of Congress. If one had to
be a graduate of a law school to be a member of the Massachusetts Bar years ago, I could not have been a member of
the Massachusetts Bar . . . It is one thing to say that an applicant must be eminently qualified, but another thing to say
that no matter how much a person might be qualified, if he
is not a college graduate that he is "barred" from consideration and appointment.[24]

McCormack's letter, with its implicit complaint of class prejudice, epitomized much of the opposition to the bill, especially in
the Massachusetts legislature. As of 1965, roughly half of the
members of the House, not far removed from working-class origins, themselves lacked college degrees,[25] and others who had
them nevertheless continued to share with the rest a sense of
class or ethnic community. In a state heavily populated by fairly
recent immigrants and their descendants, public office, both elec-
tive and appointive, has been a source of status and security for
thousands who could not find those rewards elsewhere. Members
of the legislature were reluctant to compromise a system that had
helped them to rise and could still help others. In any event, no
matter what their class, ethnic, or educational identifications,
many were pragmatic men who valued common sense and experience more than formal education.

If the reformers' effort backfired, so too did their opponents'
effort to get help from McCormack a month later. By late April,
Volpe's message having been delivered, the Public Welfare Administrators' Association was aware of the bill and seeking
changes that would protect incumbent workers. It had hired a lob-
byist and was urging members to write their representatives in the
federal and state legislatures. In one three-day period in May,
thirty-nine local directors wrote McCormack objecting to Ott's bill
and thanking him for his interest. Many of the letters were signed

by supervisors and workers as well as directors. Naively, McCormack forwarded all of them to HEW Undersecretary Wilbur J. Cohen, "in order to convey to you the opinion and position expressed by the people of Massachusetts." The Washington office, noting acidly that "the people" were all incumbent employees, in turn forwarded them to the regional office in Boston, where they were filed "for future reference . . . regarding personnel who have potentiality for promotion between now and July 1, 1967." [26] (Until that date, as a result of certain provisions in the educational-requirement directive, federal officials might exercise some discretion with respect to promotions of personnel who lacked college degrees.) Far from protecting the interests of his constituents, McCormack had unwittingly placed them in jeopardy.

The Grandfather Clause. Legislative action, set in motion by Volpe's message, continued up to the eve of the federal deadline. A bill passed three hours before midnight on June 30, almost as Ott and federal officials had drafted it, but it was challenged to the end. The central issue had to do with a grandfather clause. Welfare employee organizations and their supporters in the civil service division and the legislature accepted a degree requirement for new workers, but sought to protect the promotional chances of incumbent workers who lacked degrees. It was never clear just how many incumbents were likely to be affected, for the opposing sides differed radically on this point. Probably the most accurate estimate, which appeared in a manuscript privately prepared by a federal official for the use of NASW, was that about eight hundred workers would not be able to advance without additional education.

Before debate on the bill began, House Speaker John F. X. Davoren sent a four-man legislative delegation to Washington to ask Dr. Winston whether modifications in the federal directive were possible. The ranking members were Representative Bolling, who as chairman of the civil service committee had opposed the grandfather clause,* and Senator Beryl Cohen, chairman of the public

---

* Bolling sympathized with the bill from the start despite efforts by opponents in the legislature to persuade him that it was contrary to the interests of his

welfare committee and the reformers' principal ally in the legislature. The delegation's trip was not made for the purpose of gaining concessions. Rather, it was meant to establish at home that the federal intent had been tested and found to be firm. It helped legislative backers of the bill to limit their own responsibility. The federal government, they could say, will not give in. We have asked it to, have done what we can to resist, and now we will just have to go along with it.

The visit to the Welfare Administration, on May 13, went as expected. Dr. Winston—"a southern gentlewoman with a fist of steel," one regional official called her—took a firm line and repeated it in a written response to questions submitted by the delegation, questions that had obviously been framed by someone sympathetic to reform. But the visit to Washington had an unexpected result. After the meeting with Dr. Winston, which had been arranged by Senator Edward Kennedy's office, the group paid a routine courtesy call on Speaker McCormack. They found him aware of the issue and eager to help. With the delegation in his office, he called up HEW Undersecretary Cohen, complained about the directive, and said he wanted to see Cohen about it. The delegation went back to Massachusetts and debate on the bill was postponed pending the McCormack-Cohen meeting.

Back in Boston anxiety mounted among the reformers lest HEW give in to congressional pressure. On top of McCormack's action came a short, pointed floor speech on May 17 by Massachusetts Congressman Thomas P. O'Neill, who declared that the HEW action was a "gross injustice." He said he would "protest it vigorously" and called for adoption of the grandfather clause.[27] Backers of the bill in Massachusetts sent telegrams to Cohen urging him to stand firm and stressing the extent of support within the state for the federal position.

---

constituents. A Negro, Bolling represented a lower-class Negro district in Boston. Some tried to argue with him that raising civil service entrance standards would make it harder for Negroes to get jobs, but he seemed more receptive to the reformers' argument that better-educated welfare workers would mean better treatment for the poor. Speaking of the reformers, he said, "Some people say they are a bunch of do-gooders, but if an idea is good, it doesn't matter where it comes from." Interview, April 1, 1965. Under his leadership, the civil service committee reported the bill without a grandfather clause.

When McCormack and Cohen met on May 21, Cohen appeared to compromise HEW's position, though by how much was hard to say, so carefully was his concession worded. He said it was vital that the legislation be passed, but thereafter the department would be "prepared to make such adjustments" in its policy "as appear to be appropriate and necessary." Specifically, the Bureau of Family Services would "consider" the possibility of allowing persons who were not college graduates to become supervisors providing they passed examinations that met federal standards. In McCormack's presence, Cohen stated this position in a phone call to Senator Beryl Cohen, and he repeated it in a letter of confirmation the same day.[28]

The bill now came before the Massachusetts House. The opponents, led by Representative Charles L. Shea of Quincy, offered an amendment to make the act inapplicable to any person employed prior to July 1, 1965, and to delete provisions for mandatory hiring from district and state registers and mandatory application of hiring standards to temporary appointments and promotions. Shea and his supporters argued the need to protect the interests of incumbent workers, but they were not concerned only with particular jobs or jobholders. They believed that a principle was at stake. "We have an obligation to protect our own system," Representative Paul Cataldo of Franklin said during the debate.[29] Under this system, state jobs were distributed in conformance with values that prevailed in the Massachusetts legislature. Now the system was under attack from an alliance of federal administrators and reformers within the state, who sought to have jobs distributed according to a different set of values.

Bolling and two other members of the civil service committee who had gone to Washington—Representatives Lawrence Smith of Lawrence and William Kitterman of Pittsfield—pleaded with the House to defeat the grandfather clause. Whatever the attitude of Kitterman and Smith before the trip (proponents had doubted their sympathy), they came back strong supporters of the bill. They had gone there and obtained—mostly through McCormack's intervention—a potentially significant concession when none had seemed likely. Wilbur Cohen's letter to Beryl Cohen was read to the House. Civil service committee members, feeling themselves to be a party to this compromise, urged the House to honor it. However, the House sided with Shea, whose amendment was adopted, 119 to 86. The House agreed to reconsider the vote and Shea won again, 106 to 86. It looked as if the legislature might be willing to defy the federal directive.

Much of the debate had revolved around the credibility of the threat that funds would be withheld. Shea declared that Alabama and Mississippi had defied the federal government in fundamental matters but continued to get aid. John F. Thompson, former speaker of the House, rose to say it was nonsense to suppose that funds would be withheld. Speaking for proponents of the bill, Bolling maintained that the grandfather clause would jeopardize federal money and added that "the more money we get, the more jobs there will be." No one in the legislature argued the merits of formal education for social workers. A few members certainly believed in the value of such education, but they recognized that nothing could be gained from arguing the point before a legislature that was on the whole skeptical.

The BFS regional representative was in the House gallery during the debate, and his report of it to Washington emphasized the challenges to the administration's credibility that had come from Shea and Thompson. The regional office's role, like that of the reform lobbyists, was to bolster Washington's will, but regional officials had to do this subtly, by indirect appeals to the central executives' pride or by expressions of gratitude for acts of support. ("We feel that today you made a major contribution," the regional director wrote to Dr. Winston after her meeting with the legislative delegation.[30]) In gathering information for Washington, regional officials normally had to rely a great deal on Commissioner Ott and his lobbying allies. Reluctant to get directly involved in state politics, they had few independent opportunities for observation and intelligence gathering except when, as with the floor debates, events were exposed to public view. The active lobbyists therefore became the "eyes and ears" of the regional office. At the height of the action, the regional representative was in daily contact with Commissioner Ott and, either directly or through him, with Mrs. Fliegel.

The action of the House was not final. The bill still had to have a third reading, at which time it could be amended again. Some members may have voted for the grandfather clause with this in mind, thinking to change positions later if that seemed expedient. Thompson had urged the legislature to adopt the clause "to strengthen our bargaining position." "Maybe," he said, if the legislature took a strong stand the Massachusetts congressional delegation would "get off their butts" and "do something for a change." Thompson, like other supporters of the grandfather clause, was not satisfied with the Cohen-McCormack agreement. Cohen's concession was vague and informal. It rested solely on a personal understanding with McCormack, and, as one legislator pointed out with more realism than tact, Mr. McCormack was an old man.

Thompson's remark was a manifestation of the general anger in the House over the congressional delegation's failure to protest the directive more strongly. In letters to complaining welfare directors, congressmen denied responsibility. This was true even of McCormack, who did far more than any other congressman to help. Writing a local director on May 22, he began: "I am in receipt of your letter and several others in relation to the bill that is in the Massachusetts Legislature. As you know, this is a matter that is passed upon by the members of the Massachusetts Legislature, and not by members of the Congress." McCormack went on to stress his opposition to the action which, he said, HEW was doing "administratively." [31] Congressmen handled numerous complaints from local-agency employees routinely, that is, by sending copies of their letters to HEW and asking for comments that could be used as a basis for reply to the constituent. This had been the pattern of congressional response, too, in the conflict of 1949–50 over the extension of civil service administration to small towns.

It was the proponents of the bill who had unexploited resources of influence as the time for final action approached. The opponents had already appealed to their strongest potential ally, McCormack, and received a response that the legislature treated as unsatisfactory. They could not return to him. The proponents, by contrast, had not put forth their best effort. One of their most influential allies, the speaker of the Massachusetts House, had not brought his influence to bear on the vote.

Speaker Davoren took seriously, with Ott's encouragement, the threat that funds would be withheld if a satisfactory bill were not passed, and—although he was not necessarily in favor of authorizing educational requirements for all state jobs—he seemed receptive to the reformers' arguments as they applied to jobs in public welfare. Preferring, though, to save his influence for other matters (this, after all, was in no way an issue of his choosing), he did not at first actively help the reformers. He had not openly appealed for votes, and when the bill came before the House, neither he nor his majority leader was presiding or even present in the chamber. This gave Democratic members—in the majority—freedom to vote as they chose, and they chose to vote with Shea. Of the 119 votes for the grandfather clause, 98 came from Democrats—a result that apparently surprised Davoren, who had underestimated Shea's support. The reformers then proceeded to lobby harder than ever before, and when the bill came up again, he cast his vote against Shea's amendment; enough Democrats followed him to overturn the earlier vote. The grandfather clause was defeated, but only by four votes, 110 to 106.[32]

Senate action was anticlimactic. Senate President Donahue was for the bill; a local welfare director who approached him was told that the federal directive left no choice. An attempt to attach the grandfather clause lost, 15 to 5. When the bill was returned to the House, a last-minute series of moves by Shea to amend or delay it was beaten. Both houses completed action on June 30.

"There was a lot of suppressed resentment," Senator Cohen said not long after the vote in the Senate. "People didn't vote the way they felt." [33] Instead, legislators in both houses were responding to what they took to be a federal threat, although to the very end, federal officials themselves had issued no threats. They had not said that funds would be withheld if the grandfather clause were adopted, or even if the bill as a whole failed to pass. It was the proponents of reform in Massachusetts who said so, helped by the *Boston Globe,* which by publicizing their statements gave credence to them. The truth of the matter—that no "threat" had been made, that withholding was a remote and problematic occurrence, that it would come, if at all, only after long procedural delays—was too complex and uninteresting to make good copy, quite apart from the fact that the reporter who covered the story was too enthusiastic a supporter of the federal action to search for truths that, if found out and reported, would ill serve the reformers' cause. The availability of a mouthpiece, to play (perhaps ingenuously) the role of publicizing the presumed threat, is essential if that weapon of federal influence is to be used successfully.

If Massachusetts had failed to comply with the federal directive by the deadline, a long period of bargaining would have ensued. The actual withholding of funds would have come, if ever, only after hearings before the HEW Secretary and a finding by him that the state was not conforming to federal requirements. Yet the "threat" had a strong impact on the legislature. It was taken with enough seriousness by enough members to affect the outcome of the issue. Some, out of naiveté or ignorance, apparently took it very seriously. A few probably recognized that the threat was remote but thought it real nonetheless and frightening, in view of the state's chronic shortage of funds. Others, probably a crucial group of substantial size, did not know how to assess it but seized upon it as a rationale for voting with the leadership. House members of the majority party would prefer to vote with the Speaker, Senate members with the president, but they need a plausible defense if the vote would prove offensive to interested constituents. In this case, the threatened loss of funds was such a defense.

The Consequences. Just how much the alliance of federal administrators and Massachusetts reformers had achieved would depend on interpretation and application of the Cohen-McCormack agreement. Citing it, the civil service director in early October began sending letters to Ott asking exceptions to the degree requirement for persons who had passed examinations for social-work supervisor. Ott referred his requests to the BFS, which took six months to reply so difficult did it find the task of developing a position. Regional officials pressed for an affirmative response, fearing that if the central office did not honor the agreement Shea might still succeed in getting the legislature to pass a grandfather clause. The bureau chief replied with a limited concession. The BFS would accept the results of supervisory examinations given prior to October 1, 1965, and it agreed to accept admission of non-degree-holding candidates to one more supervisory examination providing it were administered state-wide or on the basis of districts and that appointments from the resulting register were made prior to July 1, 1967.[34]

As of that date, then, the requirement of college degrees for new caseworkers and casework supervisors was in effect without qualification. Higher personnel standards had been achieved and would not have been achieved in the absence of federal action. Although the legislature had grudgingly responded to the federal directive, it declined to remove the general prohibition against educational requirements. That bill, which depended wholly on support from within the state, was beaten in mid-May, while the federally inspired bill was beginning its tortuous way toward approval.[35]

Professionalism and State Administration

The imposition of the degree requirement was a major step toward the federal goal of professionalism, and it was soon followed by another, the bill for state administration. For the state welfare commissioner and allied reform groups in Massachusetts, the campaign of 1965 over college degrees was a prelude to that for state administration. The lobbying capacity developed for the first campaign was promptly applied to the second and augmented somewhat (for example, by enlisting participation of assistance recipients), perhaps in order to compensate for not being able this time to use the threat that federal funds would be withheld if the reform were not adopted. Though federal officials were still very closely allied with them in spirit, federal influence was not in this case at the reformers' disposal.

Sponsors of state administration saw it as a way of shifting authority and power from the almost completely unprofessionalized local agencies to the more professionalized state department. More fundamentally, it was a way of undermining localism and thus removing one of the major obstacles to professionalism.[36] If there remained any doubt of the state department's own professionalism, the reform bill helped to put it to rest.[37] The bill required the commissioner and the directors of all the community service centers, about fifty of which were anticipated, to have a master's degree in social work. A deputy commissioner and five assistant commissioners were not subject to the degree requirement or to civil service—a provision that was meant to safeguard the interests of certain incumbent state officials and that caused tension between the reformers (who were practical enough to take care of the state staff) and the federal regional officials (who pressed for maximum civil service coverage, but not too hard before the bill was passed, lest they jeopardize a reform that was very much in the federal interest).

It was hard to say where the service center directors would come from. The requirement of a master's degree in social work excluded virtually all incumbent local personnel, whether directors, supervisors, or workers. In 1966 the state department itself had only twenty public assistance staff members with MSW degrees. The House, which had been so much concerned to protect the jobs and promotional chances of incumbents in 1965, uncharacteristically showed no concern whatever for them now. No doubt this was because the question was not put to it directly. Had an effort been made on the floor to qualify or to remove the requirement for social-work degrees, a majority would surely have supported an amendment; but the local administrators no longer had an alert, committed spokesman on the floor to press for such an amendment (Shea had left in 1967 for a job with the legislature's research council). Both the leadership and the reform lobbyists were exerting strong pressure against any amendments, except a few of their own. The legislature seemed to regard the bill, as did politicians generally, as a measure to shift assistance costs to the state. A majority favored this, for it was manifestly in the interests of their local constituencies, but beyond that, they showed little interest in what was in the bill.[38]

Part III | The Consequences of
Federal Action

8 | Federal Influence: An Analysis

Federal influence has had a profound effect on the Massachusetts public assistance program. By 1965, thirty years after the start of federal aid, the program had been transformed. Assistance had been liberalized: standards of eligibility were more inclusive, grants were much higher, and a client-serving philosophy was in effect. Grants had been standardized: differences among cities and towns, substantial in 1935, were now marginal. Policymaking had been centralized: laws and rules governing the program originated entirely with the state. Both policymaking and administration had been bureaucratized: on the local (the administrative) level, appointed officials had completely superseded elected officials as administrators of public assistance, and at the state (the policymaking) level, the administrators' role in policymaking had expanded in relation to that of the legislature. To the extent that the bureaucracy was professionalized and policymaking shifted to the most professionalized part of it (to the highest-ranking officials of the state welfare department), policymaking and administration were also professionalized. There remained a residual program of assistance, general relief, of which none of this could be said, but that program had steadily diminished until it accounted for only a twelfth of the caseload. Finally, in 1967, with the adoption of state administration, the transformation was completed. Having been rendered anomalous by the course of events since 1935, the local administration of all categories and the local control of general relief were done away with.

It cannot be shown that federal action caused these changes. On the contrary, most of them were under way before federal aid began and they would certainly have continued, under the impact of urbanization and the increased political activity of interest groups within the state. It is perfectly clear, however, that the changes were accelerated and in important ways shaped by federal action. Change took place faster than it would have in the absence of federal participation, and took specific forms and directions that it might not otherwise have taken. Had federal influence not been felt, the Massachusetts public assistance program in 1965 would have been far different: less liberal, less uniform, less centralized, less bureaucratized, and less professionalized. Although the state role in policymaking and the supervision of administration would surely have grown, it would not have grown so much. It is most unlikely that state administration would have been adopted by 1967. In the absence of federal insistence to the contrary, selectmen in the smallest Massachusetts towns to this day might be administering the towns' few public assistance cases themselves, with casual clerical help from their wives.*

The purpose of this chapter is to analyze, on the basis of the Massachusetts experience with public assistance but in general terms, the nature of federal influence in grant-in-aid programs: the ends of that influence, the means of exercising it, and the degree of its effectiveness. I have assumed, consistent with the practice in public assistance, that it is state governments that receive

---

* These inferences are based partly on observation of programs in Massachusetts other than public assistance. If powerful centralizing forces were at work in the state independently of federal action, they should affect all locally run programs. Centralization should occur across the entire spectrum of local activity. This has not happened. Education, the only function that has accounted consistently throughout the cities and towns for a larger share of expenditure than assistance, has remained extremely decentralized, with policymaking and administration largely in the hands of elected local school committees and administrators appointed by them. The state education department has been very weak, and an attempt in the early 1960s to strengthen it has not made much headway. One explanation for the difference between the two programs (which would apply outside Massachusetts as well) may be that in education, in contrast to public assistance, the leading professionals have held jobs at the local level (as superintendents) rather than at the state or federal levels. The beginning of large-scale federal aid to education in the 1960s may change this. The federal Office of Education has expanded in size and gained in professional stature, and the strengthening of state departments of education has become an explicit objective.

federal grants, but the analysis is meant to apply as well to programs of aid to local governments.

Federal Objectives

The conditions attached to grants contain the most comprehensive and authoritative definition of federal objectives. In them the federal government states how far it will seek to guide the conduct of other governments. Therefore, the place to begin an analysis of federal objectives is with these conditions—with what they state and fail to state. What they fail to state is the more striking, for federal conditions cover a limited range of actions.

Political Constraints on the Setting of Conditions. In the public assistance program, federal conditions conspicuously fail to cover the questions of major substantive importance, which is to say the questions of major political importance. The states are left to make the crucial value choices—how much they will spend for public assistance and who will get it (and, by implication) how much tax revenue they will raise. Although the availability of federal aid influences their choices, and although federal law restricts in some respects the range of discretion available to them in determining eligibility, they nevertheless have had almost complete freedom in determining how poor a recipient must be and how large assistance payments shall be.

For the federal government to impose value choices on state governments it must first arrive at such choices itself. It must formulate policies that are precise and internally consistent. In general this is very difficult to do, whether or not the policy applies to grant-in-aid programs, and grant programs may magnify the difficulties because the extremely diverse interests of all state governments are directly engaged in the programs' operation. As the government with the most inclusive jurisdiction, the federal government is the only one that can enunciate common goals for shared programs, but as a resolver of conflicts—that is, as a maker of difficult value choices—it is handicapped by its very inclusiveness. It has the widest possible range of interests to reconcile. One of the functions the grant system performs is to enable the federal legislature to commit itself to serving very broad national purposes (such as "more adequate" welfare) without assuming the burden of making all of the political choices it would have to make in a unitary system (how much welfare, for whom?). The difficult choices may be left to other governments.* In the absence of powerful integrating mechanisms at the federal level—a presidential planning staff that would reconcile differences within the executive branch, a powerful party organization that would reconcile them within Congress and between Congress and the executive branch—federal policy statements for grant-in-aid programs are likely to be inconsistent, ambiguous in what they do state, and altogether silent on much that is important. This is the only way that differences of values and opinions between Congress and the executive branch (or within them) can be resolved and a *federal* position arrived at.

A second general reason for federal restraint in stipulating value choices is the necessity for buying participation in grant programs. Because participation is in principle voluntary—other governments need not accept grants unless it is to their advantage to do so—the federal government has to induce cooperation with offers of monetary incentives on favorable terms. In practice, the very great responsiveness of state governments to federal grants may seem to make this point irrelevant. Grant money is so widely sought after that opportunities for the exercise of federal influence seem to be readily available. However, the acceptance of grants would not be so prompt and widespread if the conditions accompanying them were very costly and were known to be strictly enforced. If, by acceptance of federal grants, state govern-

---

* The opportunities that the federal system provides for distributing the burden of political decisionmaking may contribute to the stability of the system as a whole or to the maintenance of the role of the federal legislature in that system. Congress' critics and its defenders both say that it is "overburdened." It would be much more so were our system not a federal one. The fact that, for all its problems, the U.S. Congress is still the most vigorous of the legislatures of the major nations may be attributed partly to the opportunities the federal system provides for responding to pressures for action while limiting the risks of the response.

ments had to accede to a wide range of federally determined value choices, the decision to accept them would become highly controversial and thus vulnerable to obstruction at the state level from groups whose interests would suffer. Congress has generally performed the function of finding the terms on which grant programs may win the widest possible acceptance while safeguarding certain basic federal interests. That Congress is highly sensitive to state and local interests means that the terms it settles on are in important respects highly permissive ones. Congressmen see to it that, for state governments, the ratio of benefit to cost in grant programs is high enough to be attractive.

Congress is not totally permissive, however. Ambivalent institution that it is, it has a conception of a federal interest as well as a good deal of sensitivity to state and local interests. The actual content of statutory conditions shows what the federal government conceives its basic interests to be. These conditions consist predominantly of requirements relating to administrative organization and methods.

Congress and the administration share a strong interest in the realization of certain administrative ends, principally efficiency and accountability. The essence of the grant system is that it entails the achievement of federal purposes by proxy. The state government becomes, for purposes of the grant program, a federal agent, and the federal government accordingly seeks to assure that it will spend funds solely for federally approved purposes. In the public assistance program, the standard of "proper and efficient operation" laid down by Congress in 1935 and 1939 expressed, at a minimum, the shared concern of Congress and the administration that federal funds should not be spent wastefully or corruptly. They should go to legally eligible, needy individuals. The requirement in the Social Security Act that "a single state agency" administer or supervise administration of the state plan was meant to assure that the locus of responsibility for spending federal funds and meeting federal conditions be clearly fixed.[1]

The stress on administrative conditions develops partly by default. It is feasible to enunciate them because they can be cast ei-

ther in value-free terms or in terms of seemingly neutral (universally held) values such as fairness. State governments or potentially interested groups at the state level, and hence their representatives in Congress, are relatively amenable to federal conditions that do not entail imposition of controversial value choices,
if only because legitimate grounds of resistance to such conditions
are relatively hard to develop. Imposition of, say, the requirement
of fairness in administration does not test the bounds of constitutional propriety. To the extent that they seek to realize substantive ends, administrators therefore are likely to do so indirectly,
through the use of administrative conditions. In the public assistance program, the requirements of state-wide operation, of a fair
hearing for applicants, and of state financial participation were
all designed in part to serve the substantive goal of adequacy.

Finally, the stress on administrative conditions develops because administrators, whose proposals to Congress and whose
day-to-day conduct are dominant in determining the content of
such conditions, attach high priority to attainment of administrative ends. Although they concentrate on such ends partly because
Congress has given them the authority to do so, it is in pursuit of
administrative ends that they are most likely to test the bounds of
congressional tolerance. When public assistance administrators
stretch statutory provisions, it is generally for the sake of reform-
ing state administrative structure or procedure. One such case was
their attempt, between 1935 and 1939, to require the states to set
up merit systems even though Congress in 1935 had declined to
enact such a requirement. In general, the pursuit of professionalization, including the imposition of the educational requirement,
was carried on without explicit sanction from Congress. Another
example was the decision to interpret the requirement of state-
wide operation as if it were a requirement of state-wide uniformity. Unlike the merit-system requirement, this never was sanctioned by Congress.[2] To be sure, "uniformity" was in part only a
means to an end. Administrators required uniform standards of
need and assistance in the expectation that payments in the poorest counties would be brought up to the standard of those in the

richest, but if uniformity of conduct toward recipients was all that they sought, they might have said so. It would have been possible to distinguish rules covering need and assistance from all other rules and to require uniformity in the former while permitting diversity in the latter. No such thing occurred. The requirement of uniformity covered everything in the state plan.

That administrators should choose to pursue primarily administrative ends may seem not to require explanation. Administrative matters, by definition, are the special object of their expertise. Not only was pursuit of administrative ends most "legitimate" for federal assistance administrators; it also served their own interests. They would find it easier to do their jobs if state practice were uniform, professionalized, and otherwise made to conform to the canons of "good administration"; the performance of review and accounting functions would be very much facilitated. Their effort was self-serving, but it was not altogether so and did not seem so to those engaged in it, for the administrative goals they were pursuing—professionalization of the public service, efficiency, suppression of "politics," rationalization of chaotic administrative structures—had been prominent in the United States as part of one widely held conception (the "reform" conception) of the public interest. Through the instrumentality of federal power, federal public assistance administrators were seeking to put reform ideals into practice at the state and local levels. Their effort complemented that of reformers who had long been independently active there.[3]

Administrative Constraints on the Setting of Conditions. In proposing conditions to Congress or elaborating with regulations those that have been enacted, administrators face not merely the political problem of what the states may be willing to conform to, but also the problem of what they have the administrative capacity to conform to. This is related to a third and similarly "administrative" problem, that of casting federal conditions in terms that will make conformance verifiable. It is essential to the federal interest both that grant programs proceed and that federal conditions be observed. A balance between these interests must be struck. Conditions must not be so demanding as to become an obstacle to the functioning of the program; at the same time, conformance must be elicited sufficiently to sustain respect for federal authority and to ensure progress toward federal goals.

To reduce the political problem of enforcement, the federal agency is likely to formulate conditions so as to make them consistent with the interests of at least one major group at the state level, typically the agency that receives grants. To reduce administrative problems, the federal assistance administration has often followed the strategy of requiring from state agencies statements of intent and methods of realizing intent rather than attempting to impose standards on the actual results of conduct. Even with respect to statements of intent and method, the federal requirements have been general rather than specific. Typically, federal public assistance administrators have required states to commit themselves to attainment of a general end (such as "service giving") and to formulate categories of policies and rules (such as "methods of assessing the staffing and assignments for service cases") to achieve that end without specifying what the policies or rules must contain, although certain characteristics of them, especially uniformity of application, have been insisted on.

At one extreme of generality and vagueness, federal requirements—as with the case of "community planning" and some other actions required by the federal directives on social services—may merely describe activities that state administrators already are engaged in, or can plausibly claim to be with minor verbal manipulations. Occasionally, the federal administration has resorted to extremes of specificity, as with the educational requirement and caseload and supervisory standards. Conformance, especially if the standard is quantified, then becomes possible to prove. Specificity entails risks, however. The more specific the language of the federal requirement, the lower the federal capacity to adapt to state peculiarities and the greater the danger that the limitations on the federal capacity to compel conformance may be exposed to view.

Ways of Achieving Federal Objectives

The Federal Government in State Politics. In giving grants and attaching conditions to them, the federal government becomes an actor in the state political system. It is a peripheral actor rather than an integral one, for it has no legitimate role within that system—no formal right to make decisions and no recognized informal right to function as a lobby. Nonetheless, it alters the environment within which the integral actors function, alters the distribution of influence among them, and thus itself becomes an actor in state politics.

The selection of subjects for the public agenda—of "issues" for consideration—is the first step in determining the content of public policy, and it is at this point in the process of state politics that federal influence begins to be felt. By offering grants for specified activities, the federal government places an item on the political agenda: should the aided activity be undertaken or not? The setting of conditions works in parallel fashion. By saying to the state that it will not give money unless a certain rule is adopted (or, if the grant program is already under way, by saying that money will cease to be given), the federal government causes the state to consider whether the required action should be taken. An issue is raised that might not have been raised in the absence of federal action. Strictly speaking, of course, the federal government does not itself place the question on the agenda of state politics. What it does is to stimulate proposals by actors integral to the state political system, such as elected executive or legislative officials, party officials, appointed administrators, or executives of pressure groups. For state political actors who independently share some or all of the federal goals, federal action creates opportunities ("excuses") for the making of proposals.

For these elected officials and for appointed administrators—who together are ultimately the objects of federal influence because they are possessors of authority to act within the state gov-

ernment—federal sponsorship reduces the cost of making a proposal and taking the subsequent action. Not only are monetary
costs transferred to the federal level; if opposition arises, state officials may be able to transfer political costs as well, by imputing
responsibility to the federal government. Moreover, federal action
increases the cost of inaction—that is, the cost of *not* proposing or
taking the actions the federal government seeks to stimulate.
Officials who do not respond to federal stimuli become vulnerable
to criticism for failing to act—for "failing to take advantage of
federal funds" or "failing to meet federal standards."

Federal influence continues to operate as consideration of the
federally stimulated proposal proceeds. The terms of the federal
offer or requirement affect the content of proposals and discussion
within the state. The proponents or action takers have as one important resource of influence, perhaps their principal resource,
the claim that action is desirable or necessary because it will secure federal funds. The "normal" distribution of influence among
political actors in the state—that is, the distribution that would
prevail in the absence of federal action—thus is altered to the advantage of those with whom the federal government is allied.

In summary, the federal government exercises influence in
large part by stimulating demands from groups within the state
and by placing "extra" resources of influence at their disposal. It
works through allies.

The State Agency as Federal Ally. Temporary allies—that is,
more or less accidental allies, intermittently active for limited
purposes—may contribute substantially to the attainment of federal objectives. In Massachusetts the federal public assistance administration has at various times and for limited purposes been
allied with the old-age lobby (the two have also been at odds) and
with professional and good-government groups such as the National Association of Social Workers and the League of Women
Voters. But the dependence of the federal government on support
within the state is such that it needs a permanent ally, one always
organized and prepared to take action, always receptive to federal
communications, and having interests thoroughly consistent with

those of the federal administration. From the perspective of the federal administrative agency, this is ideally the role of its state counterpart. As the formal recipient of federal funds, the formal channel for federal communication with the state, and a possessor of authority within the state government, the state agency has a combination of obligations to the federal administration and assets of influence at the state level that make it by far the most suitable and efficacious of potential federal allies. Much federal activity—some of it designed for that purpose and some not—contributes to making the state agency into an ally, an organization not simply accountable to the federal agency (responsible for the state's conduct and capable of reporting on it), but also *responsive* to it (disposed to make state conduct conform to federal preferences). Such activity is one of the major techniques of federal influence.

The first step in creating a state-agency ally is often to call an agency into existence. Many state and local administrative agencies, especially those in urban renewal, public housing, and antipoverty programs, have been created for the purpose of receiving and administering federal grants. The next step (likely to be more difficult with an established agency than a new one) is to shape its values and conceptions of purpose so that they are consistent with federal objectives, and to enhance its power and autonomy at the state level. To the extent that the state agency shares federal goals, is willing to commit its power to attaining them, and has power so to commit, the probability that federal goals will be achieved is greatly enhanced.

Federal patron agencies and their state counterparts might be expected to have shared values and goals without the federal agency's taking steps to assure this, if only because they share programmatic functions. The sharing of functions, however, is not necessarily sufficient to assure the congruence of a wide range of values among a high proportion of administrators in numerous governments, the governments themselves being representative of diverse value systems and regional subcultures. If federal preferences are to prevail, then, the core of shared values and goals that federal and state administrators derive from the sharing of a function must be elaborated and perfected, in ways of federal choosing, until a high degree of congruence has been achieved. The professionalization of personnel, through which a common body of values and doctrines is disseminated, has been the principal means of doing this.

To the extent the federal effort to bring about a sharing of values between governments is successful, difficulties of obtaining conformance are much reduced. The state agency becomes highly responsive to federal preferences, and responsive for what federal administrators can only regard as the right reasons. That is, it responds not just because it seeks to maximize the receipt of federal funds (and thus is willing to act as if it shared federal goals); rather, it responds because it does in fact share them. Indoctrination of the state agency is the federal administrators' only defense against the persistent and pervasive problem that arises from the tendency of state governments to agree to federally stipulated actions because doing so will enlarge the flow of federal money. At most, the spread of professionalism at the state level may altogether eliminate the problem of nonconformance. If state agencies come to share federal values and have power to embody them in state policy, they become something more than responsive partners of the federal agency. They also undertake to pursue shared goals independently. The values expressed through public action at the state level then become identical to those that prevail within the federal administration. The result is the elimination of federal-state conflict and hence the elimination of the necessity for the exercise of federal influence. The federal effort to professionalize and to render autonomous the state agency is thus in a way the ultimate adaptation to limits on that influence.

Federal action contributes to state-agency power and autonomy in various ways, of which the most obvious, in the public assistance program, has been the "single state agency" requirement. On the basis of this statutory provision, federal administrators have insisted that the agency possess enough authority to assure that federal conditions are met. Very early in the federal grant program, this resulted in amendments to Massachusetts law that much increased the rule-making powers of the state welfare department.

In the case of the "single state agency" requirement, enhancing the counterpart's power is the primary end of federal action. Although most federal actions obviously do not have this as their major goal, virtually all federal-state interaction through the grant system incidentally yields that result.

As the recipient of federal grants, the counterpart is endowed with resources that would not otherwise be available to it and that come to it more or less independently of action by the governor or legislature, upon whom it would otherwise be altogether dependent for monetary support. How much power the agency thereby gains depends on how much discretion it has in the use of federal money. This use may be closely circumscribed by federal action or by the action of the state legislature. In the Massachusetts public assistance program, the state welfare department was more a passive channel for the routinized flow of federal funds to local agencies (and ultimately to assistance recipients) than an independent allocator of the funds, the crucial decisions about allocation having been made by the legislature (once the cost-of-living formula was passed, at least). Nevertheless, the result of federal grants was to increase, in a subtle way and to an unspecifiable degree, the state agency's power vis-à-vis local agencies. The agency gained leverage in its role as rule maker and supervisor of administration, since its right to function in this role depended both on grants of authority from the state legislature and on the state's sharing of assistance costs. And the "state" share of costs, from the perspective of local agencies, was the equivalent of the state *and* federal shares combined, for the state welfare department disbursed federal grants to local agencies and had authority to supervise their spending. "Federal" money, having been so channeled, from the local perspective acquired the character of "state" money.

The stipulation of federal conditions or rules to accompany grants had the same effect. Given the nature of a federal system, federal rules can be effective within the state only after being reincarnated as state rules. Therefore the making of federal rules for the grant program stimulates the making of state rules; it stimulates the usage of the counterpart agency's authority. Again, whether the result of this process is to increase state-agency "power" depends on the particular circumstances of the rule making and the particular relationship of power. When the state rule simply repeats verbatim a federal rule and does not entail the use of state discretion, state-agency power in relation to the federal administration is decreased. On the other hand, whether the state agency exercises discretion itself (typically the case) or merely repeats what the federal administration has stipulated (less often the case), its rule-making authority within the state political system has been enhanced by usage. In Massachusetts, from the perspective of the local agencies to which public assistance rules were addressed until 1968, all rules were state rules no matter what the origin of their content. All were experienced and interpreted as manifestations of state authority. All therefore tended to enhance state power as it was exercised in relation to local agencies.*

An alliance between federal and state administrative agencies, formed and perfected through the working of the grant system, can become a powerful force in state politics, perhaps the dominant force in the making of policy for the program in question. When federal and state agencies work together, each reinforces the influence of the other, the state agency gaining as a result of the federal partnership, the federal agency being compensated for deficiencies in its ability to exercise influence directly in state affairs. The result is that a relationship of mutual dependence develops such that each accommodates itself, perhaps uncon-

---

* From the perspective of the state agency, federal efforts to enhance the agency's authority and to stimulate exercise of that authority are not unambiguously beneficial. How welcome they are depends on how highly the state agency values the ends prescribed by the federal administration; on the amount of resistance pursuit of them is likely to provoke within the state; and on the federal ability to endow the agency with resources of influence to overcome the resistance. The danger is that federal action will force the state agency into situations of conflict without sufficiently compensating it.

sciously, to the interests of the other. What the federal agency undertakes depends in part on what its state counterpart desires or can be expected to concur in, for the state agency's cooperation is essential to the realization of any federal goal. Similarly, a state agency learns to accommodate its goals to federal ones. Where, as in Massachusetts before 1968, a state agency has little independent strength within the state political system, its dependence on federal patronage becomes very great. It must rely on federal action to create opportunities for action and on the justification of "federal requirements" or the "availability of federal funds" to rationalize and legitimize all that it does. Whatever power and autonomy the Massachusetts welfare department possesses derive very largely from the relationship with its federal patron.

Federal influence, in summary, operates mainly through the agency that receives grants, and with the agency's self-serving cooperation. It operates by enhancing the role that the agency plays in the state political system and by shaping the agency's values, goals, interests, and actions. It operates primarily on the structures and processes of policymaking and administration rather than directly on the substance of policy. This may be a critical limitation, but if the influence on structures and processes is extensive and enduring enough, the result must be to influence policy outcomes as well—*all* policy outcomes, not just those in which the federal government is actively interested. If the federal government can influence the locus of policymaking authority in the state government, how the policymakers perceive opportunities for action, what values prevail among the policymakers, and what resources of influence are at their disposal, it has gone far in influencing the content of policy. It has, in any case, increased the disposition of the state to respond to federal action and to undertake, independently, actions consistent with federal preferences.

The Withholding of Funds. The ultimate resource of federal influence is the withholding of the grant, but this is almost impossible to use, for withholding serves no one's interests. Objections are bound to come from Congress.[4] Although Congress agrees with the administration on certain general statements of federal conditions when the effects on particular constituencies are impossible to foresee, withholding is a specific act, threatening to a particular constituency; this automatically brings a response from that constituency's representatives in Congress and evokes the sympathetic concern of other congressmen, who are made aware of a potential threat to their own constituencies. Even apart from the possible difficulties with Congress, administrators are reluctant to withhold funds because of the damage it might do to program goals and to relations with state governments. Given the limits on its influence, the federal administration is—or at least perceives itself to be—heavily dependent upon maintaining their good will and disposition to cooperate. Partly for this reason, it seeks to avoid direct, hostile confrontations with state governments such as the withholding of funds entails. Above all, it wishes to avoid public sanctions against the state agency (which, at least *pro forma,* must be the object of withholding), for one way of maintaining the state-agency alliance is to avoid embarrassing the agency in public.*

These objections to the manipulation of funds as an enforcement technique apply to the withholding of the entire grant, which in principle is the penalty for nonconforming policies or recurrently noncomforming administrative practices, more than to the taking of audit exceptions, which in principle is the penalty for specific nonconforming acts of expenditure. Because they are more feasible to use than withholding, the federal administration is sometimes tempted to use audit exceptions on a large scale as a substitute for withholding; that is, audit exceptions may be applied to a whole class of expenditures in an effort to bring about change in a nonconforming policy or practice, as when the regional representative decided to apply them in Massachusetts in the late 1940s to the salaries of elected board members who were engaged in administration. However, using audit exceptions in

* In doing research for this book, I found that the one restriction on the cooperation of federal regional officials was a concern that their relations with state officials might be damaged. I was given access to federal files with the understanding that I would not use them to attack or gratuitously embarrass the state agency. I was asked to use the material "objectively," a condition that I was of course happy to accept. When the completed manuscript was made available for comment, the federal office did not ask for any deletions.

this way is subject in some degree to most of the same objections, and to others besides. An audit exception is inconvenient to administer, and as a *post hoc* action that applies only to particular acts of expenditure (selected acts, in the normal case, for not all expenditures are audited) its range of effectiveness is limited. It is particularly difficult to apply to acts of omission. The difficulties of withholding or of taking audit exceptions on a large scale help to explain why the whole aim of federal enforcement activity is to bring about compliance in advance and thus to avoid confrontations in which financial penalties will have to be invoked. Federal administrators consider that they have done their jobs well when the volume of audit exceptions is low.

It would be wrong, however, to infer that the federal ability to withhold funds is of no effect. It is in fact one of the major resources of federal influence—but it is of use mainly as a potential resource. It lies at the foundation, as a weapon in reserve, of all federal enforcement activity, and the nature of that activity is such as to make the best possible use of it.

Federal enforcement is a diplomatic process. It is as if the terms of a treaty, an agreement of mutual interest to the two governmental parties, were more or less continuously being negotiated. In these negotiations, numerous diplomatic forms and manners are observed, especially by the federal negotiators. Typically they are in the position of having made a demarche. Negotiations become active when a new federal condition is promulgated or an old one is reinterpreted, or when a federal administrative review has revealed a defect in the state's administration. Negotiations are carried on privately. The federal negotiators refrain from making statements in public, for they want to avoid the appearance of meddling in the internal affairs of the states. They refrain from making overt threats. They are patient. Negotiations over a single issue may go on steadily for several years and intermittently for decades. They are polite. In addressing state officials, they are usually elaborately courteous. They make small gestures of deference to the host government, as by offering to meet at times and at places of its choosing.

The objective of the negotiating process is to obtain as much conformance as can be had without the actual withholding of funds. Because federal requirements are typically stated in general terms, administrators have a high degree of flexibility in negotiating terms of conformance. Within the broad guidelines they have laid down, they have been able to adapt to the political and administrative circumstances of each state. If the constraints of the situation so require it, federal administrators may consider conformance to have been achieved even if state action falls considerably short of the federal ideal. As long as federal requirements are vague and general, conformance, though difficult to prove, is equally impossible to disprove. The federal administration may therefore avoid outright defeat no matter what concessions it makes to state political and administrative realities. (The situation changes, of course, if federal requirements are highly specific. Federal administrators then may feel compelled to accept merely formal proofs of conformance that falsify reality and that they *know* to falsify reality, as with caseload standards in Massachusetts.)

The function of intergovernmental diplomacy in a federal system, like that of international diplomacy, is to facilitate communication and amicable relations between governments that are pretending to be equals by obscuring the question of whether one is more equal than the other. In the case of federal-state relations in the United States, that question is obscure in any event, and the function of diplomatic processes may merely be to keep it that way or to obscure, and thereby facilitate, changes in power relations. That this be done is important primarily to the federal government, for it is the aggressive, the states the defensive, actor in intergovernmental relations. It has the greater interest in seeing that change is facilitated. But perhaps the principal advantage of a diplomatic style to federal administrators (and the choice of that style is essentially their choice), is that this mode of behavior makes the best possible use of the technique of withholding funds. It enables federal officials to exploit, without actually using, this basic resource. In cases of federal-state conflict, federal negotiators keep open the possibility of withholding during the process of negotiation, referring to it in oblique and subtle terms. They seek to obscure the low probability that they will actually use it. By not making overt threats to withhold, federal administrators protect their credibility; the state is kept guessing. Diplomatic behavior is thus an adaptation to the impracticability of withholding, as well as to other constraints on federal influence, especially the widespread belief that the federal government ought not to interfere in state and local affairs. By relying so heavily on private negotiations, federal officials avoid "meddling" in public. At the same time, they avoid exposing the state agency to public embarrassment or more tangible federal penalties so that the agency's disposition to cooperate is not discouraged.

It might seem that, as time passes, the federal administration's failure to withhold funds would undermine its credibility and render withholding useless even as a negotiating weapon. In fact, the federal willingness to withhold funds itself diminishes with time. It is much easier to withhold (or delay the granting of) funds at the outset of a grant program, when the volume of the grant is low and the program not yet routinized. In the first five years of the public assistance program, the federal administration did make several attempts to withhold funds, and it was not altogether implausible, when a dispute with Massachusetts arose in 1939–40 over the merit-system requirement, that it would try to do so again. The welfare commissioner, apparently believing that it would, gave in to the Social Security Board very quickly. Ten years later, when the issue over board member–administrators arose, it was much less plausible that withholding should be tried, and by 1964–65, when the dispute over the educational requirement developed, withholding was altogether implausible. But not everyone knew this (many state legislators did not), and some people who did know it, especially the welfare commissioner, preferred to pretend that they did not. Withholding would probably not remain effective as a resource of influence were it not for the federal alliance with the state agency; when the two cooperate in pursuit of a shared goal, the state agency exploits the possibility of federal holding and vouches for the credibility of it.

The fact that the state agency is the sole official recipient of federal communications and the official interpreter of them within the state gives it an important advantage. It can make decisions about dissemination and interpretation in such a way as to facilitate attainment of its own ends. This is likely to mean, as in the dispute over the educational requirement, that the state agency will encourage the belief that a serious threat of federal withholding exists. The federal administration, which alone might provide an accurate interpretation of its own intent, refrains from doing so as a tactical necessity. Attempts to elicit clear statements of intent are unavailing, whether they come from the state agency or other sources. But whereas the federal agency refrains from issuing threats of withholding itself, it does nothing to dispel threats that others issue in its name. Its interests will best be served if those statements are believed. In these circumstances, federal intentions may be difficult for anyone to evaluate, even those who, like state administrative officials, have direct access to the federal agency and experience in the administration of grant programs. For others, such as state legislators, who have no such access and no such experience, federal intentions are virtually impossible to evaluate. In any case, it is always impossible for the opponents of federally sponsored action to demonstrate that the federal administration will *not* withhold funds.

The limited capacity of state legislators to appraise federal intentions with respect to withholding is one advantage the state agency has whenever it undertakes an action with federal sponsorship. It might be supposed, however, that opponents of federally sponsored action would get help from Congress, which is thought to be responsive to the appeals of parochial interests and skilled at overturning the acts of federal administrators. Judging from the Massachusetts experience, however, appeals to Congress appear to bring few results to those who make them. When federal and state agencies act cooperatively, they have much protection, individually or together, against unwanted intervention from legislatures at either or both levels of the federal system.

They have, of course, the usual assets of administrators confronting legislators: they are the full-time specialists in their func-

tion, while legislators have only a part-time interest in that function. For a congressman to intervene successfully once the federal
administration has committed itself to a particular action in a particular state requires an intense and sustained interest in the matter and a great mastery of administrative detail. The Massachusetts case suggests that these conditions will rarely be met. Although congressmen, in response to constituents' requests, at critical times inquired of the federal administration about its intentions in Massachusetts, these inquiries almost without exception
were routine and perfunctory. The letter from the constituent was
forwarded to the administration with a form letter from the congressman requesting a response. A response—couched in oblique,
noncommittal language that tended to minimize the degree of disruption being experienced within the state and the degree of the
federal administration's responsibility for it—then went to the
congressman, who presumably relayed it to the inquiring constituent as proof that he had acted on the constituent's request. Typically, these congressional inquiries revealed little knowledge or
specialized interest in the case on the part of the congressman,
and the replies from the administration were designed to avoid increasing either.

The only important exception to this pattern was the activity of
Congressman McCormack with respect to the directive on educational requirements. If ever there was a situation in which
congressional intervention might be effective, this seemed to be it.
Here was a congressman—the Speaker of the House, no less—
who was opposed to an important action of the administration, an
action profoundly damaging to the career prospects of perhaps
eight hundred local government employees in his state. His objection was largely spontaneous and strongly enough felt to produce
protests to the secretary and the undersecretary of health, education, and welfare. But in the end it had very little effect on the administration's action. None of this means that federal public assistance administrators are not subject in profoundly important
ways to congressional controls. What the administrators undertake to do depends heavily on what Congress has authorized and

on the administrators' guess of what Congress will tolerate. Contrary to what is perhaps the usual impression of Congress' performance, the evidence from public assistance suggests that Congress is more effective in making broad policy than in doing "casework" for particular individuals or groups of aggrieved constituents.

In addition to the defenses that administrators normally have against legislators, the grant system offers special ones, a result of the diffusion of responsibility it entails. When called to account for controversial actions, administrative agencies at both federal and state levels can escape responsibility vis-à-vis their own legislatures by attributing responsibility to a counterpart at the other level. In parallel fashion, each legislature can escape responsibility vis-à-vis its own constituents. The ability of all major official actors to deny responsibility very much reduces the chances of successful opposition.

The Results of Federal Influence

If federal influence were more extensive and more effective, state and local programs that benefit from grants-in-aid would everywhere be alike. Federal action would stimulate development of issues and otherwise influence state political processes in such a way as to bring about a uniform set of desired results. As of 1969, at least, that has not happened in public assistance. Because of the limits on the federal government's capacity to define and enforce grant-in-aid conditions, few results of state action have conformed precisely to federal intentions. On the other hand, state actions do respond in a general way to federal influence. As the Massachusetts case shows, they are different, probably very different, from what they would be in the absence of federal action. To an important degree, they reflect federal intentions.

The attainment of federal objectives depends upon certain features of a state's political system—the prevalence of values consistent with federal actions, the presence of federal allies, the power of those allies in state politics, and the prevailing ideology or political culture. Even apart from their receptivity to particular program goals, some states are more receptive than others to federal action per se. In states that tend to be receptive to government action in general and to have no ideological bias against federal action in particular, the charge of "not taking advantage of federal funds" or of "failing to meet federal standards" is potentially very damaging to politicians. In other states, where government activity in general and federal activity in particular are more resisted, the risks of nonparticipation or defiance are lower. They are still present, however: inasmuch as residents of all states contribute through taxes to the support of federal programs, and inasmuch as federal grants will go to some other state if not to one's own, the quest for federal funds can be justified on grounds of equity and self-interest even where it is at odds with ideology. Within a given state, responsiveness to federal action depends also on the content of the particular action. Massachusetts, having been unusually receptive to one objective of the federal public assistance program (adequacy of assistance) but unusually resistant to others (efficiency of administration, professionalization of personnel), illustrates the effects of federal influence in both hospitable and inhospitable settings.

Federal action in Massachusetts strengthened and stimulated those forces and tendencies in state politics that had independently produced a liberal assistance program. The increases in payments and program coverage after 1936 reflect to some degree the effects of federal influence, but the test of federal influence came over goals that were incompatible with prevailing features of state politics. The real test lay in the federal effort to reduce the power of local welfare agencies, to enhance that of the state agency, to professionalize administrative personnel, and to make administration more equitable and efficient, all of which required major change.

The federal administration achieved results gradually. In a series of conflicts, its position had to be compromised repeatedly and in important ways, and long delays in obtaining even a modest degree of compliance had to be endured as it adjusted reluctantly to the realities of politics and administration in Massachusetts. Yet by 1968 much change had been achieved. State control had superseded local control, and that was what the federal administration had sought all along.

The adoption of state administration in 1968 was the climax of the federal effort, and it was significant not simply as evidence of past success in the exercise of federal influence. By increasing the authority and power of the state agency and incorporating local agencies into it, the change had permanently altered the structure of policymaking and administration in Massachusetts: from now on, the state would be more responsive to federal action.

Public Assistance as an Example of Federal Influence

I have sought to use the public assistance program as an example of the grant-in-aid system in action and to derive from that example some general observations about federal influence in state affairs. Many students of federalism, more impressed by the differences among grant programs than the similarities, have denied that the programs constitute a "system." [5] Those who doubt that a grant system exists will similarly doubt that public assistance may be used for analytical purposes as an example of it.

I have already said that I think the regularities among grant programs are such that it makes sense to conceive of the programs as together constituting a system for the achievement of federal objectives. But the semantics of the matter (is there a system or isn't there?) may not be very important. I do not deny that other grant programs differ from public assistance in ways that are relevant to an analysis of federal influence; indeed, the differences among grant programs are such that it would be hard to defend any one choice as typical. At best, my findings have only a general applicability to other grant programs, and it may therefore be worthwhile to conclude this discussion by considering what may be peculiar about public assistance.

At least among grant programs administered by the Department of Health, Education, and Welfare, public assistance seems to have been distinguished by a large volume of federal regulation. The federal administrative agencies for, say, child welfare and vocational rehabilitation have by comparison issued very brief and general guidance to the states and have shown greater willingness to trust in the state agencies' discretion. One possible explanation is that the much greater volume of federal expenditure in public assistance, combined with the fact that the statutory formula puts no limit on spending, has stimulated a greater effort at administrative supervision. Quite simply, the monetary stakes are higher. The political stakes may be bigger too. Public assistance is not a popular program, and federal administrators may have a special incentive to try to protect themselves, by imposing numerous controls on the states, against waste, fraud, or other grounds for congressional complaint and intervention. Finally, the level of federal supervisory effort may reflect the very great gap in professional attainment between federal and state-and-local personnel. It seems likely that the federal administration is most willing to trust the state agencies' exercise of discretion when state personnel are highly professionalized. It might be argued, then, that federal influence is exercised more extensively in public assistance than in other programs, but this does not necessarily follow. Administrative regulations are only one technique of federal influence, and not necessarily an effective one. Other federal administrative agencies using other techniques (such as model state plans combined with much "consultation") may have been just as successful in shaping state conduct as the federal public assistance agency.

On the other hand, one can argue that the case of public assistance understates the extent of federal influence. It is reasonable to suppose that federal influence ultimately depends upon the capacity of federal administrators to manipulate funds—to give or withhold them depending on how closely state or local governments conform to federal expectations. If this is so, any program, such as urban renewal or model cities, that uses the method of project grants offers a greater opportunity for the exercise of federal influence than a program that, like public assistance, uses formula grants. Among applicants for, say, model-cities funds, federal administrators may pick and choose according to their preferences, deciding not only whether to grant funds but how much to grant. Public assistance administrators by contrast disburse money in accordance with a formula determined by Congress, and the fact that most of it is destined to provide subsistence to the very poor limits all the more the administrators' freedom of maneuver. They cannot penalize nonconforming governments without also punishing innocent and needy individuals. Among all administrators of federal grants, public assistance administrators therefore are perhaps least able to manipulate funds. Yet the Massachusetts case shows that this is not an insuperable obstacle to their exercise of influence. It may even be that, once Congress has determined the formula, programs using formula grants give administrators more maneuverability in their relations with state or local governments than do programs using project grants, for congressional scrutiny may subside in the former case whereas individual congressmen, seeking benefits for their constituencies, may maintain a continuing interest in the allocation and uses of project-grant funds. Apart from this, administrators of project grants may not have as much freedom to manipulate funds as they appear to have. They are under pressure to spend all the money they can as fast as they can (since that is the only way to get more from Congress), and this, combined with limits on their capacity to review both applications for funds and the actual use of funds, means that their ability to exercise influence may not be different in kind from that of agencies administering formula grants.

Public assistance, then, may not typify the extent of federal influence through grant programs, but it is hard to tell whether it deviates in the direction of exceeding or falling short of the norm. Without evidence from more programs, there is no way of knowing what the norm is. I offer the case of public assistance as a standard of comparison and a source of hypotheses for the investigation of other programs.

9 | Prospects for the Grant System: Creative Federalism?

Lord Bryce observed in the 1880s that the American Constitution contained no theory or doctrine of federalism, only those few practical provisions necessary for the founders to perform their task.[1] Doctrine developed later—characteristically, for Americans—through debate over what the Constitution meant.

As a legal doctrine, federalism was to receive a great deal of attention. Bryce referred wryly to the "mass of subtle and . . . scholastic metaphysics" that lawyers and publicists had produced.[2] The outpouring of legal theory receded after the Civil War, but the subject of federalism continued to be the special province of constitutional lawyers. Insofar as the meaning of federalism has been discussed in this country in general terms, it is mostly they who have done it.[3]

This has meant that, as explicit constitutional issues over federalism diminished in importance, the development of doctrine all but ceased. The intergovernmental sharing of functions in general, and the grant system in particular, grew up bit by bit as political institutions responded to particular circumstances in *ad hoc* fashion. This very significant change in governmental arrangements and practices took place without any systematic doctrinal justification, as have most such changes in American history.

But if there has been little doctrine, there has been much public discussion and some academic analysis from which it is possible to deduce the values that federal arrangements are expected to serve. The advantage of federalism, a system in which governmental authority is divided among a central government and regional governments, is said to be that it disperses power and permits the adaptation of political institutions and programs to the diverse needs and interests of society. Because it is a system of many governments rather than one, it is an obstacle in the way of accumulation of power by a single class or group, even a majority class or group. Thus it facilitates political pluralism. At the same time, in a diverse society, it represents an appropriate institutional response to pluralism. The existence of many governments, along with the separation of powers within governments, permits access to government by a wide variety of groups. A group that fails to attain its objectives in one sphere of government has numerous opportunities to try elsewhere. A federal system also maximizes opportunities for individual participation and encourages a sense of citizen responsibility by keeping governmental power close to its origins and facilitating public surveillance of government officials.[4] The advantage of cooperative federalism—a term that may be used to describe a system in which the divided authority is brought together again, as in the grant system, through an intergovernmental sharing of functions—is that it enables the cooperating governments to benefit from one another's special capacities while still preserving the value of political pluralism. More particularly, in the American system, cooperative federalism enables state and local governments to benefit from the superior capacity of the federal government to perceive and develop responses to nation-wide problems, to articulate widely shared program goals, and to raise taxes and reallocate revenues so as to carry out programs in an equitable fashion. The federal government, in turn, by cooperating with state and local governments, benefits from their capacity to adapt programs to local and particular manifestations of nation-wide problems and to adjust existing administrative structures for the achievement of federal purposes.

In summary, the values that the federal system is said to serve are *political pluralism,* accessibility and responsiveness of the political system to diverse group interests and to citizen participation generally, and *social efficacy,* the capacity of the political system to articulate choices and shared objectives and to achieve them through a flexible adaptation of means to ends.

Creative Federalism, Doctrine and Practice

In the 1960s there developed an increasing disposition among public officials and political pundits to ask whether the functioning of the federal system does in fact serve the values it is presumed to serve. The Johnson Administration was sufficiently concerned with this question to grope toward a formulation of explicit principles to guide the federal government in the conduct of grant programs. Outside the administration as well, liberals began to argue for decentralization, after having assumed for at least half a century the superior virtue of federal activity. The administration called the evolving doctrine "creative federalism," a term that recurred in much official speech after its introduction by the President in 1964.[5]

Creative federalism was above all a response to administrative chaos. By the mid-1960s there were more grant programs than either the givers or the receivers could keep track of. State and local officials, increasingly aware that almost any public activity might qualify for federal aid, nevertheless found it hard to ascertain just what was available, from what agency, when, and on what terms. Getting information, let alone a grant, required skill and persistence. (Specialists became known as "grantsmen," their function that of "grantsmanship.") From the federal perspective, matters were equally confusing. Inconsistencies of purpose and practice abounded. Operating bureaus ran their own programs without much direction or coordination either within or among departments. One element of the administration's new doctrine stressed the rationalization of the grant system through the consolidation and coordination of programs and administrative structures. Asked late in 1966 to explain creative federalism to a Senate subcommittee, administrative officials talked more about "manageability" than about creativity. Their main concern was with the efficacy of programs.[6]

As the name implies, however, there was more to the doctrine than a wish for better management. Another part of it stressed the importance of enhancing the scope and capacity for action (creative action, presumably) of the recipients of federal grants. Secretary of Health, Education, and Welfare John W. Gardner elaborated this element of the doctrine, in explicit defense of the value of pluralism. He told Congress:

> We have had a system—political, economic, social—characterized by dispersed power and initiative. We like that attribute of our system. But if we are to preserve it, we have to be conscious of what is happening as the old system gives way and a newer system is invented piecemeal. At every step in the development of the new system we must ask how we may preserve the dispersion of power and initiative among the various participants—Federal, State, and local government and the various nongovernmental groups and institutions.
>
> If we want pluralism in the system—and I assume we do —we are going to have to build it in consciously and systematically.

In order to preserve pluralism, Gardner argued, state and local governments had to be strengthened:

> Most State and local governments are not strong enough to play their role in an effective partnership with the Federal Government.
>
> They must be strengthened.
>
> We must revitalize the State and local leadership so that it can play its role vis-à-vis an increasingly powerful Federal Government; we must revitalize that in every way so that they can play a vital role in the partnerships without being

completely submerged and obliterated. It is the only way to preserve our position of dispersed power and initiatives.[7]

One way of achieving these objectives, the administration assumed, was by increasing the volume of grants. ("Creative federalism" was a rationale for grant giving quite as much as it was a statement of guiding principles.) Another way was to improve the quality of state and local administrative personnel. In 1967 President Johnson proposed to Congress the Intergovernmental Manpower Act, which authorized fellowships to state and local government employees and grants of up to 75 percent to help those governments in developing personnel-training plans. A third approach was to encourage the use of state and local power by constructing the terms of federal grants in such a way as to promote initiatives, and by not imposing extensive and detailed federal conditions. Gardner spoke of the need for "a more disciplined use of the categorical approach to grants-in-aid programs." [8] A definite and more daring prescription came from Walter W. Heller, who had been chairman of the Council of Economic Advisers. Heller proposed that the federal government allocate to state governments, on a per capita basis and with "next to no strings attached," 1 to 2 percent of the individual income taxable by the federal government.[9] Whatever the approach, the general aim was to promote the decentralization of functions within the federal system.

Finally, decentralization came to be stressed in another sense as well—not simply as the devolution of power to lower levels in the federal system, but as the dispersion of power among the people in general. To Richard N. Goodwin, tho had participated in the writing of the presidential speech that first referred to creative federalism, decentralization in the first sense was of value because it could be made to yield decentralization in the second sense. Goodwin wrote:

The blended goal of structure and policy alike must be to meet specific ills through methods which can in themselves enlarge the sense and reality of individual relevance and participation. The way to accomplish this, at least on the political front, is through decentralization—by assisting and compelling states, communities, and private groups to assume a greater share of responsibility for collective action. In other words, both burden and enterprise must be shifted into units of action small enough to allow for more intimate personal contact and numerous enough to widen the outlets for direct participation and control.[10]

This element of the doctrine implied the imposition of requirements of "citizen participation" in the administration of grant programs.

Creative federalism is an elusive doctrine, and its results are difficult to specify. The Heller proposal for revenue sharing, alone among the ideas developed, represented a significant departure from the grant system and, though considered by the administration and promoted by Republicans in Congress, it was not adopted. What change did occur involved modification and adaptation of the present grant system.

One such change was the increased use of project grants over formula grants. In the 1960s the practice of distributing funds to a whole class of governments in accordance with a statutory formula steadily gave way to the practice of distributing them to selected governments in response to applications for specific undertakings. As of 1966, according to the Budget Bureau, 56 percent of the grant-in-aid authorizations (226 of 399) were of the project variety, and both the number and the proportion were rising.[11] Project grants had come to be preferred on the grounds that they would better stimulate state and local creativity. Indeed, creativity was increasingly stipulated as a condition of federal aid. Money would go to those applicants whose projects were found to be "innovative."

The federal concern for better management and for coordination was reflected in a number of executive actions. The President issued an executive order giving the Departments of Agriculture and Housing and Urban Development authority to convene meetings with other federal agencies to discuss the coordination of rural and urban programs. The Vice-President was to be the liaison with state and local governments. The Bureau of the Budget created a staff to concentrate on grant-in-aid administration. The impulse to coordinate—or at least somehow to bring federal grant programs together under common administrative structures—was manifested also in legislation, notably the model-cities act, which called for local governments to combine existing federally aided programs and new programs of their own in such a way as to improve city neighborhoods. Successful applicants would get increased grants for existing programs as well as a federal contribution to new ones. Through the model-cities program, the federal government was offering localities a reward if they themselves could contrive a way of coordinating federal activities.

If creative federalism is to be found in action, the most appropriate place to look for it may be in those grant programs that developed as the doctrine was being talked about. Model cities was one such, and another, two years earlier, was the community-action program of the war on poverty. In many ways, this was the operational prototype of creative federalism. It incorporated the same stress on dispersing power and on coordinating diverse programs and institutions (that, as Daniel Moynihan has pointed put, is what the Budget Bureau thought community action meant [12]). Through the medium of federal project grants, the fight against poverty became a local activity. And it was the community-action program, with its provision for "maximum feasible" participation of those affected, that made citizen participation an ideological issue, and thus a new article of liberal faith.

Creative Federalism and the Public Assistance Program

Creative federalism was a reaction against the past. Implicit in the administration's search for new modes of grant giving was a belief that old ones had produced undesirable results. Among the authors of the antipoverty program this belief was especially strong. According to Roger Davidson, "Many in the Administration's team which drafted the bill harbored a deep antipathy toward the traditional grant-in-aid, in which federal funds were administered by the states under specified conditions. Such programs, they believed, were apt to be captured by state administrators and the private professional associations. The Department of Health, Education, and Welfare was regarded, in particular, as an agency many of whose programs had experienced such control." [13]

The public assistance program seems to have been regarded as the very model of what ought to be avoided. Contrary to the urging of the Department of Health, Education, and Welfare, drafters of the antipoverty program chose not to channel grants to the states. They offered them to private and quasi-public as well as public agencies. They avoided writing conditions into the law, preferring to preserve flexibility for applicants and, even more, for federal administrators. Far from seeking a merit-system requirement, they were positively hostile to civil service regulations. Once the program was under way, antipoverty guidelines even stressed the hiring of nonprofessionals, and administrators fought back an effort in the Senate to extend to local employees provisions of the Hatch Act, the federal ban on partisan activity by civil servants (which applied to state and local employees in public assistance and other federally aided programs).

In the next few years the antipoverty officials' implicit criticism of public assistance became increasingly explicit, as the assistance program became a growing source of political controversy. Although these issues involved matters less abstruse than the mechanics of the grant system—the program itself was in dispute—this was, for state or local officials who wished to do so, an opportune time to attack federal regulation in general. Appearing before a Senate subcommittee in 1966, for instance, New York Mayor John V. Lindsay complained that federal and state controls were hampering the city welfare agency's "creativity," which, in the context created by federal rhetoric, was the ultimate condemnation. [14]

If the public assistance program was now an example of every-thing thought to be wrong with the grant system, mere reaction against it was insufficient; reform was required. A thirty-year ac-cumulation of law and custom made this hard to do. New doc-trines could more easily be expressed in new programs than im-parted to old ones. Yet an opportunity for change arose, partly through executive choice and partly through the accident of legis-lative events.

As secretary of health, education, and welfare, Gardner more than any other member of the Johnson Administration articulated the need for change in the grant system. As a federal official he was responsible for nearly half of all grant expenditures, and in any case he had a long-standing interest in problems of organiza-tion and the structure of public institutions. Under his direction HEW began bit by bit to put creative federalism into practice. Fifteen programs of health grants to the states were consolidated into one, with only very general conditions attached. Regional of-ficials were raised in rank and authority (the preoccupation with decentralization included decentralization within federal adminis-trative structures). And a major reorganization of public welfare administration occurred which was in part designed to change the character of federal-state relations. The Welfare Administration was abolished and a new agency, the Social and Rehabilitation Service, was created in its place, with a director who, as former head of the Vocational Rehabilitation Administration, was accus-tomed to giving the states much more latitude for action than had the BPA or BFS. (The BFS was abolished in the reorganization, and its functions and personnel were distributed among several units of the new agency.) As Gardner was announcing the reorga-nization, Congress was finishing work on its own solution to the rise in ADC caseloads: the Social Security Amendments of 1967, a complicated piece of legislation that required federal adminis-trators to prepare many new guidelines for the states. Coinciding with the reorganization, the new law provided an opportunity to change the character of this guidance.

Administrative directives to implement the 1967 amendments reached the states in the summer of 1968. Simultaneously, the

SRS began a thorough revision of the *Handbook of Public Assistance Policy*. Both the directives and the new handbook sections were much more permissive than what they replaced. Policies governing provision of services in ADC illustrate the change. These may be contrasted with State Letter 606, the directive that put into effect the service amendments of 1962.

In preparing State Letter 606 (one hundred pages long), federal administrators proceeded on the assumption that they would define the activities required of the states and that the content of their directives would provide the basis for determining whether state plans and administrative activities conformed to federal policy. Thus they sought to define at length those activities that constituted the giving of services and to stipulate at least a few highly specific requirements (notably, caseload and supervisory standards). The service directive of 1968 (occupying five pages in the *Federal Register*) rested on a very different assumption.[15] It set forth federal objectives, definitions of activities eligible for aid, and plan requirements in very brief and general terms; the states were left to devise plan provisions that would meet the requirements. Guidance went little beyond the language of the federal law. Over and over the directive simply summarized statutory requirements and asserted that a state plan must show an intention to comply.

Nonetheless, the federal administration still had to lay a basis for accounting for the expenditure of federal funds and for auditing. It responded to this problem by telling the states in effect that they could lay the basis for determining conformance themselves, with provisions in their plans. Federal officials would simply check to make sure that approved plans were being complied with:

The State plans will be used by SRS as a basis for program reporting, evaluation and auditing. It is expected that States will take all necessary steps to assure that service programs are implemented in accordance with the State plan and that all Federal requirements are met. Isolated individual variations in practice from the State plan will not generally be treated as a violation of the Federal requirement although they may result in audit exceptions. Repeated or widespread failure to conform to the approved State plan is a serious matter and can lead to withdrawal of Federal funds.

To be sure, not all changes were in the direction of greater permissiveness. A few new requirements were imposed. Each state had to establish an advisory committee on the ADC and child welfare programs, one third of whose members must be "recipients of assistance or services or representatives of such recipients." The advisory committee must be given "adequate opportunity for meaningful participation in both policy development and program administration." Also, "nonprofessional positions must be established to assist in the provision of services," and "recipients of assistance or other low income persons must be given preference for such positions." Thus the liberal, reform orthodoxy of the 1930s gave way to that of the 1960s, but there could be no doubt that the new orthodoxy meant decentralization.

Decentralization by Design

It is paradoxical, if true, that pluralism can be preserved only by federal design and that decentralization must be promoted through the exercise of centralized authority. But even if this is true, will the necessary actions at the federal level be feasible? To what extent will the actions taken promote the ends they are intended to promote, and what precisely is intended? The only sure answers to these questions must come from experience, and not much of it is available as of 1969. But earlier experience with the grant system may be sufficiently relevant to permit us to make some informed guesses.

Decentralization as Devolution with the Federal System. Decentralization requires the counteracting of forces that tend to produce centralization. Some of these forces, such as the greater mobility of the population and the proliferation of national communication media, are beyond the present capacity of government to direct, even if decentralization were generally agreed to be so important an end as to justify the attempt. The more narrowly political causes of centralization are no easier to control. As long as there are substantial interest groups that perceive an advantage in appealing to the federal government, and as long as it is accessible to their appeals, pressures for centralization will persist. Furthermore, centralization through the medium of categorical grants has by now proceeded so far that it has become a self-sustaining process. The grant statutes already enacted and the federal administrative regulations already developed are attractive vehicles for the realization of various purposes through the medium of federal power; they are standing invitations to action by all who would use them. Inevitably, they tend to grow in volume and detail as the invitation is responded to.

The evolution of the public assistance program after 1936 illustrates the inertial force of centralization. Three public assistance titles of the Social Security Act, running to a combined length of nine pages, grew within thirty years into six titles that were seven times longer and imposed more numerous and detailed conditions upon recipient governments. Federal administrative regulations were growing in even greater abundance. This tendency exists in other grant programs as well, and the history of the Heller plan shows how difficult it is to deflect. Heller did not propose to do more than deflect it. Under his plan, revenue sharing would have functioned in addition to the grant system as a mode of federal support for state and local governments; he did not propose to repeal or supersede any grant programs. Revenue sharing would complement the grant system by making it easier for state and local governments to meet matching requirements: they might match conditional federal funds with unconditional ones. Yet the plan was so strongly opposed by federal administrative agencies and professional groups such as the National Education Association that the Johnson Administration never took action on it.[16]

Congressional action in 1967 shows that centralizing tendencies in the federal public assistance program have not been arrested. While federal administrators were contemplating the possibilities of creative federalism, Congress—with an eye on the ADC caseload—was writing many new and quite specific conditions into the Social Security Act. But the subsequent change in the nature of administrative guidance shows that decentralization through administrative action is to some degree feasible, given a rationale for change and an executive prepared to make the choice.

In the case of the public assistance program, the rationale rested partly on the lessons of recent experience. The service directive had severely tested the reach of federal influence. Even for those in the BFS who sympathized with the general aim of giving services along with money (and not all did), the result was discouraging. The impossibility of enforcing the wide range of federal requirements (either very general ones, like "community planning," or specific ones, like maintenance of caseload standards) became apparent. To those officials who sought a different approach to relations with the states, and to the management-consulting firm that advised them, the change in 1968 represented, not a deliberate reduction of federal influence, but an alternative and more effective strategy for exercising it. Instead of relying so heavily on explicit rules, federal administrators would henceforth seek to elicit the desired responses by stressing the objectives of federal policy and soliciting state cooperation in the preparation of programs to realize those objectives. The federal function would be informally to provide "leadership," to encourage appropriate responses with suggestion and advice.[17] This concept had prevailed in the earliest years of the public assistance program, survived in that program to some extent, and still prevailed in some other grant programs. In public assistance it had proved unstable partly because the great intergovernmental gap in professional attainment diminished the federal willingness to rely on state and local discretion, and one probable reason for the return to it in 1968 is that federal action in the interim had produced gains in the professionalization of state and local agencies. Federal influence had always been somewhat informal, in public assistance or any other program. The effectiveness of federal action depended in part on the disposition of officials or other interested political actors at the state and local levels to regard federal actions per se as worthy of emulation, on the supposition that the federal administration was especially qualified to define what constituted "correct" and "progressive" conduct. The degree of federal influence also depended on the tendency of state and local administrators to respond to the grant system with altered conceptions of their own roles. As the grant system has evolved, a "good administrator" at the state and local level has come to be defined as one who commands the confidence of federal grant givers and is skilled in obtaining funds from them, a development that has been accelerated by the shift from formula to project grants. Increasingly, his political superiors judge him, and he judges himself, on his ability to maintain good relations with the federal administration. The assistance administration's decision to rely less on formal requirements as methods of influence signified an intention to rely relatively more on intangible assets, such as professional prestige and the constraints on state and local officials produced by the very operation of the grant system.

Like federal assistance administrators, the leading proponents of decentralization formed their ideas from their own experience. These men went to Washington in the early 1960s with high hopes for the use of federal power, but they were quickly disappointed. New programs poured forth from the federal legislature only to founder, it seemed, from deficiencies in administrative capacity. Willing to concede the difficulties of direct federal administration, but dissatisfied with the results of the grant system, Heller, Gardner, Goodwin, and others began looking for ways to enlarge the administrative capabilities of state and local governments.

Theirs remained a *national* perspective. In promoting decentralization, they were looking above all for more effective ways of achieving federal purposes. Heller, in setting forth his revenue-sharing plan, was perfectly clear about this:

the Federal government simply cannot carry out large segments of its responsibilities at all—or at all efficiently—

without strengthening the states and localities. A very large part of what we do through government is done through state and local units . . .

If we want state and local governments to be efficient partners in our federalism, we have to strengthen the whole fabric of government at their levels . . . States and localities —either as they now exist, or perhaps with growing emphasis on both regional and metropolitan-area groupings—will continue to be the service centers through which important national purposes are achieved. If we don't want these purposes thwarted or diluted, we had better strengthen those operating units.[18]

Heller's case for increasing the flow of federal fiscal support rested heavily on the premise that it would increase state and local administrative competence:

[The development of state and local vitality] requires a sufficient flow of money to command the services of competent and imaginative people and to provide them with the funds to carry out their ideas. How far the revitalization process goes will depend on the financial and intellectual resources that state and local governments can command. Improvements are being made, and the caliber of state-local administration is rising. We need to accelerate that process . . .

One readily visualizes the tangible benefits [of revenue sharing]: higher salaries and hence higher caliber staffs; better performance of the jobs the Federal government subcontracts to states and localities; and a more effective attack on problems beyond the reach of Federal projects and the present system of Federal aids.[19]

Gardner's proposals for strengthening state and local government reflected the same concern. He told Congress that "the upgrading of State and local government must begin with people, and I endorse with enthusiasm the Intergovernmental Personnel Act." As an example of past success he cited the "enormously effective role" of HEW's Division of State Merit Systems in upgrading state governments.[20]

Decentralization was conceived, then, as a way of making state governments and their subdivisions better administrators of federal programs—the principal aim was to strengthen the efficacy of intergovernmental cooperation—and yet it is clear that the proponents of decentralization also sought in some sense to serve the value of pluralism. Providing money more permissively seemed one way to do this. Heller spoke of the need not only to make the states "better 'service stations' of federalism but to release their creative and innovative energies." Revenue sharing, he argued, "would provide a dependable flow of Federal funds in a form that would enlarge, not restrict, the options of state and local decision makers." [21] Gardner's search for simplified conditions of aid giving expressed the same impulse.

Still, the values of pluralism and of social efficacy are to some degree competitive. Pluralism implies the existence of a political system or set of interrelated systems (as in a federal state) so structured that it is possible to express through public action a variety of value choices. Significantly differing political outcomes, in other words, are produced simultaneously in the same society. (Government action in New York is "liberal," in Texas "conservative.") The advantage of a federal structure is that it facilitates pluralism in this sense, by creating discrete spheres and structures of political decisionmaking. The concept of social efficacy, on the other hand, presumes a more or less integrated and consistent set of values or social ends; "efficacy" implies the successful realization of these values or ends. In a federal system, the central government is the only vehicle available for the expression of such ends. If other governments cooperate in the realization of its choices, the efficacy of the cooperative action is increased to the degree that other governments independently share, or may be led by deliberate actions of the central government to share, those choices. And to that degree, the value of pluralism is sacrificed. Theory aside, experience with grant programs shows how the two values tend to conflict. In order to facilitate the realization of federally prescribed ends, the federal government promoted the professionalization of state and local personnel. To the extent it succeeded in this and in enhancing the role of professionalized administrators in state and local decisionmaking, the range of values expressed through governmental action in the society as a whole diminished; insofar as action approached the norms stipulated by professional values, pluralism was sacrificed.

That the proponents of decentralization seem not to view this as a dilemma—they think that making the states better service stations for the federal government will also safeguard pluralism—may be accounted for by the fact that for them pluralism apparently does not imply the **production** of substantially differing value choices. Rather, it implies the development, in dispersed decisionmaking structures, of a wide variety of means for the realization of a common set of ends. What they seek by decentralization is to stimulate state and local initiative in the devising of problem-solving techniques, on the assumption that the problems to be solved and ends to be served will in a general way be defined by the central government or perhaps by some sort of informal consensus among those political elites in a position to perceive the common needs of society. (Heller writes, "State and local officials need a chance to worry, not just about getting the dead cat out of the alley . . . but about how we can more effectively devote our growing abundance to our common needs, how we can get at the roots of our social failures" [22]—as if the particular and parochial concern for getting the dead cat out of the alley could not possibly command the interest of the citizen and hence the local politician.) Theirs is a conception of what might be called "administrative pluralism" as distinct from "political pluralism." Even when arguing the necessity of safeguarding pluralism, they tend to focus on the functioning of state and local administrative organizations, which they conceive of as the potential sources of new problem-solving techniques.

Heller, whose revenue-sharing plan would increase the scope of action of state legislatures as well as administrators (it therefore goes beyond the kind of reform of the grant system exemplified by the public assistance program), had to meet the argument from liberals that state governments would use their enlarged capacities in undesirable ways. They would make the "wrong" value choices. He conceded in reply that a few conditions on the shared revenues might be necessary: he was inclined to prohibit their use for highways and to specify a level of allocation to the central cities. More tellingly, he pointed out that his plan would have the advantage of substituting the (progressive) federal income tax for (regressive) state and local taxes as a source of public revenue, thereby shifting one more fundamental political choice, the pattern of taxation, up to the federal level. Finally, he argued that reapportionment would change the character of state politics. It seems clear that he would not have proposed the revenue-sharing plan if reapportionment were not "redressing the political balance in state legislatures away from rotten boroughs and lop-sided rural representation toward the urban, and especially the suburban, constituencies." [23] Liberals of this persuasion optimistically believe that reapportionment will lead to political results at the state level that will not be very different from those at the federal level, where urban and suburban interests have been relatively well represented. To some among them, like Heller, it follows that state legislatures can now be trusted with federal revenues that are only slightly restricted. Structural reform of state governments has thus fostered a willingness to experiment with decentralization. In short, the perceived decline of political pluralism has stimulated an interest in administrative pluralism.

The extent to which state and local governments are bound by federal value choices continues to depend upon the will and capacity of Congress to make such choices and to state them in precise terms, or to authorize federal administrators to do so. In the 1960s, assistance administrators renewed their interest in setting a national standard of need and payment, and thereby revived consideration at the federal level of the central political choice posed by the program. They wanted authority from Congress to set a national standard, but they did not begin by asking for that. Instead, in 1967, they called for only a modest step in that direction

—a statutory requirement that the states meet 100 percent of recipients' need as their own welfare agencies have defined it. Congress rejected even that, which illustrates how political pluralism is preserved: It is done through the action (more correctly, the nonaction) of a federal legislature in which diverse state interests are represented, and not through the design of federal administrators.

Decentralization as Dispersion of Official Power. That otherwise nonofficial persons should be given a role in official decisionmaking has become a common condition of federal aid. The urban renewal program, begun in 1949, was probably the first to incorporate such a requirement. Provision for citizen participation was one of the "seven promises" (the local administrators' term) that had to be made to the Housing and Home Finance Agency in order to qualify for a grant.[24] More recently, federal requirements typically have applied to a particular class of citizens, those directly affected by the operation of the program. These requirements represent a significant departure from the policies of earlier grant programs, and even seem to be a conscious reaction against them. The current requirement in public assistance that states employ nonprofessionals stands in stark contrast to the prior stress on professionalization. Similarly, the requirement that advisory committees be created with recipients as members compromises, if it does not reverse, the tendency of earlier policy, which was to concentrate authority in the state welfare agency. Yet these changes are not as radical as they may seem and, as devices to disperse power, are quite limited in conception.

In principle, the federal purpose has been consistent: to influence the structure of state decisionmaking processes in such a way as to produce results that will serve federal objectives. Conceptions of the particular requirements that will best do this have changed. As of the 1960s it is deemed desirable that clients should share policymaking and administrative functions with professional administrators. Thus the conception of the proper relation between the "professional" and the "client" has changed—but not the federal intention to foster a liberal, client-serving assistance program in the states. (It is possible too that federal assistance administrators were inspired by the antipoverty program to conceive of "curing the powerlessness of the poor" as one objective of the public assistance program.)

The introduction of clients into the state agency's decisionmaking structure presumably will reinforce the preference of professional administrators for a liberal program, and will increase pressure on them to take those steps toward liberalization that come within the range of their discretion. That public assistance clients and administrators will act in concert may seem implausible in the context of the late 1960s, a time in which clients have been protesting against the penury of agency programs and giving voice, in the process, to an intense hostility toward assistance administrators. The requirement of client participation thus seems to introduce a fundamentally antagonistic element into the structure of state policymaking and administration. This tension, however, is to some extent an artificial product of the political mood or style of action peculiar to an era; as an indicator of the "normal" political relations between professional givers of aid and recipients of aid, it is deceptive. Administrators of the assistance program and their clients, like administrators and clients of public programs generally, have certain essential interests in common, the main one being aggrandizement of the program. They have a common interest in increasing their claim on the supply of public revenue. When assistance agencies have given small and inadequate grants, it is not necessarily because administrators themselves were illiberal. Rather, they have been restrained by legislative action which in turn was a response, presumably, to the opinions and preferences of a popular majority. To the degree that assistance administrators and workers have been professionalized, they have favored a more liberal program and have increased benefits to recipients either spontaneously or in response to client demands, insofar as it was politically feasible to do so. Workers have sometimes engaged in protest activity in alliance with recipients.

If the federal aim were strictly to promote decentralization—

that is, to maximize the dispersion of power with respect to policy-making in public assistance—the best way to do it would be to compel the return of policymaking to popularly elected local governments; the electoral process is still the best method yet devised for dispersing power. Massachusetts before 1935 stands as a model of this kind of decentralization. But that, of course, is not at all what federal administrators wish, for there is not the slightest doubt that, if public assistance policymaking were left to elected local governments, the result would be programs much less liberal than those that have followed from the centralizing effects of federal action. This would be true even if public revenues were distributed in such a way as to equalize the fiscal capacity of localities. The outcome of policymaking at the local level would still be "conservative" by comparison to the outcome of the present system, in which decisionmaking has been elevated to the state and federal levels.* What the federal administration seeks is decentralization of a very limited sort, which is calculated to increase the policymaking role of a specific group, public assistance clients. Its action will reinforce or accelerate what is probably a normal phenomenon in politics, the tendency for policymaking to be dominated by proximately and intensely interested groups—

* Exactly why this should be true—that is, why political outcomes are more liberal as the decisionmaking unit increases in scale, as appears to be the case in American politics—deserves far more attention from students of federalism. Insofar as liberal outcomes are correlated with a high volume of expenditure, the answer perhaps lies in the superior revenue-raising capacity of the largest-scale government, but the problem is more complex than this. In public assistance, it appears that increases in scale enhance the influence in policymaking of special interest groups, principally the professional administrators, whose preferences are liberal, or at least more liberal than those of the general public. An increase in scale both requires and facilitates the formation of specialized administrative organizations, and may also make more difficult the expression of unorganized opinion. The smaller the decisionmaking unit, the easier it is for the general public to wield influence through the unconscious imposition of informal norms on the policymakers. In this sense, local politics may be more "democratic" than state or federal politics—more accurately a response to a popular or majority will—even though it may not be more democratic by any measurable indicator, such as the rate of voter participation. That this explains the greater "conservatism" of local politics follows, however, only if one assumes that the general public is more conservative than organizations of professional administrators or other organized elites that may gain from increases in scale. Again, the question is a complex one, and any attempt to analyze it must begin with an effort to specify the ways in which political outcomes at different levels do in fact differ.

the administrators and immediate beneficiaries of programs—rather than by the unorganized, remotely interested majority.

The federal requirement of recipient participation may not have much effect. The stipulation that advisory committees be set up and that a third of the members be recipients or their representatives is, like caseload standards, highly specific (though it leaves aside the question of who a "representative" might be); and, unlike caseload standards, it will probably be enforceable, for the committees can be established by the state welfare agencies. Yet the requirement (again, like caseload standards) is merely instrumental to the end actually sought, which is "meaningful participation in both policy development and program administration" for the advisory committees. As with service giving, the mode of behavior that the federal administration seeks to induce is impossible to specify, and it depends upon many circumstances beyond the control of federal administrators and perhaps even of state administrators, whose own role is determined to some extent by state legislatures. This does not mean that recipients will not play a "meaningful" role in state policymaking. Old-age assistance recipients have long done so, with no encouragement from the federal administration, and ADC recipients have begun (in Massachusetts in the summer of 1968, they persuaded, through protest activity, the state welfare department to issue rules stipulating items of furniture to which they were entitled, and earlier their activity in Boston greatly stimulated the provision of items over and above the state standard budget). However, recipients are much more likely to gain influence through the formation of private pressure groups and the development of their own strategies of demand than through federal rules about participation. The federal rules themselves, following upon the new political activity of ADC mothers, may be more a response than a stimulus to "meaningful participation."

Apart from the difficulty of enforcing requirements for recipient (or other citizen) participation in public assistance and other grant programs, there are fundamental obstacles in the way of the federal effort to promote decentralization, obstacles that lie in the very nature of the grant system.

Whatever the intention of the federal administration with respect to the distribution of power at the state and local level, of necessity it retains an interest in developing there a counterpart agency that will be responsible for fulfilling federal conditions and goals. There is an enduring federal interest in accountability for program results. In practice, this has in the past led the federal government to encourage the concentration of authority and power in the grant-receiving agency. In public assistance and other programs, such as highway construction,[25] in which the states are the recipients, the result has been to enhance the authority of state agencies (welfare departments, highway departments) in relation to their local counterparts and in relation to state legislatures. In public housing, urban renewal, and other programs administered locally, the result has been to encourage the formation of special-purpose units of government that are independent of general-purpose units and often of the local electorate (hence the complaint that federal grant programs have contributed to the "fragmentation" of local government, which in turn has given rise to efforts at repairing the situation with federal requirements for local planning).[26] The more autonomous the grant-receiving agency, and the more concentrated its authority and power, the better served is the federal interest in accountability and achievement. Unless the federal government is willing to attach highest priority to the ideological aim of dispersing power and to accept the sacrifice of achievement that will result, then the aim of dispersing power will itself have to be compromised. The dilemma is better illustrated by programs that entail the carrying out of projects, like model cities or community action, than by those that involve continuing operations, like public assistance. The federal administrative agency must face the question of whether it is more important to have widespread, nonofficial participation in the planning and execution of the project, in which case long delays will result and responsibility will be diffused, or to get the project under way promptly and have "something to show" to Congress and the public, in which case the authority to act must be concentrated. (The model-cities law requires "widespread citizen participation" and that projects start within a "reasonable" and "short" period of time.[27]) The pressure to show results is so strong in American politics that the second choice is the more likely one.

Finally, and again aside from the intention of federal administrators, the structure of the grant system is such as to put a premium on the possession of bureaucratic skills and the holding of bureaucratic office. The intergovernmental communication generated by the grant system is mainly interbureaucratic communication. Characteristically, the operation of the system involves interaction between the grant-giving and the grant-receiving administrative agencies. Critical public decisions—how to allocate funds, what actions to require of state and local governments, what responses to make to federal requirements—are arrived at through this process, which is relatively shielded from the public view and from routine participation by legislatures. Development of the grant system inevitably entails a decline in the accessibility of governmental processes to popular scrutiny and participation, and at best this decline can be only partially offset by requirements of citizen participation imposed upon the grant recipient. Participation in decisionmaking at the state or local level does not provide access to decisions at the federal level, or (what is equally important) to communications between the two.

As the functions of government expand, the search for more effective modes of administration will continue. The achievements of public action will generally fall short of the hopes and promises of the sponsors of action. Serious social problems will persist, and political activists having strong faith in the power of government to solve them ("liberals") will explain its failure to do so either by reference to the opposition of conservatives or (when that explanation is implausible, as in 1964–1968, a period of liberal dominance) by reference to flaws in the structure of policymaking and administrative institutions. Reform will be called for

—perhaps further reform of the grant system (there is no way of telling how long it will take for the interest in decentralization to run its course) or increased use of alternatives to it.

The advantages and disadvantages of the grant system are difficult to specify, for it is difficult to isolate its characteristics from more general features of the American political system. Congress, in enacting grant statutes, cannot precisely formulate statements of goals, and it may be that the necessity to "buy" the participation of state and local governments with permissive terms of grant giving is one cause of this. But the fundamental cause surely is the diversity of interests and opinions in the society and the fidelity with which Congress represents them. It may be true that the administration, in enunciating grant programs, tends to promise more results than it can deliver, and that one explanation for this is that the radical separation between those who define national goals and those who administer programs encourages unreality among those who state the goals. Still, the fundamental source of the extravagant promises in American politics surely lies elsewhere, perhaps in the President's felt need to express popular aspirations or in an optimism endemic to this political culture. It is true that intergovernmental divisions of authority make difficult the development of administrative controls to guide state and local actions toward the common goals defined by Congress. But it is also true that problems of administrative control arise largely out of a tendency to try to subject to control phenomena that are inherently uncontrollable; the problems would persist and in some ways be compounded under a system of direct federal administration. If it is easy to exaggerate the defects of the grant system, however, and to attribute to it flaws that are actually general features of contemporary American politics, it is also easy to exaggerate its advantages: as a way of dispersing power and safeguarding pluralism—supposedly its chief virtues—it is flawed by a tendency to foster powerful, self-serving intergovernmental alliances between official agencies that share values and interests as well as functions, and that gain autonomy through the system's operation.

Assuming the appropriateness of a federal system in the United States, and the necessity somehow to gain the advantages of having a central government and other governments as well, two general approaches to the sharing of governmental functions are possible. One, which was chosen by the authors of the Constitution (though it was always imperfectly carried out in practice), is to allocate functions exclusively to one level or the other. The second, which evolved through the medium of the grant system until it has become the prevailing approach, is for all major functions to be shared. The authors of the Constitution may have been right in principle. It may be that the advantages of a federal system—that is, the "right" combination of pluralism and social efficacy—can best be realized through the first kind of choice; but the particular choices made in the eighteenth century concerning the allocation of functions are of course quite obsolete, and we have had to find ways of modifying them. If we had to start again, we would have many more such choices to make, governmental functions having grown in number, and we would choose differently (in my opinion, the case for making support of the poor a function of the central government would be most compelling). We cannot do this, however. We must live with the adaptations we have devised, and keep on making more of them, in the hope that we shall be very lucky and that our adaptations will also be improvements.

Notes

Index

Notes

1. The Grant System

1. For a summary of current grant programs and analysis of basic trends, see U.S. Bureau of the Budget, *Special Analyses, Budget of the United States, Fiscal Year 1969*, 155–169. Another excellent analysis—brief, informative, and up to date—is by I. M. Labovitz, "Federal Assistance to State and Local Governments," in Tax Institute of America, *Federal-State-Local Fiscal Relationships* (Princeton, 1968), 13–43. See also Deil S. Wright, *Federal Grants-in-Aid: Perspectives and Alternatives* (Washington, 1968).

2. For criticism of centralization through the grant system, see, e.g., "The Restoration of Federalism in America," report by a Republican study group, *Congressional Record*, Feb. 1, 1968, H728–H732.

3. Commission on Intergovernmental Relations, *A Report to the President for Transmittal to the Congress* (June 1955), ch. 5.

4. The Court of course continues to have an important role in shaping the federal-state division of functions, especially in respect to civil liberties, but even in a field marked by a relatively high level of judicial activity, much depends on the independent behavior and the interaction of federal, state, and local bureaucracies. For an analysis from the perspective of the Justice Department, see Burke Marshall, *Federalism and Civil Rights* (New York, 1964).

5. The history of grant programs is conveniently available in V. O. Key, Jr., *The Administration of Federal Grants to the States* (Chicago, 1937) ch. 1; W. Brooke Graves, *American Intergovernmental Relations* (New York, 1964), chs. 14–16; and Morton Grodzins, *The American System* (Chicago, 1966), ch. 2. More generally, for a historical account of intergovernmental relations, see Daniel J. Elazar, *The American Partnership: Intergovernmental Cooperation in the Nineteenth-Century United States* (Chicago, 1962).

6. Paul H. Douglas, "The Development of a System of Federal Grants-in-Aid," *Political Science Quarterly*, 35:255–271, 522–544 (1920). For data on trends in expenditure, see Bureau of the Census, U.S. Department of Commerce, *Census of Governments, 1962: Historical Statistics on Governmental Finances and Employment* (Washington, 1964).

7. Various efforts have been made to inventory federal grant programs. The principal publications are the *Catalog of Federal Aids to State and Local Governments,* issued by the Senate Committee on Government Operations as a committee print in 1964 and kept up to date with supplements; the *Catalog of Federal Programs for Individual and Community Improvement,* issued periodically by the U.S. Office of Economic Opportunity; and, more recently, a compilation prepared by a member of Congress, William V. Roth, which appears in the *Congressional Record,* June 25, 1968, H5441ff. Roth introduced a bill providing that the President should publish annually a compendium of federal grant programs.

8. Anyone who wishes such an account—one covering the major policy issues, the interaction of parties, interest groups, public opinion, and the like—may consult Gilbert Y. Steiner, *Social Insecurity: The Politics of Welfare* (Chicago, 1966). Steiner's book focuses mainly on federal politics. There is no comparable account for Massachusetts or, to my knowledge, for any other state. Hence I hope that this book, in lieu of something more and better, will be welcome to those whose main interest is public assistance politics; but it is not at all the book I would have written had that been my interest.

2. The Sharing of the Assistance Function

1. The point is illustrated, imperfectly, by a passage from Harold Ickes' diary, citing President Roosevelt's interest in public housing projects in the fall of 1936: "He spoke especially of a housing project for Negroes that we are building in Indianapolis. He said that this was fine. He remarked also that he had driven through several streets in the Negro section near the housing project and that his picture was in the window of every house. This gave me an opportunity to tell him how much I regretted that we had not been able to go ahead with our Negro housing project in the black belt in Chicago. I told him that we had bought the land, or nearly all of it, for this project. Then, 'thinking out loud,' he developed a plan by which we might be able to go ahead with this project . . . He also told me that, if possible, he would like to go ahead with the housing projects in Bridgeport, Connecticut, and Lackawanna, Pennsylvania. He thought these projects would be of great advantage politically, and I said, 'Hardboiled Harold understands.' " *The Secret Diary of Harold L. Ickes* (New York, 1953), I, 673. The illustration is imperfect because the projects referred to were built directly by the federal government, but within a year grants-in-aid for public housing were authorized, launching the first major program that entailed direct federal aid to the cities.

2. Key, 17, 228ff.

3. "Frontiers of Control in Public Welfare Administration," *Social Service Review,* 1:99 (March 1927).

4. Social Security Board, *Social Security in America: The Factual Background of the Social Security Act as Summarized from Staff Reports to the Committee on Economic Security* (Washington, 1937), chs. 8, 13, 14, 19. See also Arthur C. Millspaugh, *Public Welfare Organization* (Washington, 1935).

5. Arthur M. Schlesinger, Jr., *The Coming of the New Deal* (Boston, 1959), 301–311; *Report to the President of the Committee on Economic Security* (Washington, 1935); Frances Perkins, *The Roosevelt I Knew* (New York, 1946), 278–301; Edwin E. Witte, *The Development of the Social Security Act* (Madison, 1962), 3–41.

6. Sophonisba P. Breckinridge, *Public Welfare Administration in the United States* (Chicago, 1938), 628.

7. Jane P. Clark, *The Rise of a New Federalism* (New York, 1938), chs. 6, 7, 8.

8. For a recent comment on its significance, see Daniel P. Moynihan, "The Crises in Welfare," *The Public Interest* (Winter 1968), 12.

9. Arthur J. Altmeyer, *The Formative Years of Social Security* (Madison, 1966), 36; Social Security Board, *Second Annual Report, 1937*, in Breckinridge, *Public Welfare Administration*, 1079–1086.

10. Mark P. Hale, "The Process of Developing Policy for a Federal-State Grant-in-Aid Program, as Illustrated by the Work of the Social Security Board, 1935–46," *Social Service Review*, 31:290–310 (Sept. 1957).

11. U.S. Advisory Commission on Intergovernmental Relations, *Statutory and Administrative Controls Associated with Federal Grants for Public Assistance* (Washington, 1964), 61–71.

12. Altmeyer, 79–80, 119–20; Mark P. Hale, "Some Aspects of Federal-State Relations," *Social Service Review*, 28:126–136 (June 1954); Kathryn D. Goodwin, "Administrative Review in Public Assistance," *Social Security Bulletin* (Oct. 1943), 5–16; William L. Mitchell, "The Administrative Review in Federal-State Social Security Programs," *Social Security Bulletin* (July 1946), 10–13; U.S. Welfare Administration, *Public Assistance under the Social Security Act: Serving People in Need* (Washington, 1966), 14. For a fuller discussion of the form of federal-state relations in the conduct of grant programs generally and the assistance program in particular, see the cited works by Key, Clark, and Hale, and Ruth Raup, *Intergovernmental Relations in Social Welfare* (Minneapolis, 1952).

13. The first commissioner, Robert W. Kelso, served as president of the National Conference of Social Work and was the author of a textbook on public welfare administration as well as a scholarly history of poor relief in Massachusetts. His successor in 1921, Richard K. Conant, held office for fourteen years, during which he took an active part in professional affairs, including the founding of the American Public Welfare Association in the early thirties. He later became dean of the Boston University School of Social Work. Both men had law degrees from Harvard.

14. Regional representative (hereafter abbreviated reg rep), BPA, to

associate director, BPA, May 5, 1937, Mass. File 661, in Assistance Payments Administration Regional Office, Boston (hereafter abbreviated RO). Although some documents have been destroyed or are missing, much regional office correspondence with Washington headquarters and the Massachusetts welfare department is preserved there, along with internal office notes and memoranda.

15. *The History of Public Poor Relief in Massachusetts, 1620–1920* (Boston, 1922), 92.

16. *Ibid.*, 66.

17. *Ibid.*, 143.

18. Mass. Department of Public Welfare, Manual of Laws (Dec. 1932), ch. 118A, sec. 4.

19. On the welfare department in the 1930s, see Mass., *Report of the Special Commission on Taxation and Public Expenditures*, part II [Haber Report], House No. 1702 (Boston, 1938); William Haber, "The Public Welfare Problem in Massachusetts," *Social Service Review*, 12:179–204 (June 1938); and William Haber and Herman M. Somers, "The Administration of Public Assistance in Massachusetts," *Social Service Review*, 12:397–416 (Sept. 1938).

20. Ch. 402, *Acts of 1930;* the OAA statute is ch. 118A of the *General Laws.*

21. Ch. 593, *Acts of 1941.*

22. Ch. 597 and ch. 729, *Acts of 1941.*

23. Ch. 489, *Acts of 1943.*

24. Ch. 415, *Acts of 1946.*

25. Haber Report, chs. 3 and 4; Alton A. Linford, *Old-Age Assistance in Massachusetts* (Chicago, 1949), 124–134; Charles Stauffacher, David Bell, and G. Burnham Lyons, "The Problem of Public Relief in Massachusetts," mimeograph, Oct. 1, 1940 (Widener Library, Harvard University), 31–36.

26. McCarthy's reaction appears in the *Boston Globe* of Feb. 4, 1938. He was responding both to the Haber Report itself and a *Globe* series by Louis M. Lyons that was based on the report. McCarthy's reply was mimeographed by the Welfare Department and a copy ("Reply to Welfare Report") is available in its library. He wrote: "The relief statutes contain sections referring to supervision by the State Department. These sections make nice reading, but in practice they are of questionable value. To state the problem frankly—the state should be empowered by proper legislative enactment and legal safeguards to carry out in fact actual and real supervision" (4).

27. Mass., *Annual Report of the Department of Public Welfare* (1939), 2–8.

28. Mass. Department of Public Welfare, *Manual of Laws, Rules, Policies and Procedures for the Administration of Public Assistance* (Sept. 27, 1939), and Mass. Department of Public Welfare, *Manual of Public Assistance* (Nov. 1, 1943). Copies of the 1939 manual are in the library

of the state welfare department. As of 1967, the only original copy of the 1943 manual I could find was in the files of the department's Office of Policies and Procedures, preserved there by Francis M. Kelly. See also "The Development of a Manual of Policies and Procedures," a master's thesis at the Boston University School of Social Work by Rosa Rabinow, on preparation of the 1943 manual. A copy is in the state department's library.

29. The high volume of appeals in Massachusetts and of reversals of local decisions should not be taken as an index of local deviation from state intent. That intent has often been vague, and local agencies, in the absence of explicit state rules to guide their decisions, might themselves stimulate appeals in order to evoke from the state a definitive interpretation of its own rules. See Mass. Department of Public Welfare, *Report of a Study of Appeals in Disability Assistance* (April 1965), report on file in Bureau of Research and Statistics.

30. *Meeting the Problems of People in Massachusetts* (Boston, 1965).

31. The crucial question in the legislature arose over an attempt by opponents of state administration to substitute for the reformers' bill one that would have provided for the state assumption of assistance costs while leaving administration with local units. The vote against the substitute was 22–13 in the Senate and 122–99 in the House.

32. SSB Division of Plans and Grants to regional director, Boston, Dec. 7, 1938, Mass. 610, RO. Unfortunately, the Current Activities Reports of the BPA regional representative, which might reveal how he handled this recommendation in discussions with state officials, have been destroyed. Nothing in the files indicates that he conveyed it to the state in writing.

33. Neil P. Fallon (regional commissioner, SRS) to Mary Switzer (commissioner), Oct. 5, 1967, Mass. FS-5, RO.

3. Adequacy of Assistance

1. *U.S. Statutes-at-Large*, vol. 49, ch. 531 (1935); italics added. The Social Security Act with amendments is frequently issued as a public document, with the title *Compilation of the Social Security Laws*. Through the 1940s, it was issued by the Federal Security Agency. Since then it has appeared as a congressional document, usually of the House of Representatives. For example, see House Document 312, 89 Cong., 1 sess. (1966).

2. BPA, State Letter 108, Sept. 15, 1948.

3. An exception occurs in Title 19 (Medical Assistance), passed in 1965, which provided that a state must pay 40 percent of the costs and by July 1, 1970, 100 percent of them, unless it adopted a formula for distributing federal and state funds "on an equalization or other basis which will assure that the lack of adequate funds from local sources will not re-

sult in lowering the amount, duration, scope, or quality of care and services available under the plan."

4. U.S. House, *Economic Security Act*, Hearings before the Committee
on Ways and Means, 74 Cong., 1 sess. (1935), p. 975.

5. U.S. Senate, *Economic Security Act*, Hearings before the Committee
on Finance, 74 Cong., 1 sess. (1935), 70–78; the quoted passages appear
at 77 and 73. Witte's interpretation of the southerners' motives is in his
The Development of the Social Security Act, 143–144. Rep. Smith was explicit about the race problem (House hearings, 976).

6. Altmeyer, 105.

7. Congressional Quarterly, *Congress and the Nation, 1945–1964*
(Washington, 1965), 1273–1283; Steiner, 50–59; Altmeyer, 104–113.

8. As of October 1967, all states participated in the OAA, ADC, and
Aid to the Blind programs; all but one (Nevada), in DA; and all but five
(Alaska, Florida, Mississippi, Missouri, and South Carolina) in either
MA or MAA.

9. Richard E. Dawson and James A. Robinson, "The Politics of Welfare," in Herbert Jacob and Kenneth N. Vines, eds., *Politics in the American States* (Boston, 1965), 371–409; and Thomas R. Dye, *Politics, Economics, and the Public: Policy Outcomes in the American States* (Chicago, 1966), 124–128.

10. Jacob and Vines, 404–405; Dye, 143–144.

11. The ADC law, originally passed as ch. 763, *Acts of 1913*, constitutes ch. 118 of the *General Laws of Massachusetts*; the OAA law, originally passed as ch. 402, *Acts of 1930*, constitutes ch. 118A. The Department of Public Welfare has issued, irregularly, a manual of laws in which
statutes pertaining to public welfare are collected. The last such manual
was published in 1956.

12. Linford, 80.

13. The Committee on Economic Security did collect state expenditure
data as of 1935, and its findings are the source of the figures given in
Chapter 2, p. 18. There is no way of being sure that the data its staff developed then, before federal aid began, are comparable to the series
begun by the state welfare department in 1936. If they are, then the average monthly cash grant for OAA dropped between 1935 and 1936 (from
$26.08 to $24.85) while that for ADC rose (from $51.83 to $59.18).
This anomaly reinforces doubts about the validity of comparison.

14. The data are from the Bureau of Research and Statistics, Mass. Department of Public Welfare, which maintains this series on posting cards.

15. State laws passed in 1935–36 provided that federal grants would
be passed along to the cities and towns. Although local governments used
the new funds to cut their expenditure per OAA and ADC recipient, the
drop in local expenditures after federal aid began, amounting to $3.6 mil-
lion between 1935 and 1939, was nowhere near as great as the increase in
state and federal expenditures, which amounted to $21.6 million. Only a
fraction of the increased federal and state expenditure was substituted for

local expenditure; most of it went for broadened coverage. (Annual reports of the Mass. Department of Public Welfare. The last published report is for 1939.) Whereas payments per OAA and ADC recipient did not rise significantly after the start of federal aid, the number of recipients did, a development that will be analyzed later.

16. The Public Welfare Administrators' Association, the organization of local agency directors, often introduced bills to benefit OAA recipients, an activity that may have had its origins in a desire for self-preservation. In the 1940s the old-age lobby and local administrators were anything but political allies. The lobby tried to have administration of old-age assistance removed from local welfare agencies and transferred to a separately established office under a deputy commissioner within the state welfare department. In 1946 it went so far as to put this proposal before the state electorate with an initiative petition, and the proposal lost by only 32,000 votes out of 1,100,000 (Linford, 98–101). Thirty years later, a loose alliance with local administrators having developed in the meantime, the old-age lobby was against the reformers' proposal for state administration.

17. *Annual Report of the Department of Public Welfare* (1936), 2–3; Linford, 256–260.

18. Rotch to Charles H. Alspach, reg rep, Jan. 30, 1941, Mass. welfare commissioner's files (hereafter abbreviated cmsr's files). These files, which are arranged chronologically, consist almost entirely of federal-state correspondence and hence are a major source for this book.

19. Alspach to Rotch, March 6, 1941, cmsr's files.

20. Linford, 266–270.

21. *Ibid.*, 272, 287–296; Mass., *Special Report of the Commissioner of Public Welfare in Regard to an Investigation and Study of the Administration of the Old Age Assistance Law and of the Benefits Received by Recipients of Such Assistance*, House No. 1475 (1942).

22. Cf. Ellen J. Perkins, "Unmet Need in Public Assistance," *Social Security Bulletin*, April 1960, 3–11, and U.S. Commission on Civil Rights, *Children in Need: A Study of a Federally Assisted Program of Aid to Needy Families with Children in Cleveland and Cuyahoga County, Ohio* (Washington, 1966), 8–11.

23. From annual reports of the state welfare department.

24. *Annual Report of the Department of Public Welfare* (1932), 12.

25. Mass. Department of Public Welfare, *The Aid to Dependent Children Law, Rules Relating to the Administration of the Aid to Dependent Children Law and Rules Relative to Notice and Reimbursement, Revised January 1, 1937*, in John F. Kennedy School of Government Library, Harvard University. I was not able to find an earlier set of mothers' aid rules, but the department's annual reports make it clear that aid had previously been barred to mothers of illegitimate children. Nor was illegitimacy the only offense that caused aid to be cut off. Others listed in a sample year were "habitual immorality or intoxication," illegal sale of liquor,

larceny, neglect of children, keeping male lodgers, and neglect of homes. *Annual Report* (1929), 9–10.

26. From annual reports of the state welfare department and unpublished data in the files of the department's Bureau of Research and Statistics.

27. Since my purpose in this chapter is not to describe and explain the behavior of the state's caseload, but rather to identify the most general consequences of federal attempts to promote adequacy, I will not attempt here an analysis of the reasons for the recent large increase in the ADC caseload. This increase, which has occurred across the nation, is much in need of study. For the federal administration's explanation, see John M. Lynch, "Trend in Number of AFDC Recipients, 1961–65," *Welfare in Review*, May 1967, 7–13.

28. The first data on provision of medical care in public assistance were developed by a federal survey in 1946 of twenty states, of which Massachusetts was one. At that time it ranked eighth among the twenty in average monthly medical expenditure per OAA case and fifteenth per ADC case. Ruth White, "Expenditures for Medical Services in Public Assistance," *Social Security Bulletin*, Aug. 1952, 7–12. Following adoption of a state-wide medical care plan in 1954, the Massachusetts ranking rose sharply. Data on state medical vendor payments, along with other public assistance program statistics, have been published in federal serials: the *Social Security Bulletin* and, after 1963, *Welfare in Review*.

29. The state policy manual of 1943 instructed local officials that "standards for the provision of medical care . . . should be established," and that "local plans should be developed to the end that each community may have a plan that is best adapted to its particular situation."

30. Ch. 441, *Acts of 1945*.

31. The plan appeared as State Letter 68, Dec. 31, 1953. It seems originally to have been conceived as one to put the method of vendor payments in effect uniformly throughout the state. Following the federal agreement in 1950 to share in medical vendor payments, a number of states adopted this method. Massachusetts was following a trend. Interview, Francis M. Kelly, July 10, 1967; interview, Virginia M. Vahey, January 31, 1968; House No. 3070, 1957, 78–81; and miscellaneous notes and memoranda in file, "Medical Plan Data," Bureau of Research and Statistics, Mass. Department of Public Welfare.

32. House No. 3328 (1960).

33. Interview, Endicott Peabody, Feb. 26, 1968. A search of governors' annual messages and addresses from 1945 to 1964 revealed few references to public assistance.

34. A letter in 1947 from Commissioner Tompkins to Governor Robert Bradford suggests the awkward, anomalous character of its position (the letter was written to request an interview with the governor, whose time has not usually been available for audiences with the welfare commissioner no matter who the incumbent in either position): "You are un-

doubtedly aware that the department's legislative program was directed toward preventing any major public welfare legislation, particularly in the field of Old Age Assistance, during the most recent session of the Great and General Court. Rather, we emphasized your Inaugural Message which requested the creation of a recess commission which would provide comprehensive study of the entire public welfare structure." Aug. 8, 1947, files of Office of Policies and Procedures, Mass. Department of Public Welfare.

35. *Boston Globe,* Aug. 12, 1966, 1; Aug. 21, 1966, 17; Aug. 24, 1966, 1.

36. For federal attempts to appraise the impact of federal funds on state expenditures and size of payments, see Ellen J. Newman and Saul Kaplan, "Effect of Increased Federal Participation in Payments for Old-Age Assistance, 1940–41, and Aid to Dependent Children, 1940–42," *Social Security Bulletin,* April 1943, 18–21, and Ellen J. Perkins, *State and Local Financing of Public Assistance, 1935–1955,* Public Assistance Report No. 28 (Washington, 1956), 18ff.

37. Data here and in the following two tabulations are from the Bureau of Research and Statistics, Mass. Department of Public Welfare.

4. Equity of Administration

1. Altmeyer, 80–82; U.S. House, *Amendments to the Social Security Act,* Hearings before the Committee on Ways and Means, 79 Cong., 2 sess., 1946, 785ff, esp. 790; Joel Gordon and Olivia J. Israeli, "Distribution of Public-Assistance Funds within States," *Social Security Bulletin,* Dec. 1939, 23–28; and Byron L. Johnson, "Intrastate Equalization in Financing Public Assistance," *Social Security Bulletin,* June 1945, 6–13.

2. Medicaid, enacted in 1965 as Title XIX of the Social Security Act, was the first public assistance program to include a requirement of equalization in the distribution of state funds.

3. Federal assistance administrators paid much attention in the mid-1940s to the definition of program goals for guidance of the states. Besides calling the conference of 1946, they twice prepared lengthy formal statements of program objectives and distributed them to state public assistance agencies. See "Public Assistance Goals: Recommendations of the Social Security Board," *Social Security Bulletin,* Nov. 1944, 2–8, and "Public Assistance Goals for 1947: Recommendations for Improving State Legislation," *Social Security Bulletin,* Dec. 1946, 8–16. A summary of the conference is contained in State Letter 82, Aug. 11, 1947.

4. Altmeyer, 175, 191–92; U.S. House, *Social Security Act Amendments of 1949,* Hearings before the Committee on Ways and Means, 81 Cong., 1 sess., part I (1949), 3, 9; see esp. the exchange between Altmeyer and Rep. Carl T. Curtis, 72–73.

5. For an account of the passage of this requirement and its subsequent significance for federal-state relations, see Steiner, 90–99.

6. State Letter 452, Jan. 17, 1961; Steiner, 99–101; Winifred Bell, *Aid to Dependent Children* (New York, 1965), ch. 9.

7. Handbook Transmittal No. 77, March 18, 1966.

8. See Mary B. Newman, "The General Court: An Instrument of the People of Massachusetts," in Robert R. Robbins, ed., *State Government and Public Responsibility*, vol. 4: *Papers of the 1962 Tufts Assembly on Massachusetts Government* (Medford, Mass., 1962), and League of Women Voters of Massachusetts, *The Great and General Court: The Legislature of the Commonwealth of Massachusetts* (Boston, 1965).

9. Interview, Patrick A. Tompkins, June 28, 1967.

10. Bureau of Government Research, University of Massachusetts, *Proceedings of the 1961 Public Welfare Workshop* (Amherst, 1961), 18–19. The reference to Newburgh applies to Newburgh, New York, whose city manager in the early 1960s devised controversial rules to reduce the city's assistance caseload. See Joseph P. Ritz, *The Despised Poor: Newburgh's War on Welfare* (Boston, 1966).

11. House No. 1475 (1942), 38–55, 80–86.

12. The difference is, of course, that Congress could redefine the terms of its obligation at will, whereas the Massachusetts cities and towns were subject to the will of the state legislature.

13. Even general relief was subject to standardizing influences, insofar as local assistance officials were freed by federal and state action from local control and reoriented toward superiors in the state and federal bureaucracies. The state suggested that its standard budget be applied in general relief, and some local places did this. Had general relief been entirely free of state and federal influences, the contrast between it and ADC would be even greater.

14. Derived from data in the Bureau of Research and Statistics. The category "rural towns" in the table consists of 232 places with populations below 10,000. "Cities" are the 29 places (27 cities and two towns) with at least 100 ADC cases as of July 1965. The remaining 90 local places (12 cities and 78 towns) were divided among the other three categories according to median family income as of 1959. Those with medians of $7,000 or more were classified as urban upper-middle-class towns; those between $6,000 and $6,999 as middle-class; and those below $6,000 as lower-middle-class.

15. The tables are based on expeditures reported by local agencies to the state welfare department's Bureau of Research and Statistics, but field research indicates that the reported differences were substantially greater than the actual differences. For a detailed explanation, see Martha Derthick, "Intercity Differences in Administration of the Public Assistance Program: The Case of Massachusetts," in James Q. Wilson, ed., *City Politics and Public Policy* (New York, 1968), 243–266.

16. *Public Assistance Policy Manual of the Massachusetts Department of Public Welfare*, revised 1965, ch. 4, sec. a.

17. For a much more detailed analysis, covering vendor payments (both medical and nonmedical) as well as cash grants, see Derthick, "Intercity Differences." A federal official, reading a manuscript draft of this book, commented: "Massachusetts never has complied with the 1946 policy on need as it related to special needs. This was and is true of many states. The lack of compliance relates to: (1) special items are not mandatory; (2) special circumstances are not spelled out; (3) standards for special items are not supplied. Had this been done there would have been ever greater uniformity within the State." More generally, for an analysis of how assistance administrators use their discretion, see Alan Keith-Lucas, *Decisions about People in Need* (Chapel Hill, 1957).

18. For a perceptive analysis of these problems and their implications for the ADC program, see Grace M. Marcus, "Reappraising Aid to Dependent Children," *Social Security Bulletin*, Feb. 1945, 3–5. Miss Marcus concludes that ADC, "as a category, is fundamentally defective."

19. Sue S. White to Thomas H. Eliot, "Massachusetts State Plan for Aid to Dependent Children," Jan. 6, 1936; Walter V. McCarthy, Mass. welfare cmsr, to Frank Bane, exec dir SSB, Feb. 25, 1936; Edward B. Williams to BPA, March 20, 1936; dir BPA to McCarthy, April 24, 1936, all in Mass. 621, RO. This file contains much other correspondence on the subject.

20. March 24, 1950, cmsr's files.

21. Nov. 5, 1947, cmsr's files.

22. Reg PA rep to chief of the program operations division (hereafter abbreviated chf prog opns div), Dec. 9, 1960, A.R. Mass. DPW, July 1, 1954–Dec. 31, 1960, RO. Putting mothers on general relief instead of ADC did not necessarily save the city money in the particular case, for although general-relief grants were lower the city bore a higher share of the cost. Rather, it was a way of expressing disapproval of the recipient's conduct, and perhaps—as the regional representative's statement suggests—a way of discouraging poor migrants from settling in the city.

23. Reg PA rep to chf prog opns div, Feb. 2 and May 12, 1961, and replies, Feb. 16 and May 29, 1961, in Mass. DPW 621, 1959–1961.

24. State Letter 452, Jan. 17, 1961.

25. Reg PA rep to Mass. cmsr, March 24, 1950, cmsr's files.

26. "Report of Administrative Review Findings for the Annual Period October 1, 1948–September 30, 1949," reg PA rep to Mass. cmsr, Feb. 3, 1950, cmsr's files.

27. The final version is "Report of Findings for the Administrative Review of Aid to Dependent Children in 18 Cities in Massachusetts for the Period June 1, 1959–May 31, 1960," RO; the earlier version, from which the quotations here are taken, is cited in note 22.

28. Ralph T. Jones, "Inter-City Differences in the Enforcement of Sup-

port in Cases of Aid to Families with Dependent Children in Massachusetts" (unpublished seminar paper, Harvard University, 1966).

29. Reg FS rep to Henry Weissman, Dec. 6, 1965, Mass. OA-6, "Complaints against Springfield Welfare Department (1965–1966)," RO. My account is based on the contents of this file and an interview with George F. Reilly, director of the state welfare department's Springfield district office, June 17, 1966.

30. Reg FS rep to Mass. cmsr, April 26, 1966, Mass. OA-6, RO.

31. *Meeting the Problems of People in Massachusetts*, 6.

32. Author's notes from Ott's testimony at hearings on S. 804, before the legislature's Committee on State Administration, March 13, 1967. Legislative hearings in Massachusetts are not published or even transcribed.

5. Efficiency of Administration

1. Social Security Board, *Compilation of the Social Security Laws, Including the Social Security Act Amendments of 1939* . . . (Washington, no date [1940?]), 2.

2. As an example, here are the comments of Jane Hoey, BPA director, at a conference among federal public assistance officials and Massachusetts Commissioner of Welfare Arthur G. Rotch in January 1940:

"Miss Hoey: . . . You . . . have set up presumably in Massachusetts standards for personnel. . . . Presumably, we have in the plan personnel standards, have we not, Mr. Alspach, for town employees, minimum standards of education, training, and experience?

"Mr. Alspach [BPA regional representative in New England]: I don't think we ever reached local employees. . . .

"Miss Hoey: You were supposed to have that in your plan . . . We asked for that, and I had presumed we had it in the plan. What does the plan say?

"Mr. Davis: I think some of the State employees are covered, but the local employees are not covered.

"Miss Hoey: We certainly asked for it. I didn't know we didn't have it, or I would have been asking for that long ago, because no plan has been approved for some time without minimum standards for personnel."

"Conference before the Board, Massachusetts Public Assistance Merit System, January 23, 1940," cmsr's files; hereafter abbreviated SSB-Rotch Conference.

3. U.S. House, *Social Security*, Hearings before the Committee on Ways and Means, 76 Cong., 1 sess. (1939), 2362, 2394, 2397. On the federal conflict with Illinois, see Arthur P. Miles, *Federal Aid and Public Assistance in Illinois* (Chicago, 1941), 249–250.

4. *Social Security*, Hearings (1939), 2.

5. Steiner, 87ff; Altmeyer, 75ff.

6. Acting dir BPA to exec dir SSB, "Massachusetts—Progress Report —Department of Public Welfare," Sept. 18, 1945, and memo, reg rep BPA to dir BPA, "Massachusetts Progress Report," July 8, 1946, in Mass. 660, RO; "Massachusetts Public Assistance Personnel Review Narrative, Local," 1945–1946, in Mass. 651.2, RO.

7. House No. 1475 (1942), 109.

8. SSB-Rotch Conference. The statement was disingenuous. Evidence in the regional office files shows that they had major problems with at least one other state, Minnesota. For one example of federal-Minnesota conflict over merit-system rules, see Paul N. Ylvisaker, *The Battle of Blue Earth County*, No. 25, Inter-University Case Program (University, Ala., 1955).

9. Telegram, Hoey to Pearson, Jan. 20, 1940. The telegram quotes excerpts from the phone conversation. Mass. 650, RO.

10. SSB-Rotch Conference.

11. McCormack to Rotch, Feb. 14, 1940, and Altmeyer to McCormack, Jan. 29, 1940, cmsr's files. Apparently it did not occur to Rotch to solicit McCormack's help. Rotch was a Republican, a Yankee gentleman, and a member of the civic elite, who was anxious to maintain civil and cooperative relations with federal officials. To "play politics" in the matter, especially if that meant soliciting the intervention of a Democratic member of Congress, would probably not have been to his taste.

12. In issuing the rules, Rotch had advice from the Social Security Board's attorneys, who set forth the legal foundation for his action in a lengthy memorandum. They argued that "the will of the State as a whole to join with the Federal government in its program has been amply attested. The mere fact that certain essential powers, such as the appointive power and similar administrative functions, are exercised by local administrative units engaged in the State-wide program should not hamper the State in conforming with the Congressional policies." "Memorandum of Law on the Application of a Merit System to Local Old-Age Assistance and Aid to Dependent Children Personnel in Massachusetts," enclosure to reg PA rep to cmsr, Jan. 29, 1940, cmsr's files.

13. *Acts of 1941*, chs. 593 and 597.

14. In the federal view, the ideal merit system was one that covered all administrators without exception. Federal administrators made this plain in 1941 when a question arose over extension of civil service to the agency director in Boston. The city's corporation counsel, Robert Cutler, appealed to Commissioner Rotch for an exception. The magnitude of the Boston agency's work, Cutler wrote, "raises its administrator out of the category of a mere administrative official into the category of an officer whose recommendation as to policymaking would have great weight." Citing an analogy to federal cabinet officials, he argued that "in major cities the heads of great departments—charged with carrying out the policies of

the city administration—ought not to be subject to civil service." Rotch passed Cutler's appeal on to the regional office, which referred it to Washington with the explanation that Boston's inquiry developed when officials there learned that the welfare director in New York was exempt. The regional representative asked how he was to explain this anomaly. The BPA central office replied that, though federal standards did not provide for the exemption of big-city directors, it was true that exemptions were in effect in New York, San Francisco, and Baltimore. The SSB had not chosen to regard this as evidence of nonconformity, but it had not approved these deviations either and hoped to remedy them. (At least in New York, it never has.) If it appeared feasible to get Boston to conform, the regional office should insist on its doing so. The regional representative had already reported to Washington that the demand for an exception was "not insistent." The incumbent director had just passed the civil service examination and was "quite happy about it." Cutler to Rotch, Dec. 13, 1940, cmsr's files; reg PA rep to chf field div, Jan. 10, 1941; chf State Technical Advisory Service to reg dir SSB, Feb. 4, 1941; in unnumbered file RO (Mass. 650 series?).

15. Chf plans and grants div (Gertrude Gates) to dir BPA, May 16, 1942, unnumbered file, RO. Ironically, the result of extension of the merit system in 1940–41 was actually to increase the number of towns that did not employ a worker. In eight towns that had employed one, incumbents were disqualified as a result of failure to pass the civil service examination and they were not replaced.

16. This is the most likely explanation, and there is evidence to support it. Late in 1940, after the Social Security Board had approved the department's merit-system rules, the bureau notified the regional office that this approval was not to be construed "to include specific approval of the exemption of any positions not exempted under the Federal standards," but the regional representative apparently did not transmit this message to Commissioner Rotch. About a month later, after reviewing a draft of the state welfare department's proposed revision of the civil service law, the bureau's central office wrote the regional office, "While we have not previously questioned the practice of having a board member perform the duties of agent . . . such a provision written into the law would raise a question of conformity." Again, the regional office apparently either did not transmit this position to the state or did not insist upon obtaining conformance to it, and the central office failed to follow up its own instructions with close supervision of regional office action. Memo, Mary M. Dailey, PA analyst, to reg PA rep, "Chapter 402, Acts of 1941—Massachusetts," Jan. 23, 1945, Mass. 610, RO. This document is an analysis of the disputed provisions of the Massachusetts civil service law and of BPA action on them.

17. At first there was the question of how merit-system coverage should be achieved. This brought Rotch to Washington for the conference in January 1940, and it persisted in various forms for two years while his au-

thority to act was challenged in the courts and defended through legislative action. Before long a second major issue developed over a proposed blanketing-in of all incumbent workers as of 1940, whether or not they had passed the examination, and this was preoccupying federal officials in Boston and Washington at the time when a challenge to use of board member–administrators might have been made. See Chapter 7.

18. Approval of plan material may have been qualified more frequently in Massachusetts than in most other states. The regional office, in an angry memorandum to the central office, complained in 1966 that this was so: "In relation to your memorandum of April 14, 1966, discussing deficiencies in the approved State plan relating to fraud, we bring to your attention that the plan was accepted for incorporation in Central Office after the Regional Office had outlined in detail the ways in which the plan did not meet Federal requirements. For Massachusetts only, it has been the practice for years for the Central Office to accept for incorporation provisions of the state plan which do not meet Federal requirements and, thereafter, to continue to ask the Regional Office to negotiate amendments. The Regional Office tries to push the agency to amend plans that do not meet minimum Federal requirements. This is a time-consuming and difficult process." Reg FS rep to chf prog opns div, April 26, 1966, Mass. OA-1, RO.

19. Reg PA rep to cmsr, Nov. 6, 1940, cmsr's files. In 1942, Miss Hoey herself wrote Commissioner Rotch: "We believe it is necessary . . . that there should be available for every locality in Massachusetts, no matter how small, the services of a worker with civil-service status . . . It is anticipated, therefore, that the State Department of Public Welfare will take the necessary action through its supervisory authority, or through other means, to establish mandatory standards as to organization and staff needs in each of the local boards of public welfare, such staff to be appointed in accordance with . . . the State civil-service law." May 1, 1942, cmsr's files. The regional office seems not to have followed this up.

20. The region's welfare commissioners seem to have regretted the departure of Miss Schopke's predecessor and tried to get the Social Security Board to replace him with one of his subordinates in the regional office. The Rhode Island commissioner wrote letters to Board Chairman Altmeyer and to BPA Director Hoey, and enlisted other New England commissioners in his effort. "We might have a regional meeting," he suggested to Commissioner Rotch, and then added:

"I am sure you will agree that the regional representative of Public Assistance is a position of such importance that the self-interest of all of us is deeply involved. I am also of the opinion that in a region of this kind, we should have something to say with respect to whom the Social Security Board appoints to a position in this highly important field of federal-state relationships.

". . . We have, especially in the past two years, seen a great deal of . . . and have come to value her technical qualifications and fine approach most highly.

"In any event, [she] knows the problems and varied patterns as they exist in the respective New England States and is not, as they say in Maine, 'an outlander.' In my opinion this is a highly important factor. Without reflecting upon New England in any way, we still have some of those peculiar characteristics which O'Neill so drastically painted in his drama 'Strange Interlude' which centered about New England character.

"As I said to Harry in my letter, when I was Chairman of the Unemployment Compensation Board we had quite an unhappy experience when the Social Security Board sent a very good man to New England who came from, I believe, Minnesota, who had difficulty in understanding us and we certainly had difficulty in understanding him."

C. J. France to Rotch, Aug. 2, 1944, cmsr's files. This effort was unsuccessful. The new regional representative was unmistakably an "outlander," having spent the seven previous years as the regional representative covering Texas, Louisiana, and New Mexico, and having worked before that in Ohio and New York.

21. Acting pers rep to reg auditor, Dec. 5, 1947, Mass. 650-D, 1940–1949, RO. Most of the documents relating to the issue of the exempt administrators are in this file.

22. *Ibid.*

23. Reg atty to reg auditor, Dec. 19, 1947, Mass. 650-D, 1940–1949.

24. Reg PA rep to chf, fld sec, prog opns div, May 29, 1947, and chf STAS to reg pers rep, July 28, 1947, Mass. 650-D, 1940–1949.

25. "Submittal for Commissioner's Consideration Requesting Guidance on Problems with Massachusetts," Feb. 19, 1948, Mass. 650-D, 1940–1949.

26. Reg PA rep to cmsr, Jan. 28, 1948, cmsr's files.

27. Reg PA rep to cmsr, Dec. 9, 1948, cmsr's files.

28. BPA dir to cmsr, May 17, 1948, cmsr's files.

29. Cmsr to gov, June 2, 1948, cmsr's files.

30. Cmsr to BPA dir, June 23, 1948, cmsr's files.

31. BPA dir to cmsr, Aug. 18, 1948, cmsr's files.

32. Reg PA rep to chf, fld sec, prog opns div, Aug. 19, 1948.

33. Reg PA rep "current activities report," Jan. 6, 1941, unnumbered file, RO. (This file brings miscellaneous RO documents from 1940–1942 together with a covering memo, "Massachusetts Elected and Appointed Officials Not Covered under Civil Service Now Serving as Visitors with Respect to Public Assistance Programs," Jan. 22, 1945.)

34. Reg PA rep to chf, fld sec, prog opns div, Oct. 22, 1948, Mass. 650-D, 1940–1949.

35. Reg PA rep to chf, fld sec, prog opns div, Dec. 2, 1948, Mass. 650-D, 1940–1949.

36. Dir BPA to cmsr, Dec. 16, 1948, cmsr's files.

37. Acting admin SSA to Lodge, Mar. 7, 1949, Mass. 650-D, 1940–1949.

38. *Third Report on Laws of the Commonwealth Relating to Public Welfare by Special Commission to Study and Revise the Laws Relating to Public Welfare,* House No. 2276 (1949).

39. A federal official comments: "Yes, at *public* hearings, but we testify repeatedly at closed sessions in most States including Massachusetts. We have been instrumental in the enactment of progressive legislation and in obtaining appropriations in several States."

40. Joseph T. Mulcahy and Mary J. Melville to Kennedy, Jan. 26, 1949; Kennedy to cmsr SSA, Feb. 4, 1949; cmsr SSA to Kennedy, March 14, 1949; all in cmsr's files.

41. Cmsr to cmsr SSA, Apr. 12, 1949, cmsr's files.

42. Reg PA rep to cmsr, Nov. 12, 1946, Sept. 19, 1947, and June 6, 1949; dir BPA to cmsr, May 17, 1948, and Aug. 17, 1949; and "Memorandum of Meeting with Miss Jane Hoey and Other Federal Security Administration Representatives, April 12, 1948"; all in cmsr's files.

43. Dir BPA to cmsr, Aug. 17, 1949, cmsr's files.

44. Reg dir SSA to gov, Dec. 6, 1949, cmsr's files.

45. Bresnahan to files, Jan. 19, 1950, Mass. 650-D, 1950– , RO.

46. Gov to dir BPA, June 16, 1949, Mass. 650-D, 1940–1949.

47. Gov to cmsr SSA, Feb. 8, 1950, Mass. 650-D, 1950– .

48. Dir BPA to cmsr, Jan. 6, 1950, cmsr's files.

49. Reg PA rep to cmsr, with enclosure, Feb. 2, 1950, cmsr's files.

50. *Worcester Telegram,* Feb. 21, 1950.

51. *Quincy Patriot-Ledger,* April 5, 1950. This and the preceding citation are from clippings in a scrapbook in the state welfare department's library.

52. Reg PA rep to chf prog opns div, Feb. 16, 1950, Mass. 650-D, 1950– .

53. Miss Hoey told Miss Schopke that it would be necessary before passage of the act to get written commitments from Tompkins and Civil Service Director Greehan on three points: (1) that the Civil Service Commission would give state-wide open competitive examinations for the newly created jobs; (2) that it would in the future certify district lists when there were not enough names on a local register, and that selection from such lists must be mandatory; (3) that the public welfare commissioner would direct a combination of towns in accordance with state staffing standards when a town's caseload did not warrant a full-time worker. The regional office copy of this letter bears a worried notation, apparently Miss Schopke's, that says: "Is this the absolute minimum? If state does not provide for . . . ('3') what will Wash[ington] do?" Dir BPA to reg PA rep, Feb. 20, 1950, Mass. 650-D, 1950– . Despite Miss Schopke's reservations, she promptly transmitted these three points to Tompkins, although in doing so she described them as conditions to be met if (that is, after) the proposed legislation were enacted. The assurances would have

to be submitted then for incorporation in the Massachusetts state plan. Reg PA rep to cmsr, Jan. 18, 1950, cmsr's files. Neither the federal nor state files contain a reply to this. It is possible that Tompkins never made one and that, once the legislation was passed, federal officials forgot about or elected to ignore their demand.

54. Cmsr to dir BPA, Jan. 18, 1950, cmsr's files.

55. Whether in open or executive session is not clear from the records. In testimony before the House Ways and Means Committee in 1939, Altmeyer had stated the Social Security Board's policy on such appearances: "I would say that the policy . . . is not to have [our] representatives appear before any State legislative committee, or to discuss social-security matters with any individual State legislator, except upon request, and then we prefer that the request be in formal fashion from a duly organized committee of the State legislature having to deal with the particular problem, so that our relations can be public, orderly, and a matter of record." *Social Security*, Hearings, 2255.

56. "Statement to be Made by Mr. Bresnahan before the Committee on Public Welfare of the Massachusetts Senate . . . ," enclosure to reg PA rep to cmsr, May 9, 1950, cmsr's files. The covering letter shows that the statement was delivered.

57. "Statement to be Made by Mr. Bresnahan before the Committee on Public Welfare . . ." draft, enclosure to reg PA rep to chf prog opns div, April 28, 1950, Mass. 650-D, 1950– .

58. Acting reg PA rep to chf prog opns div, July 19, 1950, Mass. 650-D, 1950– . See also acting reg PA rep [Margaret K. Morcom] to cmsr, July 21, 1950, cmsr's files.

59. Frances Burkhalter, BPA, for Jane M. Hoey, Sept. 26, 1950, Mass. 650-D, 1950– .

60. Reg auditor to reg dir, March 17, 1953, Mass. 661, RO.

61. Using an anonymous questionnaire, in 1968 I asked local directors to report on the role of welfare boards in the hiring of casework personnel. The question and their responses are as follows (179 directors out of 256, or 70 percent, replied to the questionnaire, but this particular question was addressed only to those in agencies where there was more than one professional employee—where, that is, the role of "director" was differentiated from that of "worker") :

Which of the following statements best describes the attitude of your board toward the hiring of casework personnel in recent years (say, the past five) ?

They leave appointments strictly up to the director.	61
They are interested in appointments and want to pass judgement on candidates, but their interest is not self-serving or otherwise "political."	61

One or more members has tried to interfere in appointments for the purpose of getting jobs for friends or other favored persons.   9

62. Of 169 local directors who responded to a question about the attitudes of elected officials in their city or town toward state administration, only 49 said that the officials were "strongly opposed to it." The question and responses are as follows:

Which of the following statements best describes the attitude of elected executive officials (selectmen, mayors, and councillors in manager cities) in your city or town(s) towards the bill for state administration of welfare?

They were (he was) in favor of it.   39

They (he) did not care one way or the other.   11

They (he) were somewhat opposed to it, but not enough to put much pressure on members of the legislature.   70

They (he) were strongly opposed to it, and tried hard to prevent passage of the bill.   49

6. The Giving of Services

1. *Services in Public Assistance: The Role of the Caseworker*, Public Assistance Report No. 30 (Washington, 1957) 1.

2. Grace F. Marcus, *The Nature of Service in Public Assistance Administration*, Public Assistance Report No. 10 (Washington, 1946), 2. Miss Marcus wrote (26–27):

"Good public policy demands that opportunity for individuals to carry their personal responsibilities be the more carefully safeguarded because these personal responsibilities are of such a nature that no external organization, public or voluntary, can undertake them with equivalent adequacy and economy . . .

"In every case load there are some situations in which poverty, chronic illness, or marital conflict produce a bewildering number of consequences, such as bad housing, undernourishment, insufficient household equipment, slovenly housekeeping, negligence in the training and supervision of the children, or unregulated management. In such situations the agency is tempted to shift from providing [monetary] assistance . . . to regulating or managing the individual's affairs . . .

"When the agency sees that its main task is to provide assistance, the relations of workers to individuals in need may follow a sounder course and the latent capacity of these people to take hold of their own affairs may have a chance to assert itself."

See also Jane M. Hoey, "The Significance of the Money Payment in Public Assistance," *Social Security Bulletin,* Sept. 1944, 3–5. Only a year before publication of Miss Marcus' pamphlet, the BPA had published another— *Common Human Needs,* by Charlotte Towle, a professor at the University of Chicago—that was as ambitious and optimistic in its claims for service giving as Miss Marcus' work was cautious and prudent.

3. House, 1949 Hearings, 110ff, 531ff. In 1946 the administration's proposals to Congress included a request for authority to give services to nonrecipients, but this was a minor part of the administration's program and received little consideration in Congress. Monsignor O'Grady objected to federal matching of services in child welfare rather than public assistance, but Congress may not have attached much importance to this distinction.

4. The amendments of 1956 are P.L. 880, 84 Cong., *U.S. Statutes-at-Large,* vol. 70, 807; those of 1962 are P.L. 543, 87 Cong., vol. 76, 172.

5. See Gilbert Steiner's discussion of the "withering-away fallacy," *Social Insecurity,* ch. 2.

6. On the political history of the 1962 amendments, see Steiner, 34ff, and Charles E. Gilbert, "Policy-Making in Public Welfare: The 1962 Amendments," *Political Science Quarterly,* 81:196–224 (June 1966).

7. U.S. House, *Public Welfare Amendments of 1962,* Hearings before the Committee on Ways and Means, 87 Cong., 2 sess. (1962), 166.

8. U.S. Senate, *Public Assistance Act of 1962,* Hearings before the Committee on Finance, 87 Cong., 2 sess. (1962), 109.

9. See the analysis in Gilbert, 216ff. The problems as perceived by a federal administrator are discussed in Eunice Minton, "The Relationships of State Commitments to the Progressive Framework of the Social Services Policies," unpublished manuscript of a speech given in 1964 to state public assistance administrators and program development staff. I am indebted to Professor Gilbert for a copy.

10. This was accomplished by defining categories of problem cases and stating services that were appropriate to each category. Among the categories were, for example, "aged and disabled individuals in need of protection," "families disrupted by desertion or impending desertion," "children in need of protection." Among the prescribed services, the following, for "families disrupted by desertion or impending desertion," are typical: "Services to help such families and their children in respect to: maintaining ties or effecting reconciliation with the deserting parent; support from the absent parent; problems in recent desertions; dual responsibilities of remaining parent; serious problems of children resulting from loss of the parent; stresses conducive to desertion; and, including the use of available specialized agency and community resources in respect to serious problems, e.g., marital conflicts of young couples, repeated deser-

tions, adjustments of newly reconciled parents, children's behavior problems or overburdening resulting from loss of the parent, and emotional disturbance of the remaining parent." State Letter 606, Nov. 30, 1962. In the BFS *Handbook*, this was in part IV, 4500.

11. *Ibid.; Handbook*, IV, 4244.3.

12. Mass. State Letter 69 was issued on Jan. 5, 1954. For one outgrowth of rising federal interest in services at this time, see SSA, *Services in the ADC Program* (no date, 1957?), which was a digest of state and regional discussion of a federal draft report on ADC services issued jointly by the BPA and Children's Bureau in 1954.

13. House, 1962 Hearings, 424ff. The states had not, however, made many claims for federal matching of services under the BPA policy of 1943, and Tompkins was the only state commissioner to appear before the Ways and Means Committee except for Ellen Winston of North Carolina, who was representing the American Public Welfare Association.

14. Administrators' Letter 124, March 15, 1962; State Letter 145, July 2, 1962; Administrators' Letter 128, Aug. 27, 1962; State Letter 149, Aug. 28, 1962. The state welfare department's Office of Policies and Procedures maintains a file of administrators' letters and state letters.

15. Acting reg FS rep (Ruth M. Pauley) to chf prog opns div, Sept. 5, 1962, and asst chf prog opns div (Phoebe M. Bannister) to acting reg FS rep, Sept. 27, 1962, with penciled notation, in Mass. DPW 621 Plans (1962), RO. My account of federal-state negotiation over services is based on the contents of this file, supplemented by a few documents from the files of the state welfare department's Bureau of Research and Statistics.

16. Interview, Patrick A. Tompkins, June 28, 1967.

17. At one point in the negotiations, the BFS central office seems to have suggested as much. In a memorandum to the regional office, it observed somewhat casually that it might be a good time for Massachusetts to review its administrative structure. Whether the regional office explicitly conveyed this message to Ott is not clear from the records. (A federal regional official comments: "Certainly not! That was a gratuitous and unwarranted suggestion which was ignored as it deserved. To pass it on would only have created irritation and delayed progress.")

18. State Letter 145B, June 12, 1963.

19. From annual statistical reports (mimeographed) of the state welfare department's Bureau of Research and Statistics.

20. From files of the Bureau of Research and Statistics. Comparable data are not available for succeeding years.

21. *Ibid.*

22. Observations about workers, other than data from questionnaires cited below, derive largely from visits to local agencies. In 1966 I spent a week each in three city agencies, reading records at a desk within the office or accompanying caseworkers on home visits, and—whether inside or outside the office—talking with workers about the giving of services.

23. I administered questionnaires to 265 workers in eleven agencies

(Boston, Brockton, Cambridge, Chelsea, Lynn, Medford, Pittsfield, Quincy, Somerville, Springfield, and Worcester). These agencies were selected—along with two others that declined permission to administer the questionnaire—principally on the basis of geographical distribution from a list of the twenty-three that had ten or more workers as of 1966 (I arbitrarily excluded from selection, without regard to location, the five agencies of the twenty-three in which I had otherwise observed worker behavior). In all cities but Boston, responses were obtained from all workers carrying categorical caseloads except those who were on leave as of the day the questionnaires were administered. In Boston, they were administered to veteran workers, a sample derived by choosing every Nth name from a list of the department's workers but excluding those who had been hired since 1963, until a total of fifty names (twenty-five workers assigned to family cases, twenty-five to the adult categories) had been obtained. (Six workers were absent because of illness or vacations when the questionnaire was administered, so that forty-four responses were obtained.) Oversampling for veteran workers in Boston had the advantage of producing a larger total number of veteran-worker responses, which were the responses most relevant to my inquiry, but it meant that Boston would be overrepresented in the tabulation of the responses. Though Boston accounts for about a fourth of the workers in the state, it accounted for nearly a third of the veteran-worker responses to my questionnaire. (It was Boston workers who, more than others, tended to report an "increase in service giving" as the single most important change in workload; see note 29 below for an explanation.) The agencies in which the questionnaire was administered accounted for 54 percent of the workers in the state.

The questions about changes in workload, with responses, are as follows. Although these questions were addressed to all workers, the responses presented are for veteran workers only.

What would you say has been the single most important change in your workload in the past five years (or since you began casework, if you have been employed less than five years)? Please check *one.*

Increase in size of caseload	24
Decrease in size of caseload	3
Increase in time spent on determining eligibility, need, and amount of assistance	2
Decrease in time spent on determining eligibility, need, and amount of assistance	7
Increase in paperwork	66
Increase in service giving	23

Other (please specify)   0

Response not tabulable   15

In the past five years (or since you have been a caseworker, if you have been employed less than five years), would you say that the time available to give services has

Increased	22
Decreased	92
Stayed about the same	23
No response	3

24. In 1958 the Boston welfare department hired Community Research Associates, a welfare consulting firm, to conduct a demonstration project with ADC cases. The project was intended to show the efficacy of services in the public assistance program. (A number of such projects were conducted in different parts of the country in the late 1950s and early 1960s. The reports of their results provided much of the rationale for the 1962 amendments.) The project involved assigning five highly motivated and well-educated workers to work intensively with ADC cases. As an effort in problem solving, the project was a disappointment. The cases showed no significant change. Moreover, workers who were given a load of cases with severe problems found the assignment depressing. According to Doris Burke, head social-work supervisor in the Boston department, morale sagged (interview, June 28, 1965). The project is reported in Boston Welfare Department, "Aid to Dependent Children Project: New Directions as Reported by Community Research Associates," Feb. 1960.

25. In the questionnaire referred to above (note 23), workers were asked to estimate the proportion of an average day spent on paperwork (as distinct from home visits and office work other than paperwork). The median answers in the eleven agencies ranged from 30 to 60 percent, the average median being 45.5 percent. Surprisingly, this very rough estimate supplied by workers themselves is not far different from the figure arrived at by one elaborate and objective time study done in sixteen local agencies in New York in the fall of 1962, which concluded that 38.4 percent of the caseworker's time was "required for recording findings of interviews and consultations about applicants for or recipients of assistance, and for executing the forms, reports, and other documents called for." Byron T. Hipple, Jr., *Local Public Welfare Administration in New York State* (Albany, [1963?]), 6.

26. The question, with responses, is as follows:

The following are thought to be some of the most important obstacles to rehabilitation of recipients by public assistance agencies. Please rank them (1, 2, 3, 4, 5) in their order of importance, as you see it.   *Rank "1" responses*

Lack of professional training for caseworkers.	17
Recipients' resistance to intervention in their lives.	11
Lack of time for casework (because of excessive case-loads, paperwork, etc.).	157
Shortage of help from other agencies, such as family service associations, mental health clinics, child welfare and vocational rehabilitation agencies.	18
The difficulty of changing human behavior.	42
Not tabulable.	20

27. In fact, the federal administration was trying to do so, for example by urging state and local agencies to simplify methods for determining eligibility and amount of assistance. See Gladys O. White, *Simplified Methods for Determining Needs,* and *Simplified Methods for Consideration of Income and Resources,* published by the BFS respectively in 1964 and 1965. The drive for simplification in the 1960s was in contrast to prevailing doctrine in the 1940s, when the most delicate and precise possible calculation of resources and needs was regarded as good professional practice.

28. Case records had to include the findings of a social study (the worker's "diagnosis" of the case) and a "treatment plan." For several years (until, after an administrative review in 1966, the federal regional office recommended discontinuance) workers had to maintain for each ADC family a five-by-eight-inch classification card, on which they evaluated with symbolic letters (A, good; B, fair; C, poor) each member of the household in ten "basic social areas," such as homemaking, mental health, and rehabilitation potential. They had to fill out semiannually, for each service case, a social-service record form that the state had devised to meet federal reporting requirements. They had to keep on a state-prescribed form a daily account of work units according to categories of assistance (OAA, ADC, etc.) and "service" or "other" cases within each category (although this was not much more demanding than what they had had to do before the services directives went into effect). Finally, and most important, they came under pressure from state field representatives and local administrators to keep fuller narrative records.

29. For information on the directors' questionnaire, see note 61, Chapter 5. The same question addressed to workers brought the following responses from veteran-workers in the eleven agencies. Workers were much more likely to answer that service giving had increased than were directors, but this difference diminished when responses from Boston workers were extracted.

Since 1962 the federal and state governments have placed increased stress on giving services. Which of the following statements best describes what your agency has done since then?

	N	%	N (Boston excluded)	%
We give more services than we did before.	55	40.1%	29	31.1%
We give services just as we always did, but now we record them more fully.	21	15.3	16	17.2
There has been no change at all. We give services and record them just as we always did.	15	10.9	6	6.4
We give fewer services than before. Paperwork has grown so fast that we have less time to give services than we used to.	46	33.5	42	45.1

Interviews with respondents in Boston indicated that many of them interpreted the giving of services to include—or to be the equivalent of—authorizing expenditures above the basic monthly cash grant for such items as taxi fares or furniture. The giving of such extras, which had always been relatively frequent in Boston as compared to other local agencies, became much more frequent in the late 1960s, apparently in response to demands from newly organized ADC mothers. Non-medical vendor payments (a rough measure of payments for such extras), which were made at the average rate of $3.93 per ADC case per month in the first five months of 1965, were made at the average rate of $18.56 per ADC case per month in the first five months of 1968. Until 1968 the political activity of ADC recipients was largely confined to Boston, however, and so was a sharp rise in this particular form of service giving.

30. BFS, "Administrative Review of Social Services for Massachusetts Department of Public Welfare: State Agency Profiles of Program and Administrative Planning for Social Services, Region I, May 1966," RO.

31. BFS, "Report of Administrative Review Findings, Review of Social Services, for Massachusetts Department of Public Welfare, Fiscal Year 1967, Region I," RO.

32. The federal-state correspondence is in SS Mass. Social Services, RO. My sources are the contents of that file and conversations with Commissioner Ott.

33. State Letter 966, April 12, 1967.

34. Laura B. Morris, "Report of a Study of Service in the ADC Program in Massachusetts Urban Communities before February 1, 1954," Nov. 1954, MS in files of Mass. DPW Bureau of Research and Statistics.

7. Professionalization of Personnel

1. Altmeyer, 36.

2. *Social Security,* Hearings (1939), 2382, 2394.

3. National Social Welfare Assembly, *Salaries and Working Conditions of Social Welfare Manpower in 1960: A Survey Conducted by the United States Department of Labor, Bureau of Labor Statistics, in Cooperation with the National Social Welfare Assembly, Inc., and the United States Department of Health, Education, and Welfare* (no date), 55; see also U.S. Department of Health, Education, and Welfare, *Public Social Welfare Personnel, 1960* (Washington, 1962).

4. On the civil service system in Massachusetts, see George C. S. Benson, *The Administration of the Civil Service in Massachusetts* (Cambridge, 1935), and League of Women Voters of Massachusetts, *The Merit System in Massachusetts: A Study of Public Personnel Administration in the Commonwealth* (Boston, 1961). Educational data are from the federal survey cited in note 3.

5. The division wanted to maximize the potential supply of recruits so as to facilitate its function of keeping jobs filled; the legislature's interest was in protecting the utility of one source of patronage. Many, probably most, members of the Massachusetts legislature rely heavily on patronage to win support from their constituents. Patronage has taken many forms —special license plates, fixing traffic tickets (until a no-fix law took effect in 1966), appeals from civil service examinations, pay raises, life tenure for particular jobholders, liquor licenses, early admission to institutions, and jobs (in general, not particularly in welfare agencies). The legislature's interest in jobs has been the basis of a symbiotic relationship between it and the Division of Civil Service. Legislators are constantly in and out of the division's offices, which are located on the first floor of the Capitol building, to inquire about job vacancies and the timing and results of examinations. The legislature's Committee on Civil Service usually has acted in close cooperation with the division and depended on it for staff support and advice in the drafting of laws. The division in turn has depended on the legislature to produce detailed laws of its own liking. The division director normally sits with the committee in its meetings. When the division and the legislature resisted the proposals of reformers, it was hard to distinguish the interests of the one from those of the other, or to discern the direction of influence between them.

6. Cmsr to reg PA rep, March 7, 1941, Mass. File 654.2, RO.

7. Reg atty to exec dir Office of General Counsel, Oct. 21, 1940; OGC to reg atty, Oct. 24, 1940; dir BPA to reg PA rep, Oct. 31, 1940; and reg PA rep to cmsr, Dec. 26, 1940; all in Mass. 653, RO.

8. Reg PA rep and pers cons to chf, fld sec, prog opns div, and chf STAS, March 7, 1941, with enclosures, Mass. 653.

9. Each year several hundred people appeal examination marks to the Civil Service Commission, often with the aid of their representative in the legislature. A high proportion of the appeals is granted. See League of Women Voters of Massachusetts, *Merit System*, 40ff.

10. There are major discrepancies between my account of these events and that which appears in Linford, 116ff. Linford states (117n) that through the appeals process "the percentage of failures was reduced from about 55 to something like 5." It seems clear from the contents of the federal files, especially Mass. 654.2, that this overstates the proportion of initial failures and understates the proportion of eventual failures—and thus very much exaggerates the impact of the appeal process.

11. Cmsr to reg PA rep, March 14, 1950, cmsr's files.

12. Reg PA rep to cmsr, March 27, 1950, and cmsr to reg PA rep, March 28, 1950, cmsr's files.

13. Cmsr to reg PA rep, Dec. 23, 1943, Mass. 654.2.

14. Exec dir SSB to cmsr, May 2, 1944, cmsr's files.

15. U.S. Department of Health, Education, and Welfare, *Analysis of Appointments, Public Assistance Caseworkers and Employment Security Interviewers* (Washington, 1963).

16. Interview, June 7, 1965.

17. Reg FS rep to cmsr, Dec. 2, 1964, Mass. DPW PL-3, RO. The federal directive is Handbook Transmittal No. 35, Oct. 23, 1964.

18. "Commissioner Ott's Meeting with Federal Agency Representatives—Federal Handbook Transmittals Nos. 35 and 36—December 9, 1964," Mass. DPW PL-3.

19. Cmsr to gov, Jan. 27, 1965, with enclosure, Mass. DPW PL-3.

20. The associate regional representative with responsibility for Massachusetts, Ruth M. Pauley, had a deep interest in the extension of social services that long antedated the amendments of 1956 or 1962, and she felt, as did all professional social workers in Massachusetts, that the state's civil service system stood in the way. A resident of the state since 1952, when she came to the regional office from Washington, she had been active in the League of Women Voters, had contributed substantially (though anonymously) to a League study that promoted civil service reform, and had urged formation of Citizens for Advancement of the Public Service. As a federal official, she watched all efforts at civil service reform in the state with great interest, and as a citizen she participated in them to the extent consistent with official propriety.

21. Here and throughout this account of action on the educational-requirement directive, I am relying heavily on information gathered from participants while the action was in progress. These events occurred after

research for the book had begun, and I gathered evidence as it developed, attending legislative hearings and debates, collecting documents, and interviewing numerous participants. Two years later, as research for the book was coming to an end, I also consulted the regional office files, which supplemented and confirmed data gathered earlier from other sources.

22. Mass. DPW PL, "Educational Requirements," RO.

23. Alves to McCormack, April 17, 1965, Richardson's files.

24. McCormack to Alves, April 22, 1965, Richardson's files.

25. This is a guess based on data from a biographical guide to the legislature. Of 239 listings for House members, 159 contained information on education. Among the 159, 94 members, or 59 percent, had attended college.

26. McCormack to HEW undersecy, May 24, 1965; HEW undersecy to reg dir, July 9, 1965; reg FS rep to reg dir, July 23, 1965; all in Mass. PL, "Educational Requirements, HB 3652 (Speaker McCormack's Letters)," RO.

27. *Congressional Record*, vol. 111, 89 Cong., 1 sess., 10930–1.

28. HEW undersecy to Beryl Cohen, May 21, 1965, Mass. DPW PL, "Educational Requirements."

29. A journal of proceedings in the Massachusetts legislature is published, but it is only a record of actions. It does not, like the *Congressional Record*, include a transcript of speeches. Quotations are from my notes.

30. Acting reg dir to welfare cmsr, May 13, 1965, Mass. DPW PL, "Educational Requirements."

31. McCormack to Stanley R. Lipp, welfare dir, Dedham, author's files.

32. The Speaker's power over the House comes from several sources. He presides and is leader of the majority party. He has some influence over distribution of state jobs, handles campaign funds for the majority party's candidates for the House, and, most important, assigns members of both parties to committees. Very often, majority party members take their voting cues from his conduct on the rostrum. He may cast a vote and, when he does, it is a signal for party members to follow. If fully exploited, these powers enable him to control the House. Thompson, Davoren's predecessor, used them so successfully that he was called the "Iron Duke." Davoren, elected in a reaction against such rule, was much less exacting, but he could not fail to be influential.

33. Interview, June 28, 1965.

34. Cmsr to reg FS rep, Sept. 20, 1965; reg merit-system rep to reg FS rep, Feb. 8, 1966; reg FS rep to reg dir et al., Feb. 15, 1966; dir BFS to reg FS rep, April 18, 1966; all in Mass. PL Personnel (State), RO.

35. Two years later, however, the legislature did give the director of civil service discretionary authority to impose educational requirements.

36. The debates over state administration showed how sharply the attitudes of local administrators differentiated them from the cosmopolitan, professionally oriented people who were pressing for reform. Challenged

to yield to state administration, local administrators typically declared in defense of themselves that "we know our people"—in their eyes a uniquely valuable qualification that could not be acquired in a college classroom but only by long residence in the same community. "We are taxpayers and homeowners." Thus they expressed a tangible stake in the local community's welfare. Local administrators and workers reacted strongly against state administration not just because they were attached to their jobs (as the reformers often seemed to think), but because they were attached to jobs in particular places. State administration threatened them with the prospect of reassignments and transfers that might compel them to leave their community of residence or undertake a long daily trip. To the reformers, their localism was incomprehensible and socially undesirable. In the reformers' view, welfare workers should be glad to move from place to place in search of professional advancement. To the professional, the local administrators' self-defenses could only be taken as self-indictments, evidence that local administrators failed to share the professional decisionmaking criteria of impartiality and objectivity. The claim to "know our people" suggested partiality in administration, for particular persons who were judged by local standards to be deserving and against others who were judged not to be. It suggested also a reliance on intuition rather than objective evidence in the determination of eligibility and other aspects of administration. To claim the virtue of taxpaying status was still more suspect in the eyes of the professional. It confirmed his belief that local, unprofessional administration was penurious and dominated by a desire to keep people off the rolls and control the tax rate. Senator Cohen replied sarcastically to local administrators on the Senate floor. "They know the people, all right, Mr. President—they know all the *wrong* people," Cohen declared. Apparently he meant that they knew the presumably conservative community leadership better than they knew the poor.

37. The strength of the bill was due in large measure to the conviction of the guiding spirit of reform, the chairman of the MCCY, Dr. Martha M. Eliot, retired from a long career with the Children's Bureau, of which she had been chief between 1951 and 1956. As assistant chief in the 1930s, she had been at the chief's side in testimony on the Social Security Act and, thirty years later, back home in Cambridge, she was still pursuing with utmost firmness the principles that the Children's Bureau had stood for since its founding. Foremost among them was the principle of professionalism.

38. Oddly, the legislature actually strengthened the bill's provisions for professionalism. As originally drafted, the bill would have permitted a waiver of the MSW requirement in the initial appointment of service-center directors. The waiver was dropped in the Senate on the motion of Cohen, acting in response to the reformers. The Public Welfare Administrators' Association did not press for restoration in the House. Its strategy was to defeat the whole bill and substitute one that would increase the

state's rule-making and supervisory authority (by extending it to general relief) and provide for 100 percent state financing without calling for state administration. That bill was defeated in both the House and the Senate. In 1968, however, the waiver was restored. The PWAA sought to delete the requirement, and, as a compromise, Senator Cohen agreed to the restoration of the waiver.

8. Federal Influence: An Analysis

1. The federal goal of accountability might have been made the subject of a separate chapter in Part Two of this book. However, as a goal instrumental to the attainment of all federal goals, it is inseparable in practice from the pursuit of others. By itself, is an independent objective of federal action, it received relatively little attention from the BPA. Thus, explicit and implicit description of the federal effort to make the Massachusetts Department of Public Welfare accountable to the federal administration is given throughout Chapters 3–7, as well as in Chapter 2.

2. I think this the single most important instance of the exercise of administrative discretion in the public assistance program. In his book Altmeyer says that the most important decision the administration made was to insist on applying a standard of need in public assistance cases, i.e., to resist the pressure of the Townsend Movement for pensions to the elderly poor (60–61). This was without doubt an immensely important question, and the administrators' conceptions and preferences were very influential in shaping public policy; but the actions of the administrators had a clear foundation in the statute, which provided from the outset that aid should go to "needy" individuals, and which provided after 1939 that in determining grants the states should take into account income and other resources of the applicants. What distinguishes the administrators' actions in the uniformity matter is that they acted despite Congress' failure to respond to their request for a statutory requirement of uniformity.

3. In Banfield and Wilson's terms, they were striving to realize the middle-class conception of the public interest. "The logic of the middle-class ideal requires that authority be exercised by those who are 'best qualified,' that is, technical experts and statesmen, not 'politicians.' The logic of the middle-class ideal implies also . . . particular regard for the public virtues of honesty, efficiency, and impartiality . . . The middle-class ideal favors centralization of authority in an ever-wider sphere. In order to treat all elements of a situation in a coordinated way [and in order to achieve efficiency and impartiality on the widest possible scale] . . . the . . . administrator must cross over any jurisdictional boundary." Edward C. Banfield and James Q. Wilson, *City Politics* (Cambridge, 1963), 330, 335–336. This was precisely the ideal, or set of ideals, that animated federal public assistance administrators.

4. See U.S. Senate, *Proposed Cutoff of Welfare Funds to the State of*

Alabama, Hearings before the Committee on Finance, 90 Cong., 1 sess. (1967), for a recent example.

5. For example, Labovitz, "Federal Assistance to State and Local Governments," 42.

9. Prospects for the Grant System: Creative Federalism?

1. James Bryce, *The American Commonwealth* (London, 1889), I, 315.

2. *Ibid.*

3. The only book on the theory of American federalism is, inevitably, a summary of constitutional doctrine: Walter H. Bennett, *American Theories of Federalism* (University, Alabama, 1964). American political scientists have also discussed in abstract terms the nature and role of federalism in intercultural contexts and have sought to construct theories of why and how federalism develops and is maintained. See, among others, Arthur W. Macmahon, *Federalism: Mature and Emergent* (New York, 1955), esp. part 1; Arthur W. Macmahon, *Delegation and Autonomy* (New Delhi, 1961); William H. Riker, *Federalism: Origin, Operation, Significance* (Boston, 1964); and selections in Aaron Wildavsky, ed., *American Federalism in Perspective* (Boston, 1967), esp. essays by David B. Truman and Morton Grodzins on federalism and the party system.

4. See esp. Paul Ylvisaker's discussion of a "rationale for an areal division of governmental powers" in Arthur Maass, ed., *Area and Power* (Glencoe, 1959), 32; George C. S. Benson, *The New Centralization* (New York, 1941), and "Values of Decentralized Government—1961," in *Essays in Federalism* (Claremont, 1961); and Nelson A. Rockefeller, *The Future of Federalism* (Cambridge, 1962).

5. In addition to sources cited below, see Congressional Quarterly, *Guide to Current American Government,* Fall 1967, 97–105; Max Ways, " 'Creative Federalism' and the Great Society," *Fortune,* Jan. 1966, 121ff; Alan L. Otten, "Sharing Power: Administration Favors A Bigger Local Voice in Many U.S. Programs," *Wall Street Journal,* March 16, 1966, 1; Daniel P. Moynihan, "The Politics of Stability," *New Leader,* Oct. 9, 1967, 6–10, and "The New Racialism," *Atlantic Monthly,* Aug. 1968, 35–40.

6. U.S. Senate, *Creative Federalism,* Hearings before the Subcommittee on Intergovernmental Relations of the Committee on Government Operations, 89 Cong., 2 sess. (1966), part 1.

7. *Ibid.,* 268.

8. *Ibid.,* 269.

9. Heller's proposal is set forth in *New Dimensions of Political Economy* (Cambridge, 1966), ch. 3, esp. 144–147. He had advanced it even before leaving the administration, and it was the subject of a study by a presidential task force headed by Joseph M. Pechman. See Alan L. Otten

and Charles B. Seib, "No-Strings Aid for the States?" *The Reporter*, Jan. 28, 1965, 33–35.

10. "The Shape of American Politics," *Commentary*, June 1967, 36.

11. *Special Analyses, Budget of the United States, Fiscal Year 1969*, 164.

12. "What Is 'Community Action'?" *The Public Interest*, Fall 1966, 3–8, and *Maximum Feasible Misunderstanding: Community Action in the War on Poverty* (New York, 1969).

13. Roger H. Davidson, "'Creative Federalism' and the War on Poverty," *Poverty and Human Resources Abstracts*, 1:5–14 (Nov.–Dec. 1966).

14. Lindsay testified: "We have attempted bold new approaches in a number of programs, perhaps none so important as those in the welfare department. Two major demonstration projects have been designed . . . Unfortunately, the creativity of the welfare department and the support of the city administration are insufficient to try out these concepts. The necessary approvals at the State and Federal levels have not yet been granted . . . Every detail of every innovation or change in welfare procedure must be approved by State and Federal officials. Mere inaction at the State and Federal levels has blocked our efforts to achieve significant procedural improvements. We find this unreasonable and unnecessary. A more rational approach would be to grant to the city broad powers of procedural innovation subject to a veto by either the State or Federal Governments. The burden of action should be placed on those who would seek to restrict experimentation and innovation." U.S. Senate, *Federal Role in Urban Affairs*, Hearings before the Subcommittee on Executive Reorganization of the Committee on Government Operations, 89 Cong., 2 sess. (1966), 556.

15. *Federal Register*, vol. 33, July 17, 1968, 10234–9.

16. Otten and Seib, and Richard F. Janssen, "Sharing Revenues: A Plan to Divert Part of Federal Tax Take to States Hits Snags," *Wall Street Journal*, Nov. 17, 1964, 1.

17. Interview, E. J. Rubel of Harbridge House, Inc., Boston, consultants to the SRS, July 26, 1968.

18. *Heller*, 121, 123–124.

19. *Ibid.*, 138–139, 169.

20. *Creative Federalism*, Hearings, 272, 269.

21. *Heller*, 168, 169.

22. *Ibid.*, 168.

23. *Ibid.*, 118.

24. J. Clarence Davies, *Neighborhood Groups and Urban Renewal* (New York, 1966), 28.

25. On federal-state relations in the highway program, see Philip H. Burch, Jr., *Highway Revenue and Expenditure Policy in the United States* (Rutgers, 1962), ch. 10.

26. Advisory Commission on Intergovernmental Relations, *Impact of*

Federal Urban Development Programs on Local Government Organization and Planning, committee print of the U.S. Senate Committee on Government Operations, 88 Cong., 2 sess. (1964).

27. U.S. House, Committee on Banking and Currency, *Basic Laws and Authorities on Housing and Urban Development (Revised Through January 15, 1968),* 90 Cong., 2 sess. (1968), 282.

Index